maranGraphics'™
Simplified Computer Guide for Microsoft®

Windows™ 3.1

Richard Maran and
Ruth Maran

maranGraphics Inc.
Mississauga, Ontario, Canada

Distributed in United States
by Regents/Prentice Hall

Telephone: 1-800-223-1360
Fax: 1-800-445-6991

Distributed in Canada
by Prentice Hall Canada

Telephone: 1-800-567-3800
Fax: 416-299-2529

Distributed Internationally
by Simon & Schuster

Telephone: 201-767-4990
Fax: 201-767-5625

Published 1992.

Canadian Cataloguing in Publication Data

Maran, Richard
MaranGraphics' simplified computer guide, Windows 3.1

Includes index.
ISBN 0-13-001074-X

1. WINDOWS (Computer program). I. Maran, Ruth, 1970- . II. Title.

QA76.76.W56M38 1992 005.4'3 C92-094200-8

Acknowledgements

Special thanks to John Hodgins and Allan Watson of Microsoft Canada Inc. for their support and consultation.

To the dedicated staff at maranGraphics Inc. and HyperImage Inc., including Monica DeVries, Matthew Korchinski, Béla Korcsog, Jim C. Leung, Robert Maran, David Pearson and Dave Ross for their contributions.

To Eric Feistmantl who was always there to solve our technical and operational problems.

To Maxine Maran for providing the organizational skill to keep the project under control.

Trademark Acknowledgements

Art Director & Cover Design:
Jim C. Leung

Layout & Colorization:
Béla Korcsog

Illustrations:
Jim C. Leung
Dave Ross

Film generated on maranGraphics' Linotronic L-330 imagesetter at 2540 dpi resolution.

Table of Contents

TYPICAL TWO-PAGE FORMAT

This guide uses a unique two-page format, with text and graphics tightly integrated on each two-page spread. This means each spread can present a great deal of condensed information in an accessible way.

A typical spread is shown at the right. Notice how the topic is presented as a screen-by-screen flow that shows exactly what you see at each step. Red lines and callouts emphasize the key points of each step.

Another unique element is the visual key system, at the right and top edges of each spread.

The key at the right edge shows all the chapters in the guide. The current chapter is highlighted in red type.

The key at the top shows all the topics in the current chapter. The current topic is highlighted in red type.

With this visual key for guidance, you can see in a flash where you are in the guide.

STARTUP ON A SPECIFIC APPLICATION

Move an Application to the Startup Window

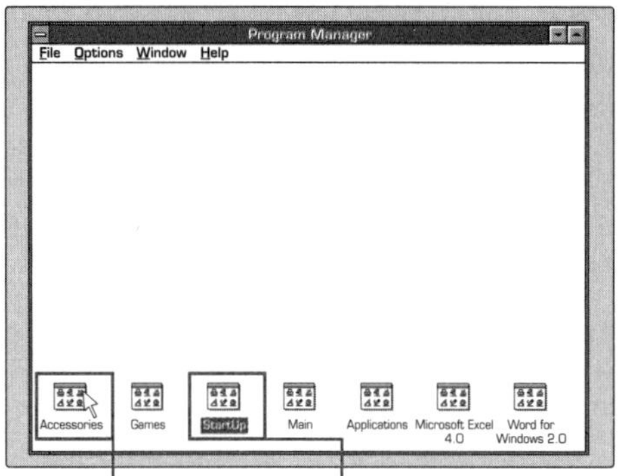

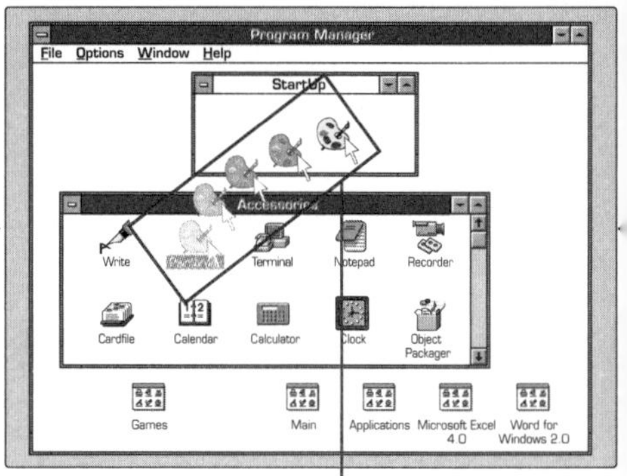

One or more applications can be automatically started when you open Windows.

If you always use the same program(s) after launching Windows, this can be a very convenient feature.

1. Double click the **Startup** Group window to open it.
2. Double click the Group window (example: **Accessories**) which contains the application you want to automatically start when Windows is opened.
3. Resize the windows as shown above.
4. Move the mouse over the desired Program item icon (example: **Paintbrush**). Click and hold down the left button as you drag the icon into the **Startup** Group window.

Start an Application when you Open Windows

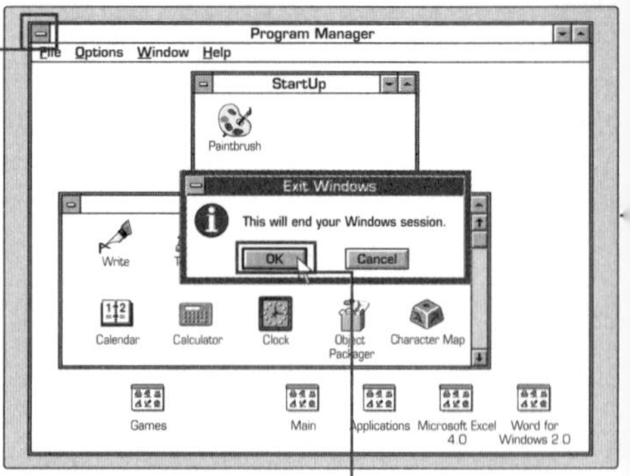

1. To exit Windows, double click the **Program Manager**'s Control menu box and the **Exit Windows** dialog box appears.
2. Click the **OK** button.

24

■ All topics in the current chapter are displayed. The current topic is highlighted in red type.

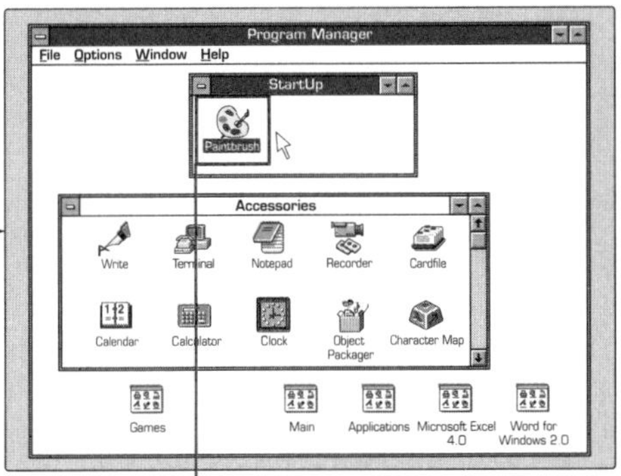

5 Release the button and the icon (example: **Paintbrush**) stays at its new position.

*Note: Multiple program item icons can be dragged into the **Startup** Group window.*

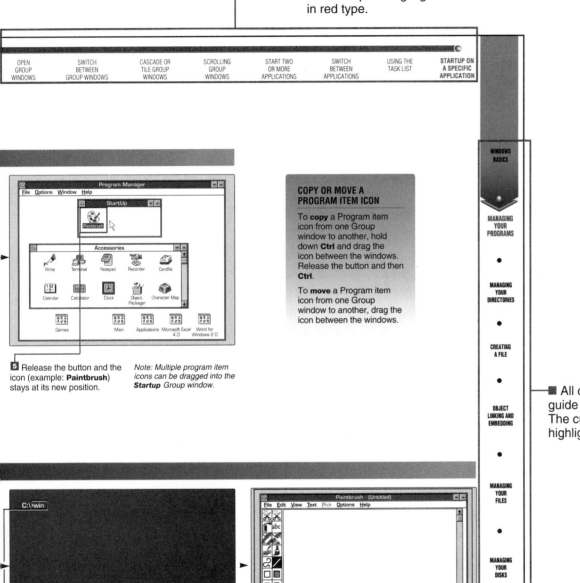

COPY OR MOVE A PROGRAM ITEM ICON

To **copy** a Program item icon from one Group window to another, hold down **Ctrl** and drag the icon between the windows. Release the button and then **Ctrl**.

To **move** a Program item icon from one Group window to another, drag the icon between the windows.

3 Type **win** and then press **Enter** to start **Windows**.

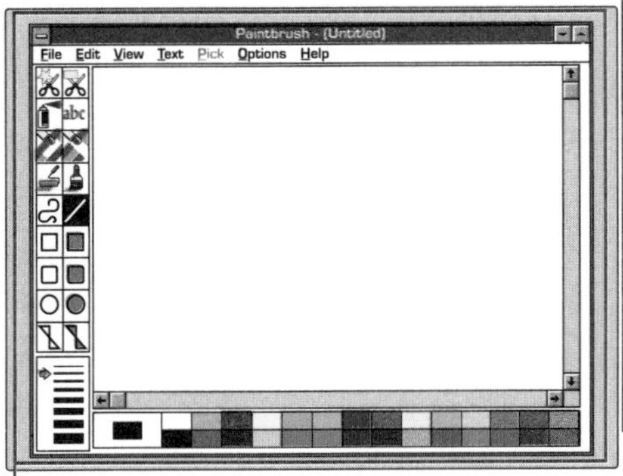

■ The application (example: **Paintbrush**) is automatically opened.

Note: To close an application, double click its Control menu box ⊟ *.*

WINDOWS BASICS
MANAGING YOUR PROGRAMS
MANAGING YOUR DIRECTORIES
CREATING A FILE
OBJECT LINKING AND EMBEDDING
MANAGING YOUR FILES
MANAGING YOUR DISKS
HELP

■ All chapters in the guide are displayed. The current chapter is highlighted in red type.

START WINDOWS

1 To start Microsoft® Windows™ 3.1 from MS-DOS, type **win** and then press **Enter**.

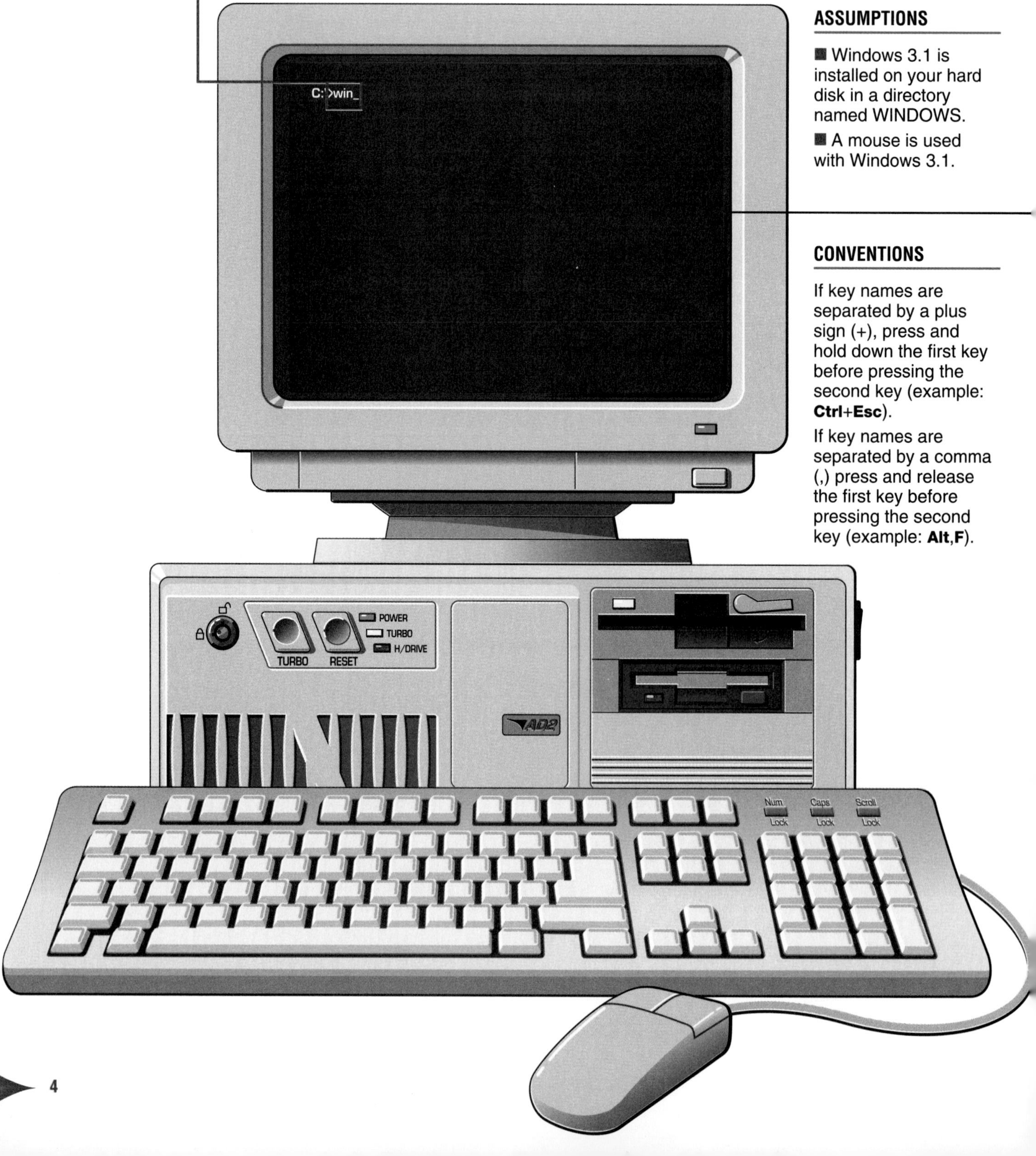

ASSUMPTIONS

- Windows 3.1 is installed on your hard disk in a directory named WINDOWS.
- A mouse is used with Windows 3.1.

CONVENTIONS

If key names are separated by a plus sign (+), press and hold down the first key before pressing the second key (example: **Ctrl**+**Esc**).

If key names are separated by a comma (,) press and release the first key before pressing the second key (example: **Alt**,**F**).

Windows

Windows allows you to increase your productivity and work more intuitively with the computer.

Windows can run multiple programs at the same time, help manage and organize your files, and copy information (or objects) between applications.

Windows contains Program item icons. These icons represent programs.

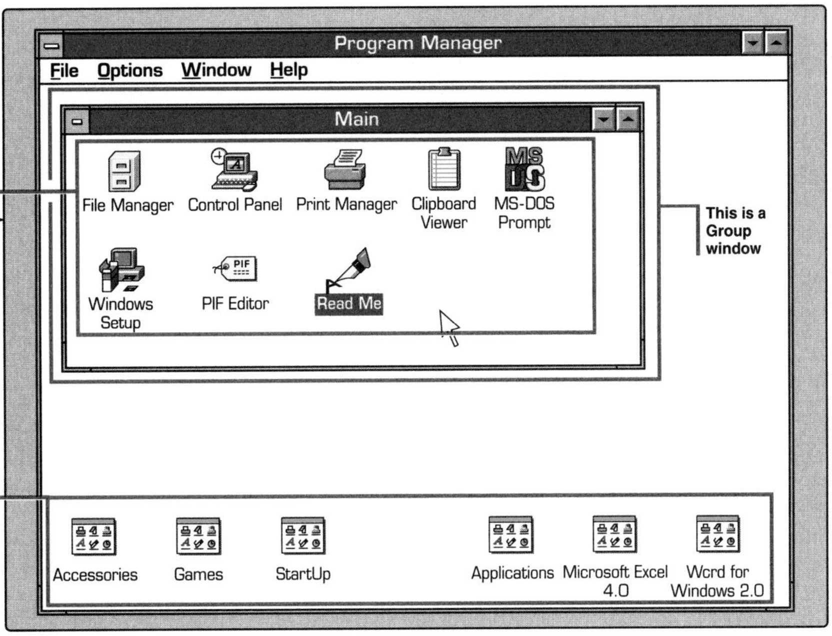

These are called Group icons. A Group icon can contain up to 50 Program item icons.

The entire computer screen is called the desktop. Multiple windows can be displayed on the desktop.

Note: The terms "program" and "application" are used interchangeably.

Windows 3.1 includes built-in intelligence. After you type **win** to start the program, it checks your computer's hardware and memory and then starts Windows in the appropriate mode.

TWO OPERATING MODES OF WINDOWS 3.1

STANDARD MODE

The Standard Mode starts when the computer is an 80286 machine (or higher) with no less than 640K of conventional memory and 256K of extended memory.

386 ENHANCED MODE

The 386 Enhanced Mode starts when the computer is an 80386 machine (or higher) with no less than 640K of conventional memory and 1024K of extended memory.

MOVE AND ARRANGE ICONS

MOVE A WINDOW

Move an Icon

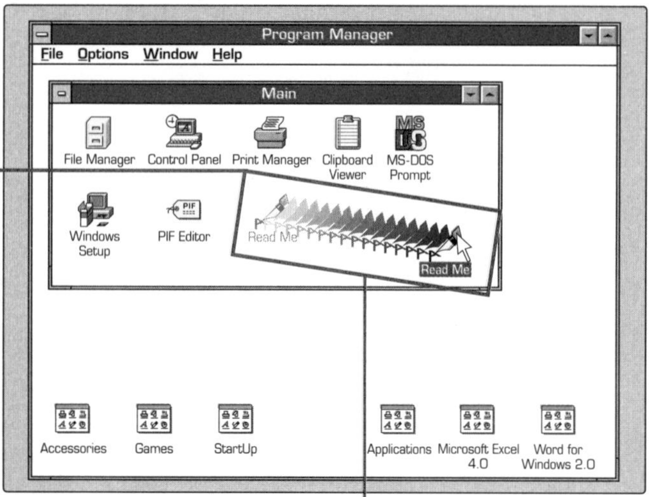

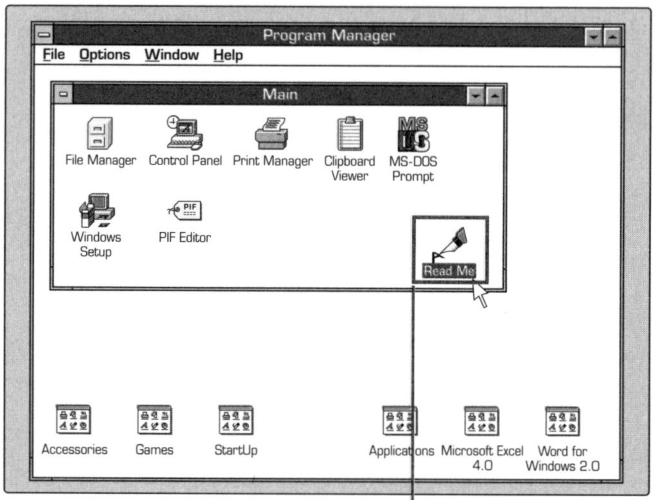

1 Move the mouse over an icon (example: **Read Me**). Click the left button and hold it down.

2 Still holding down the button, drag the icon to where you want it positioned in the window.

3 Release the button and the icon stays at its new position.

Note: All icons on the desktop can be moved this way.

*Note: An icon will not stay at its new position if **Auto Arrange** is **on**. For more information, refer to page 12.*

Move a Window

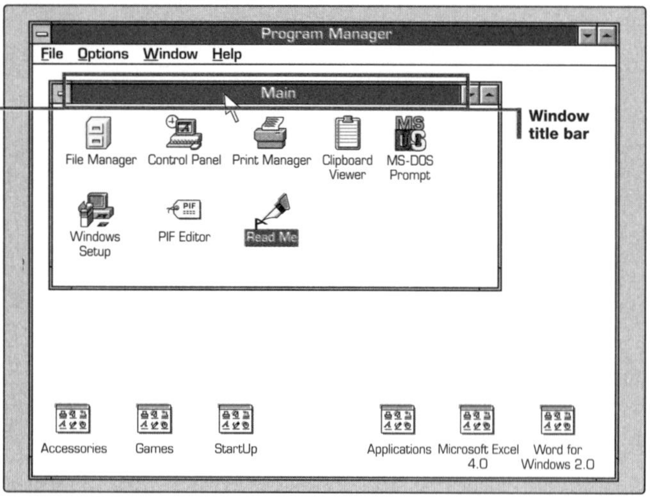

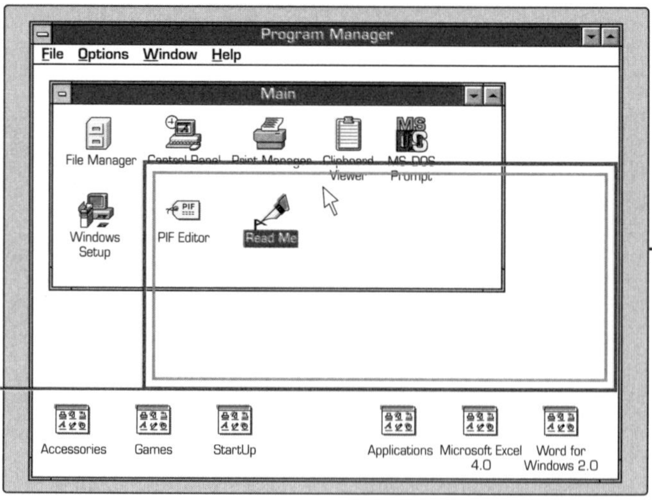

1 Move the mouse over any part of a **Window title bar**. Click the left button and hold it down.

2 Still holding down the button, drag the window to where you want it positioned.

*Note: You cannot move any Group window outside the **Program Manager** window.*

Arrange Icons

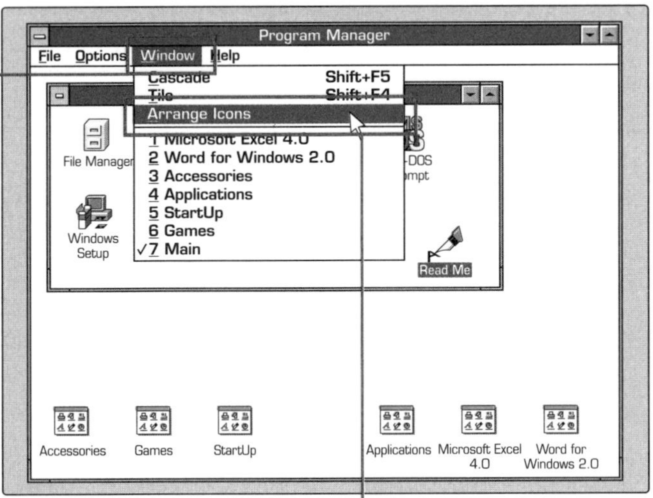

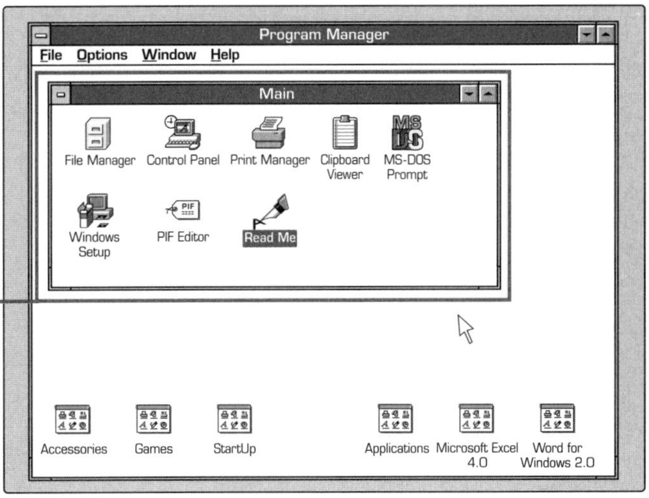

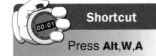

1 To arrange icons in the **Main** window, move the mouse ⇖ over **Window** and click the left button. Its menu appears.

Note: To cancel a menu, press ***Esc*** *twice.*

2 Move the mouse ⇖ over **Arrange Icons** and click the left button.

Shortcut

Press **Alt**,**W**,**A**

■ All the icons in the window are displayed in an orderly fashion.

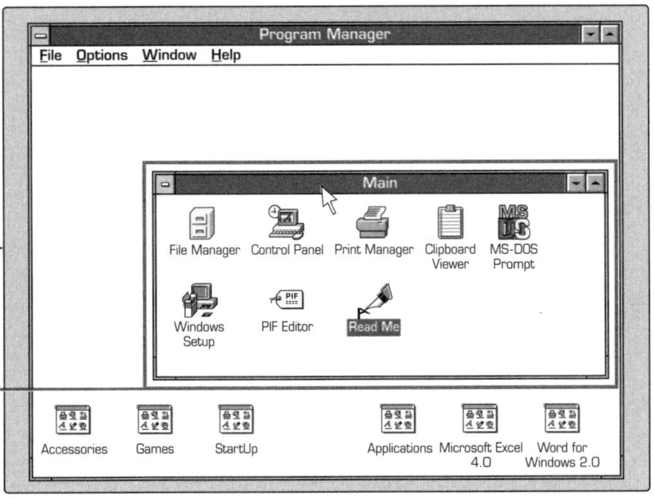

3 Release the button and the window jumps to its new position.

Note: If you press ***Esc*** *before releasing the button, the move is cancelled.*

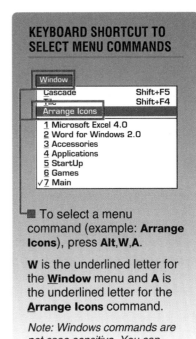

KEYBOARD SHORTCUT TO SELECT MENU COMMANDS

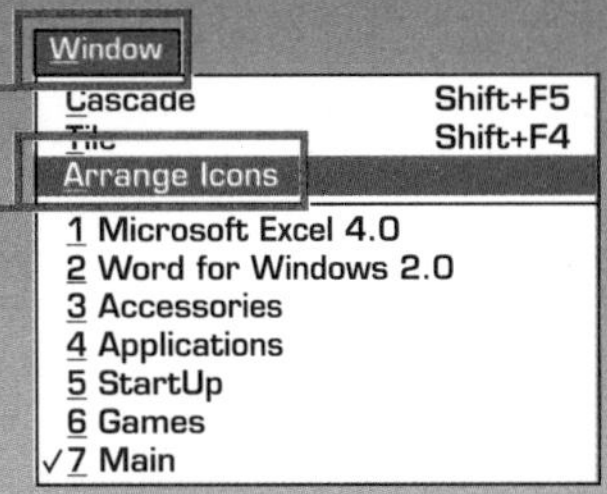

■ To select a menu command (example: **Arrange Icons**), press **Alt**,**W**,**A**.

W is the underlined letter for the **Window** menu and **A** is the underlined letter for the **Arrange Icons** command.

Note: Windows commands are not case sensitive. You can press ***Alt***,***W***,***A***, *or* ***Alt***,***w***,***a***.

CHANGE A WINDOW'S SIZE

Horizontally

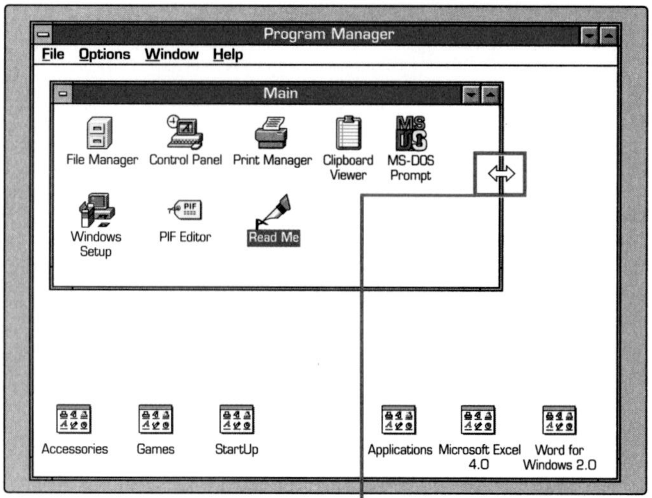

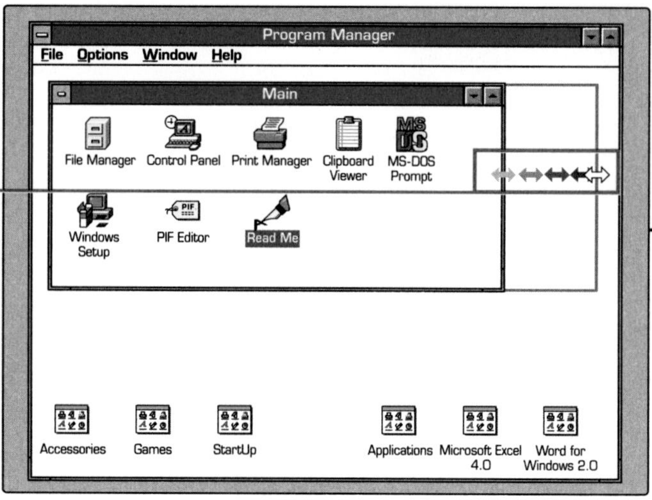

The ability to size each window independently is very useful when working with multiple windows on the desktop.

1 Move the mouse ↖ to the right edge of the window and it turns into ⇔.

2 Click and hold down the left button as you drag the edge of the window to the desired size.

Horizontally and Vertically at the Same Time

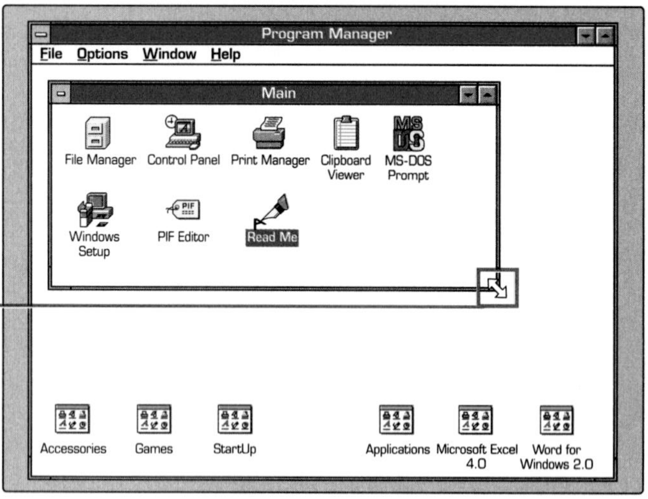

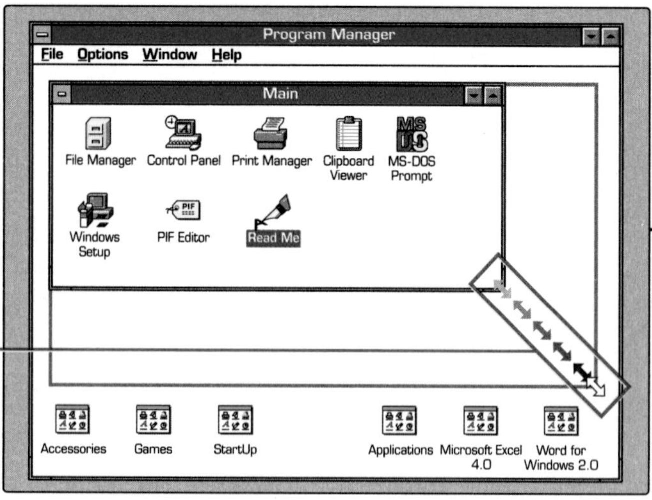

1 Move the mouse ↖ to the bottom right edge of the window and it turns into ⇘.

2 Click and hold down the left button as you drag the edge of the window to the desired size.

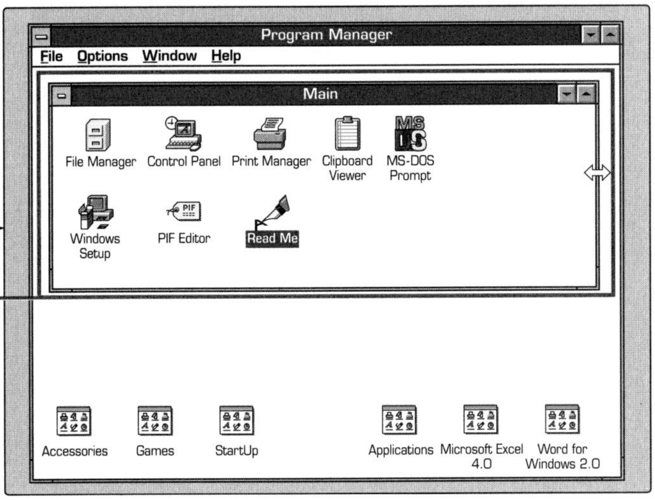

3 Release the button and the window is resized.

Note: If you press ***Esc*** *before releasing the button, the resizing is cancelled.*

Vertically

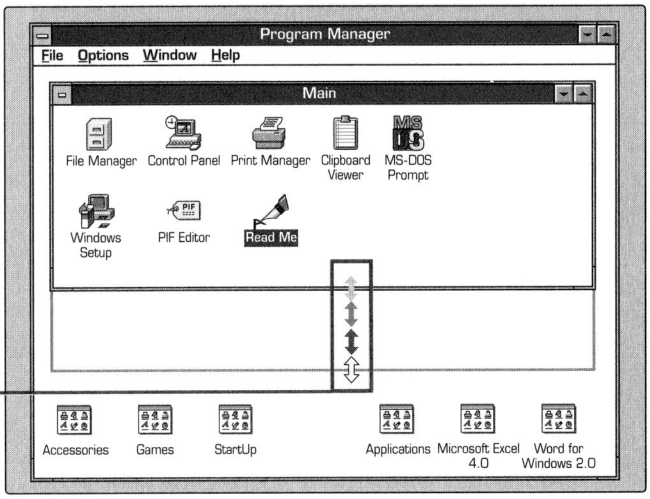

1 Use the same method to resize the window vertically (except drag the bottom edge of the window).

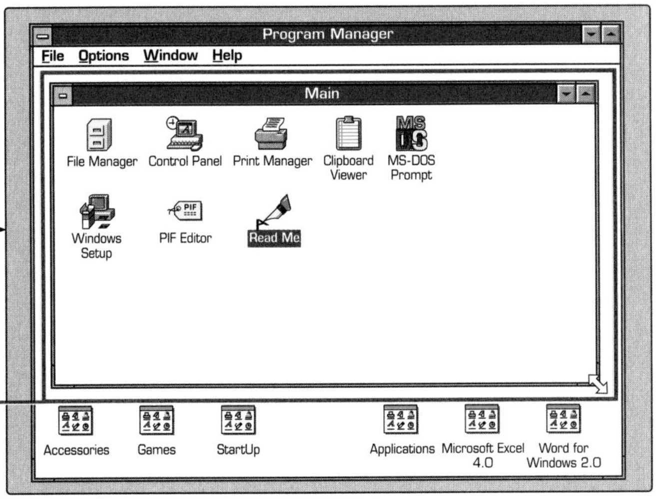

3 Release the button and the window is resized.

Note: If you press ***Esc*** *before releasing the button, the resizing is cancelled.*

Note: You can change a window's size to make it larger or smaller from any corner.

If resizing a window hides some of the Program item icons, click ***Window****. Then click* ***Arrange Icons****. This will rearrange and display all icons in the resized window, but will only work if the window is large enough to accommodate all the icons.*

MINIMIZE AND RESTORE ICONS

Minimize a Window to an Icon

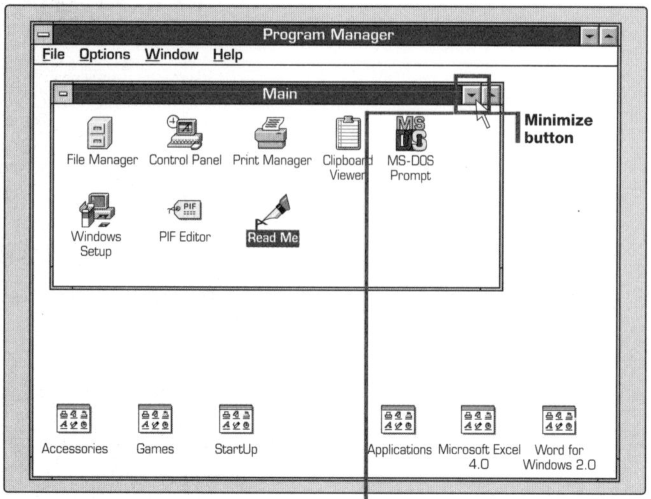

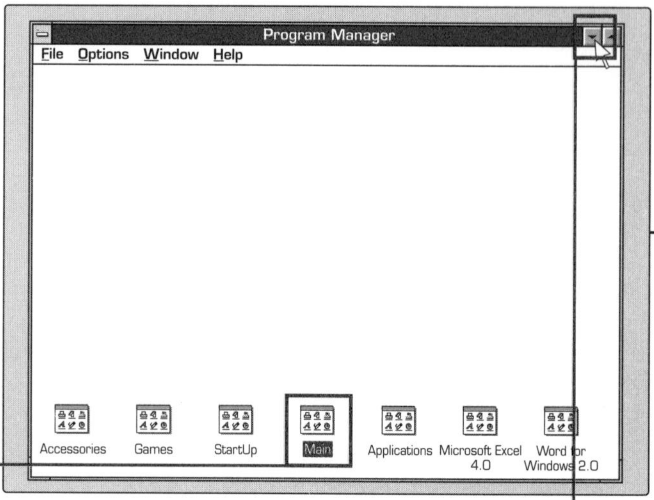

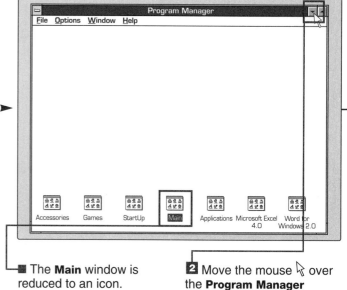

When you are finished working with a window, it can be minimized to give you more working space on the desktop.

1 Move the mouse over the **Main** window's **Minimize** button, and click the left button.

■ The **Main** window is reduced to an icon.

2 Move the mouse over the **Program Manager** window's **Minimize** button, and click the left button.

Restore an Icon to a Window

1 To restore an icon to a window, move the mouse over the icon and click the left button twice in quick succession.

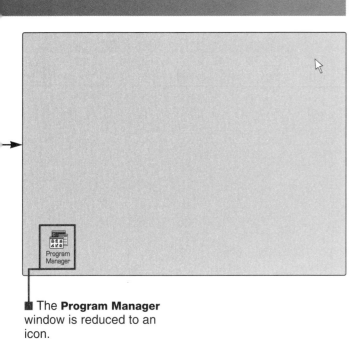

■ The **Program Manager** window is reduced to an icon.

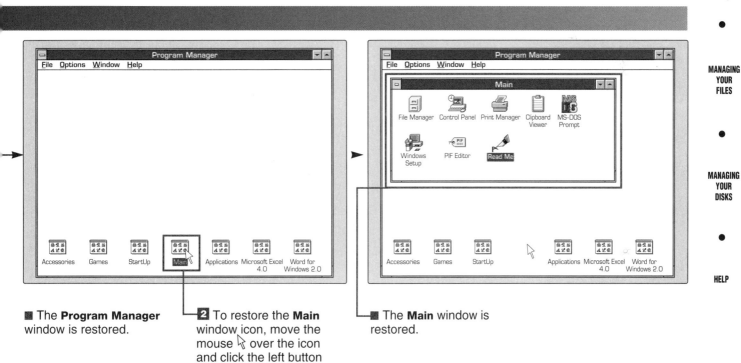

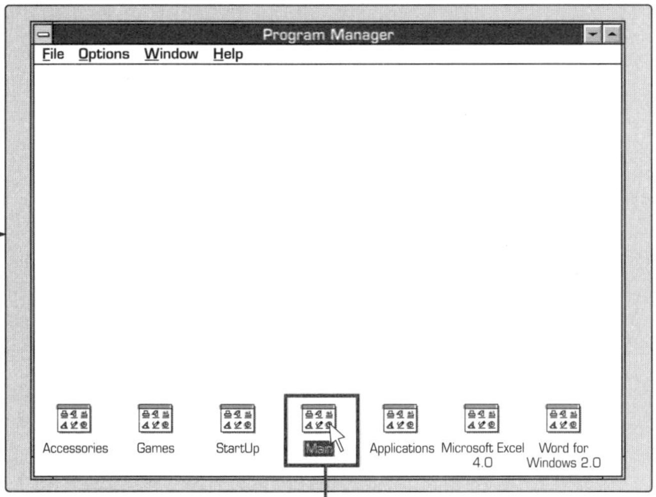

■ The **Program Manager** window is restored.

2 To restore the **Main** window icon, move the mouse ↖ over the icon and click the left button twice in quick succession.

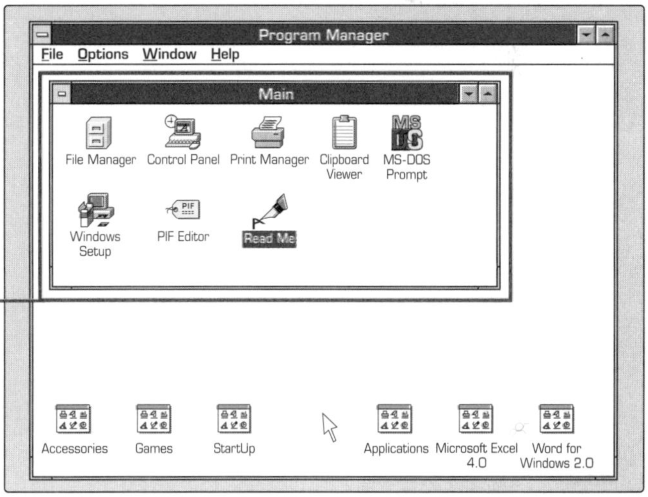

■ The **Main** window is restored.

MAXIMIZE AND RESTORE A WINDOW

AUTO ARRANGE ICONS

Maximize and Restore a Window

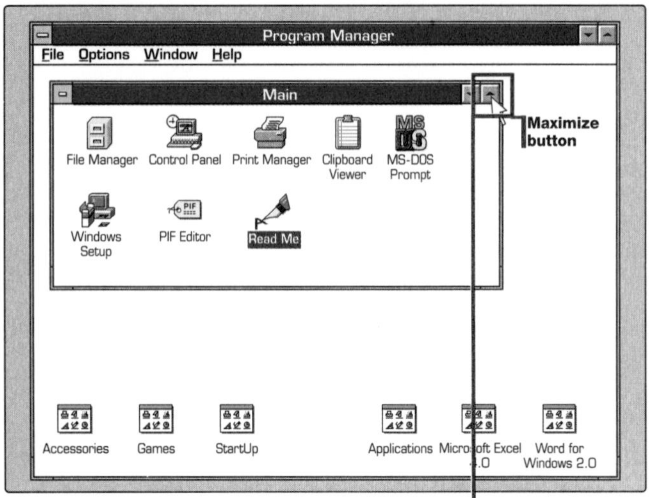

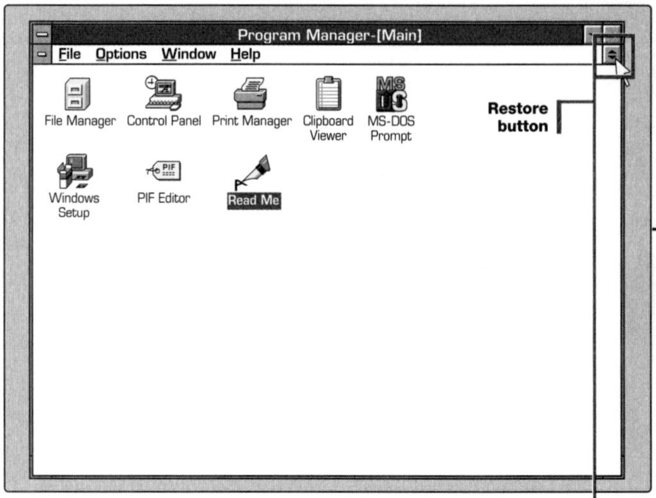

When working in a window, it can be enlarged to create a larger working area.

1 Move the mouse over the **Main** window's **Maximize** button, and click the left button.

■ The **Main** window is enlarged to occupy the complete area within the **Program Manager** window.

2 Move the mouse over the **Restore** button, and click the left mouse button.

Auto Arrange Icons

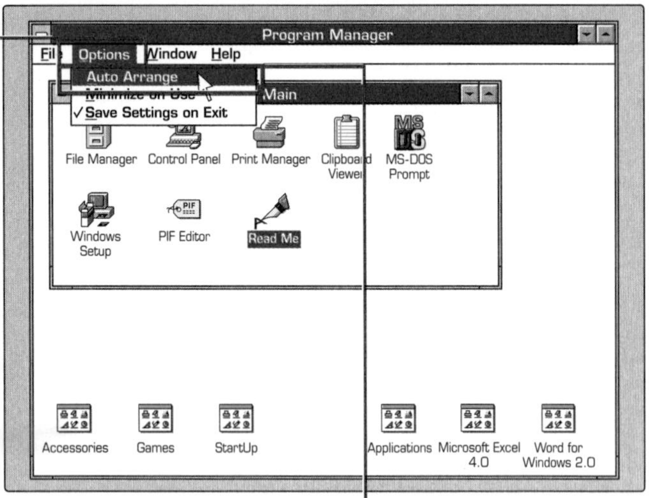

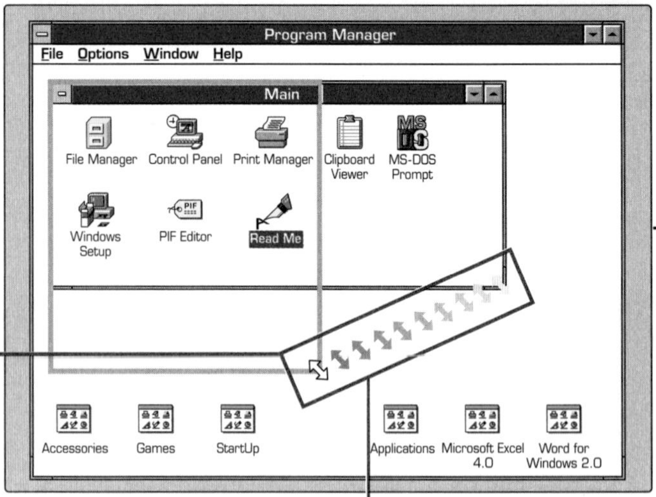

The Auto Arrange mode automatically rearranges Program item icons whenever you resize a window.

1 Move the mouse over **Options** and click the left button. The **Options** menu appears.

2 Move the mouse over **Auto Arrange** and click the left button to turn it **on**.

*Note: If a checkmark (✓) is in front of **Auto Arrange**, it is already **on**.*

3 Move the mouse to the right edge of the window and it changes to ⤡.

4 Click and hold down the left button as you drag the edge of the window to the desired size.

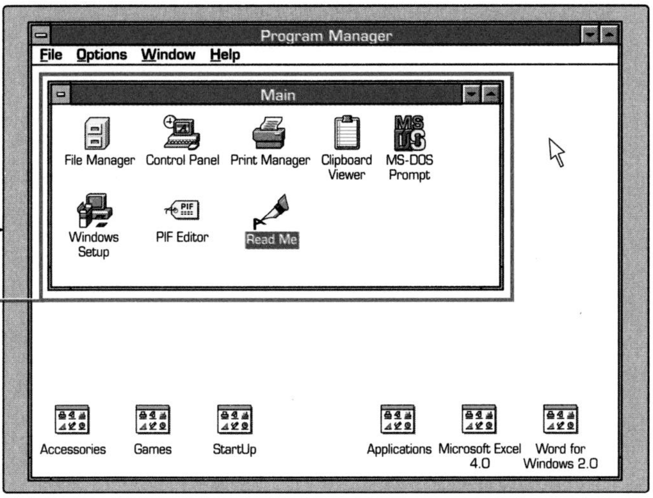

■ The **Main** window is restored to its previous size.

*Note: The **Program Manager** window can be enlarged to occupy the entire desktop and then restored in the same way.*

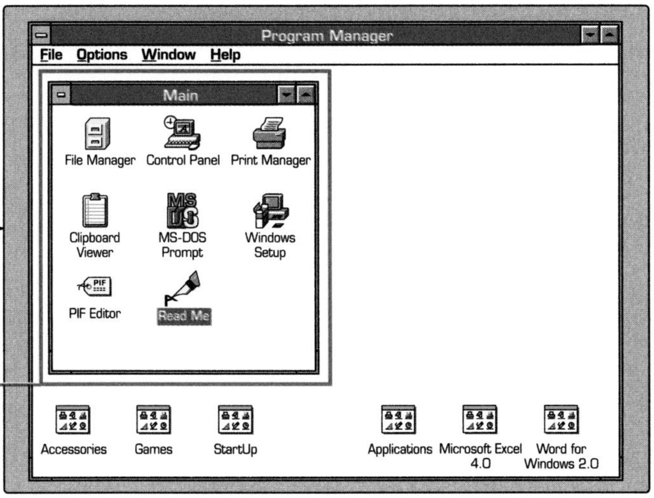

5 Release the button and the Program item icons are automatically rearranged within the window.

1 To check if the **Auto Arrange** mode is **on** or **off**, move the mouse over **Options** and click the left button.

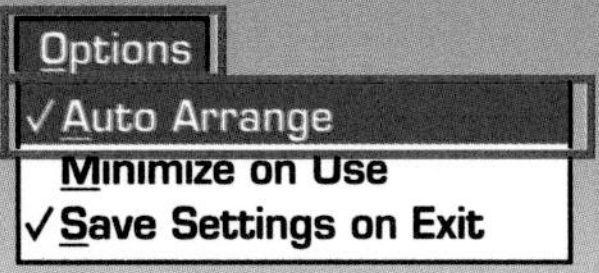

■ The checkmark (✓) in front of **Auto Arrange** indicates it is **on**.

*Note: To close the **Options** menu, press **Esc** twice.*

SAVE SETTINGS ON EXIT

EXIT WINDOWS

Save Settings on Exit

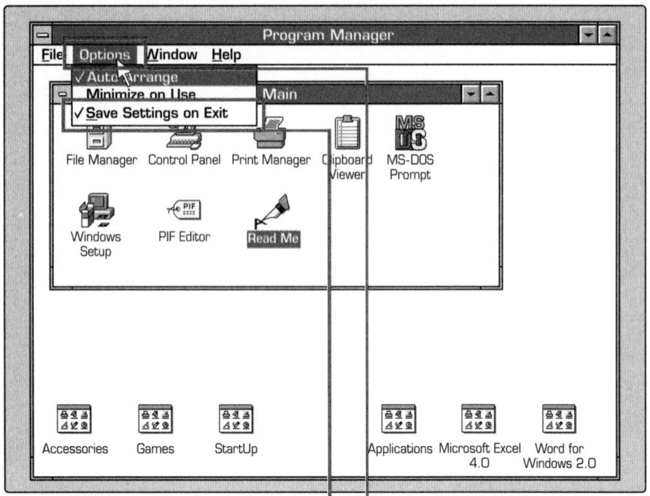

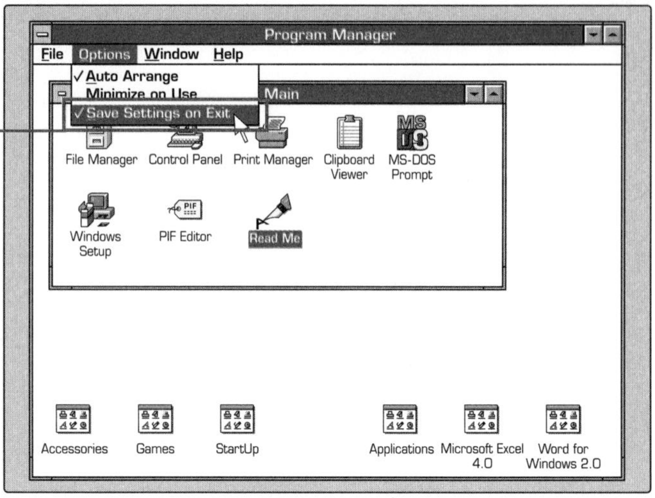

If Save Settings on Exit is on, the current arrangement of Group windows and icons is saved when you exit Windows.

1 To check if **Save Settings on Exit** is **on** or **off**, move the mouse over **Options** and click the left button.

■ The checkmark (✓) in front of **Save Settings on Exit** indicates it is **on**.

2 To turn it **off**, move the mouse over **Save Settings on Exit** and click the left button.

Note: To keep it on, press ***Esc*** *twice to close the* ***Options*** *menu.*

Note: For the remainder of this book, ***Save Settings on Exit*** √Save Settings on Exit *is* ***on****.*

Exit Windows

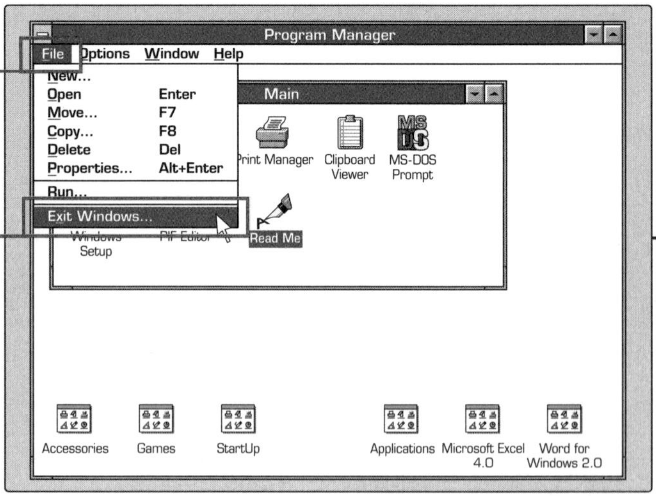

Always exit Windows **before** turning off the computer.

1 Move the mouse over **File** and click the left button.

2 Move the mouse over **Exit Windows** and click the left button.

Shortcut

Press **Alt+F4**

Using the Mouse

For the rest of this guide, the following shortcuts are used:

- "Move the mouse over **xx** and click the left button" becomes: **Click xx**
- "Move the mouse over **xx** and click the left button twice in quick succession" becomes: **Double click xx**
- "Move the mouse over **xx**. Click and hold down the left button as you drag **xx**" becomes: **Drag xx**

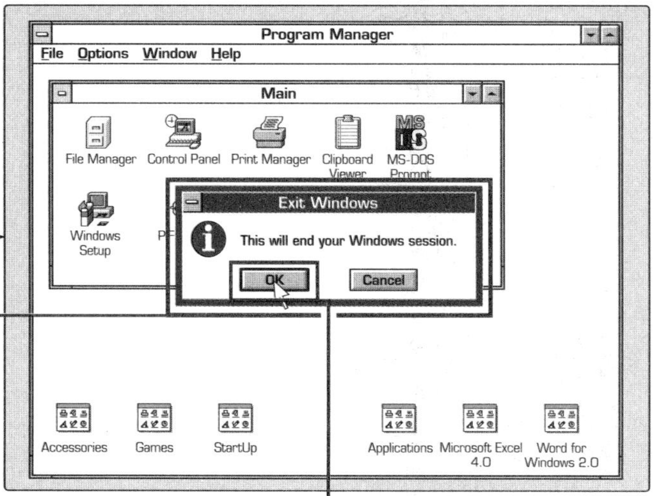

- The **Exit Windows** dialog box appears.

3. To exit Windows, move the mouse over the **OK** button and click the left button, or press **Enter**.

Note: To cancel the Exit command, press ***Esc****.*

- You are returned to the DOS command prompt.

OPEN GROUP WINDOWS

SWITCH BETWEEN GROUP WINDOWS

When you start up Windows the first time, the **Main** Group window is open.

1 To open another Group window (example: **Accessories**) double click its icon.

These icons represent programs and are called Program item icons. Each program is started by double clicking its Program item icon.

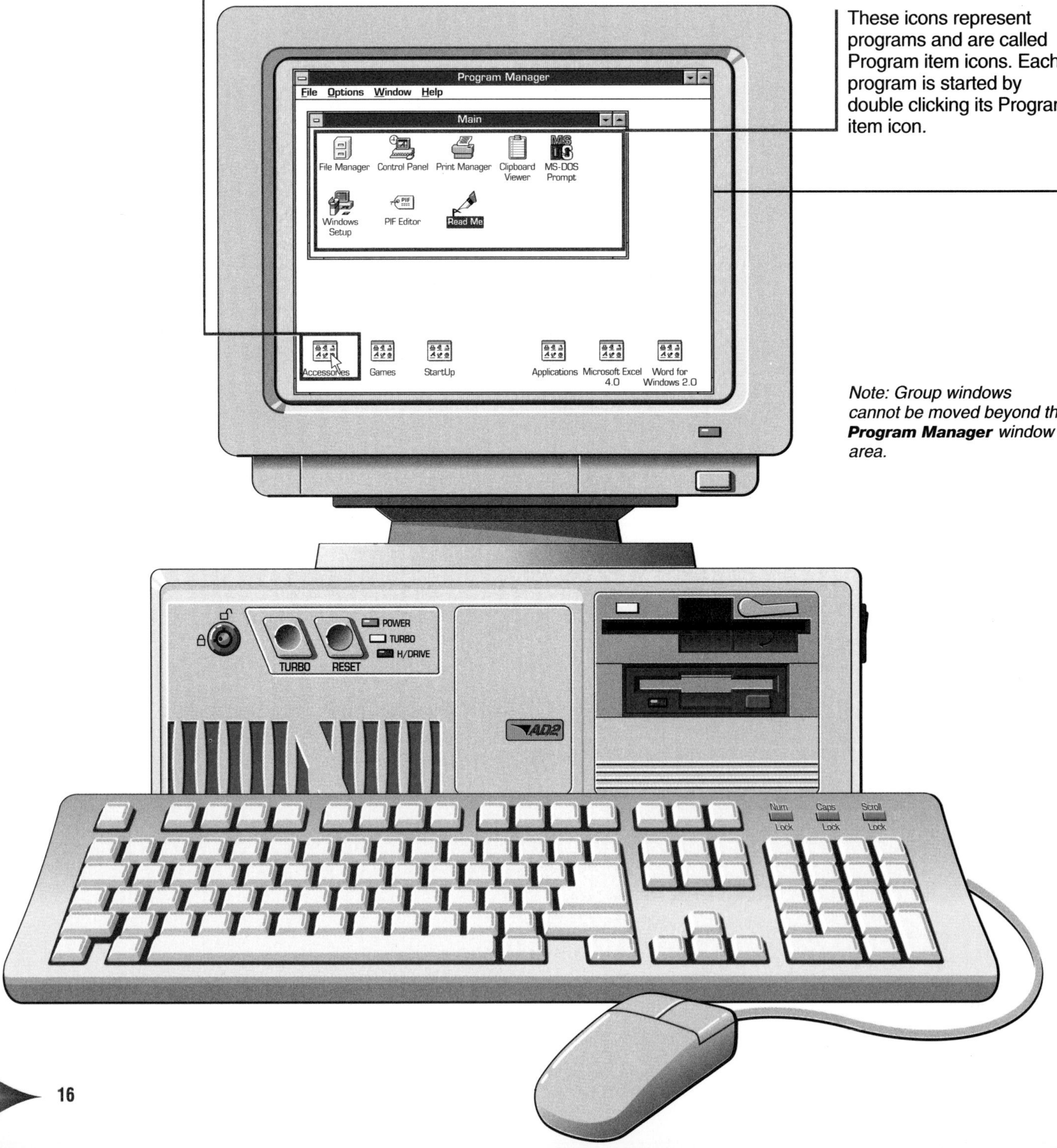

*Note: Group windows cannot be moved beyond the **Program Manager** window area.*

Open Group Windows

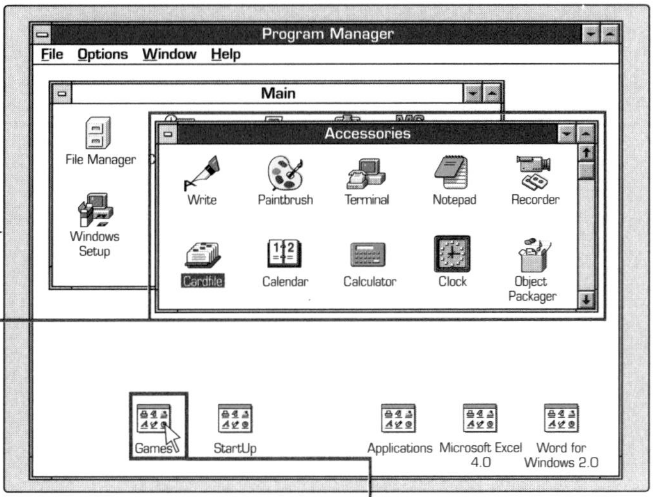

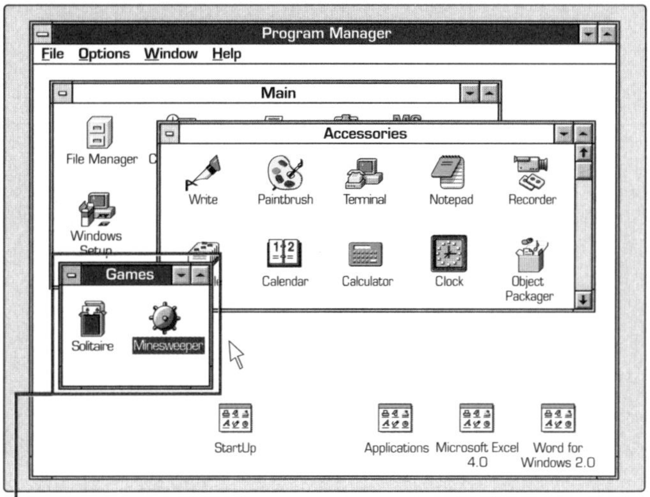

■ The **Accessories** Group window opens and becomes the current or active window.

2 To open the **Games** Group window, double click its icon.

■ The **Games** Group window opens and becomes the current window.

Note: The current window is identified by the dark title bar. Program Manager commands only work on the current window.

Switch Between Group Windows

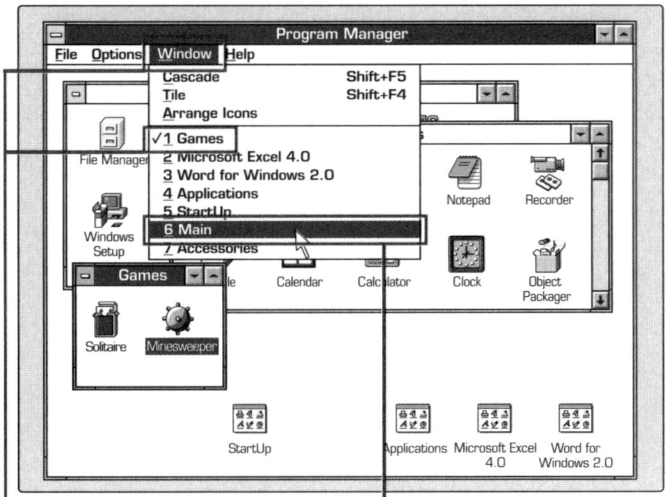

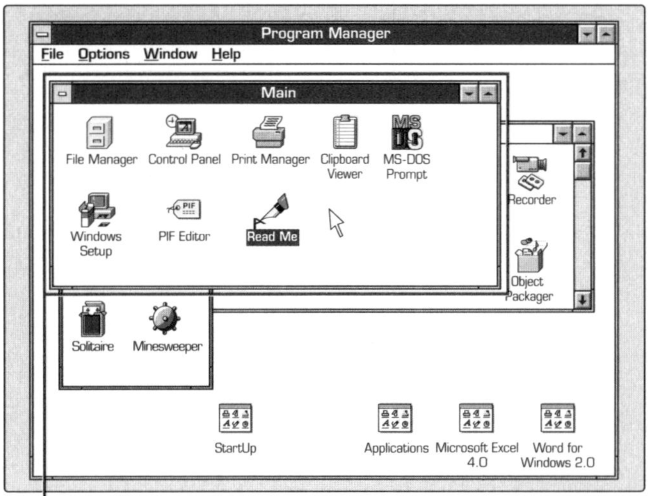

1 Click **Window** and its menu appears.

■ The (✓) in front of **Games** indicates its Group window is current.

2 To switch to another Group window (make it the current window), click its name in the **Window** menu (example: **Main**).

■ The **Main** window becomes the current window.

Note: This feature is useful when the Group window you want to make current is ccmpletely covered by another Group window.

Shortcut

Click in any window to make it current.

CASCADE OR TILE GROUP WINDOWS

SCROLLING GROUP WINDOWS

Cascade Group Windows

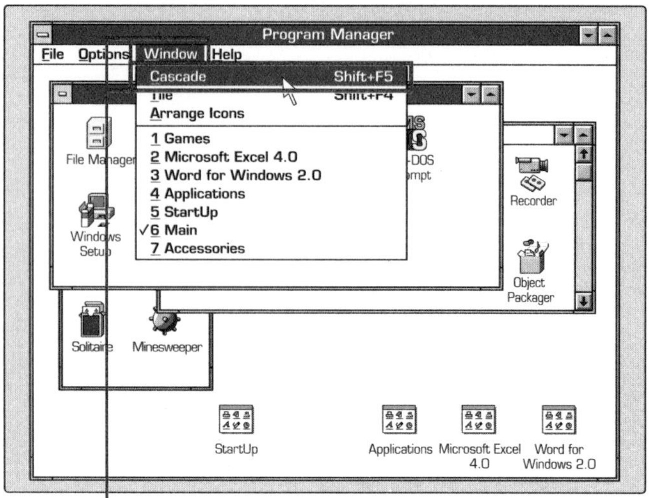

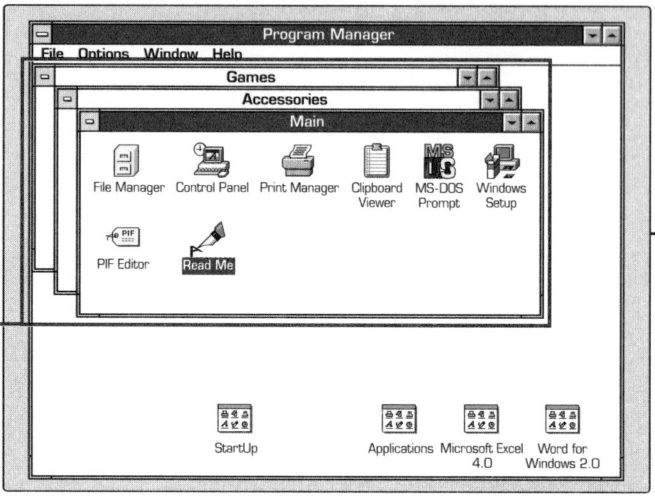

If several Group windows are open at the same time, some of them may be hidden. To view all the windows, you can use the Tile or Cascade commands.

1 Click **Window** to open its menu.

2 Click **Cascade**.

■ The Group windows are cascaded.

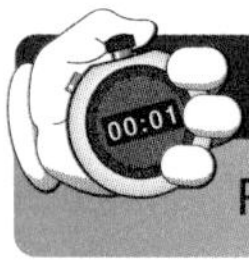

Shortcut

Press **Shift+F5**

Scrolling Group Windows

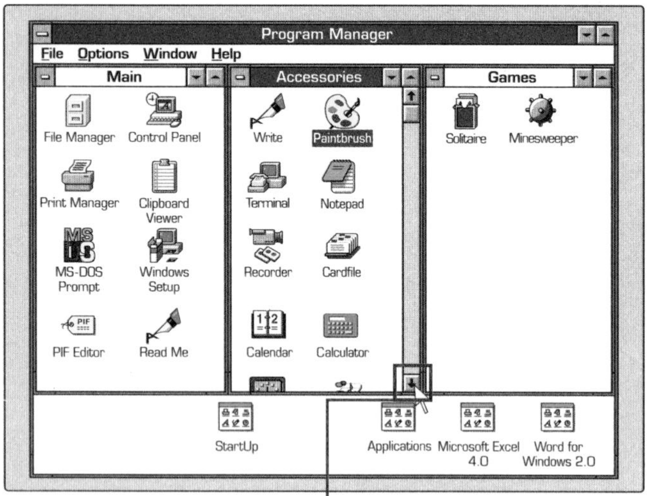

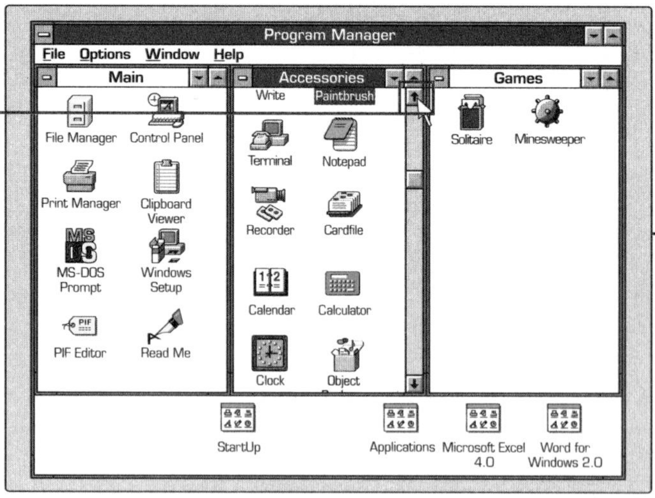

A Group window may not be large enough to display all its Program item icons.

To view the rest of these icons, you must scroll through the Group window.

Scroll down

1 Move the mouse over the down scroll arrow and click the left button.

Scroll up

1 Move the mouse over the up scroll arrow and click the left button.

Tile Group Windows

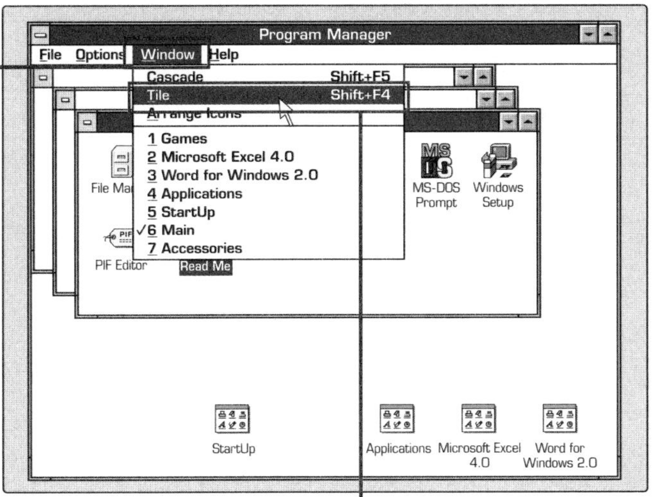

1 Click **Window** to open its menu.

2 Click **Tile**.

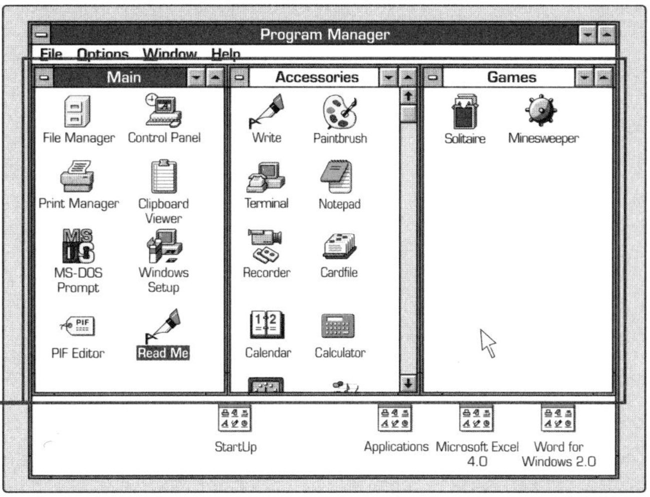

■ The Group windows are tiled.

Shortcut

Press **Shift+F4**

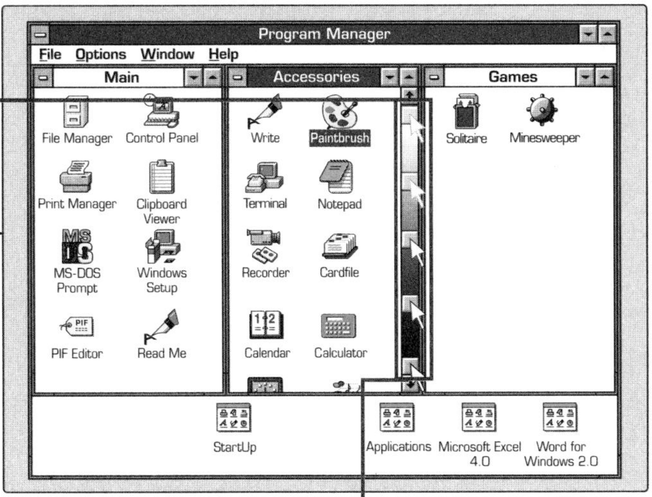

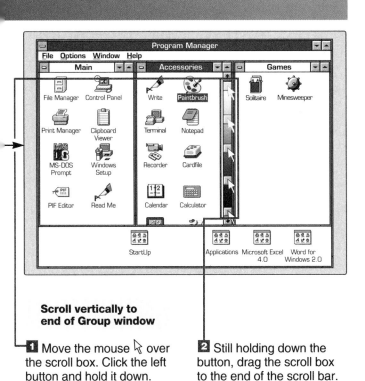

Scroll vertically to end of Group window

1 Move the mouse over the scroll box. Click the left button and hold it down.

2 Still holding down the button, drag the scroll box to the end of the scroll bar. Release the button.

TO CLOSE A GROUP WINDOW

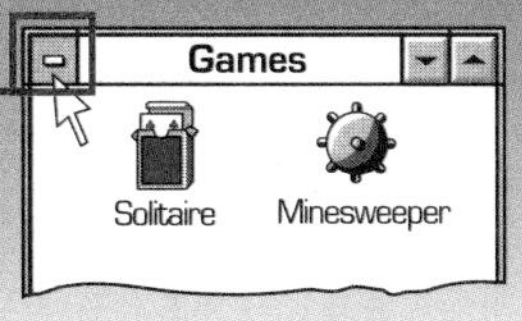

1 Double click its Control menu box ▭.

START TWO OR MORE APPLICATIONS

SWITCH BETWEEN APPLICATIONS

Start Two or More Applications

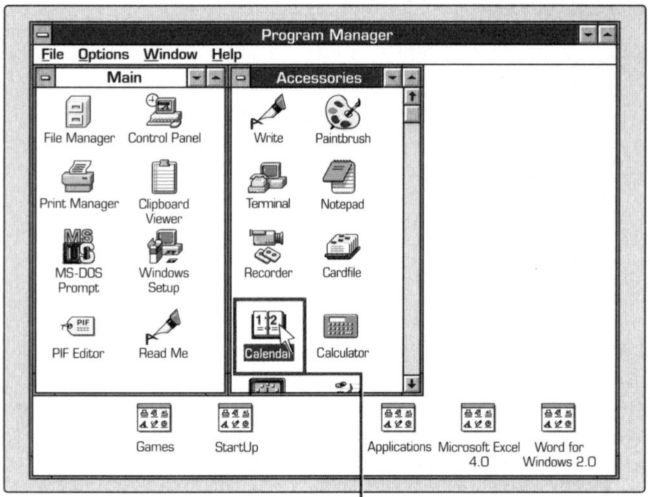

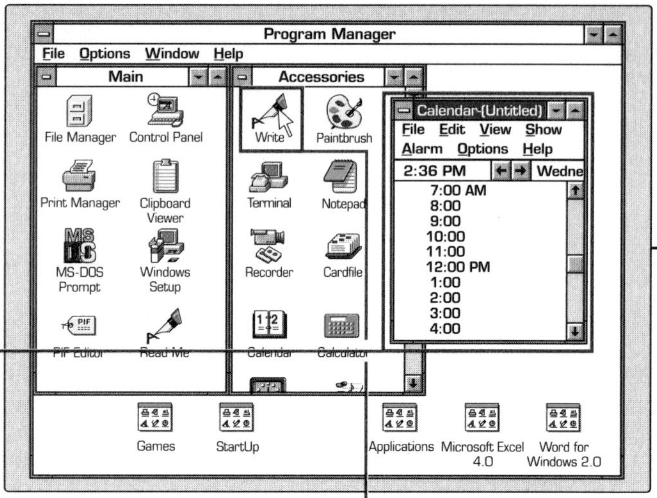

Windows can run two or more applications at the same time. For example, you can make appointments while writing a letter.

1 To start an application (example: **Calendar**), double click its icon.

2 Resize and move the application window (example: **Calendar**) as shown above.

Note: To resize a window, refer to page 8.

3 To start another application, double click its icon (example: **Write**).

Switch Between Applications

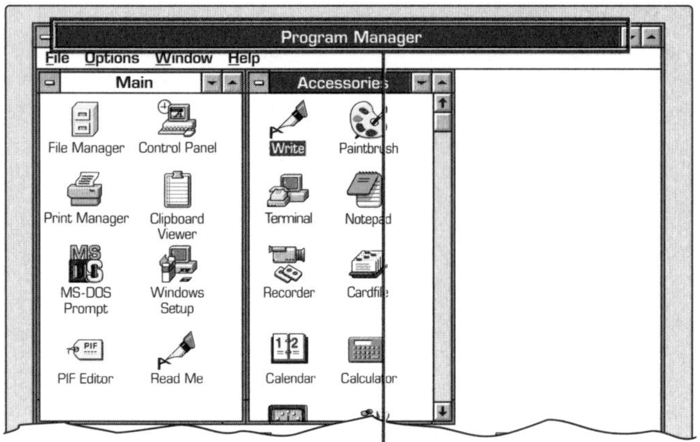

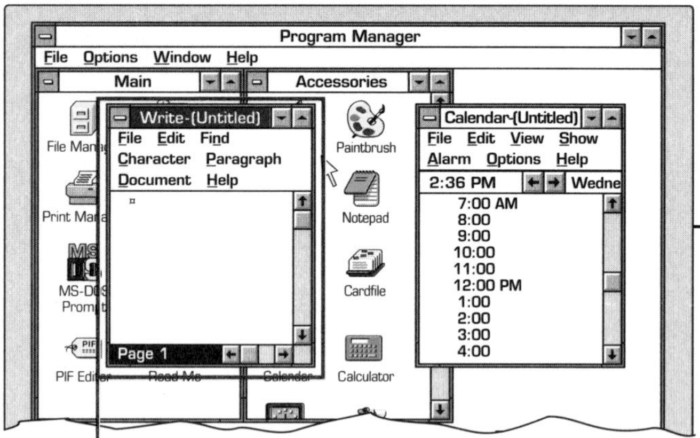

If several applications are open at the same time, some of them may be hidden. By switching between your applications you can view each one in turn.

■ The current (or active) application is indicated by a dark title bar (example: **Program Manager**).

*Note: The active application runs in the foreground. Other applications (example: **Calendar** and **Write**) run in the background.*

1 Press **Alt+Esc** until the application (example: **Write**) you want to switch to becomes active.

Shortcut

To make an application active, click in its window. This only works if the application is visible on the desktop.

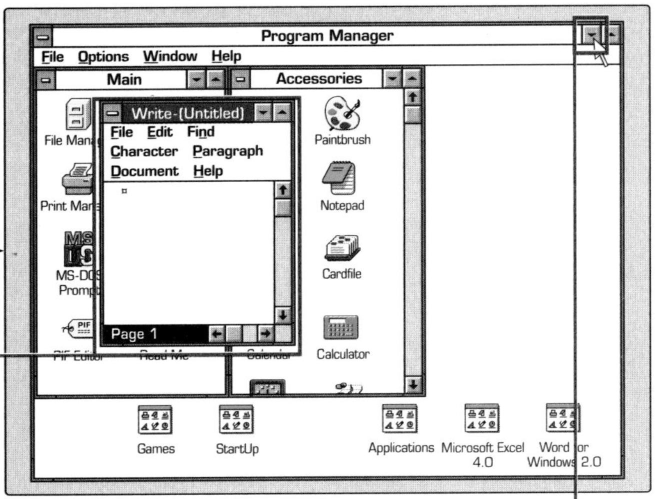

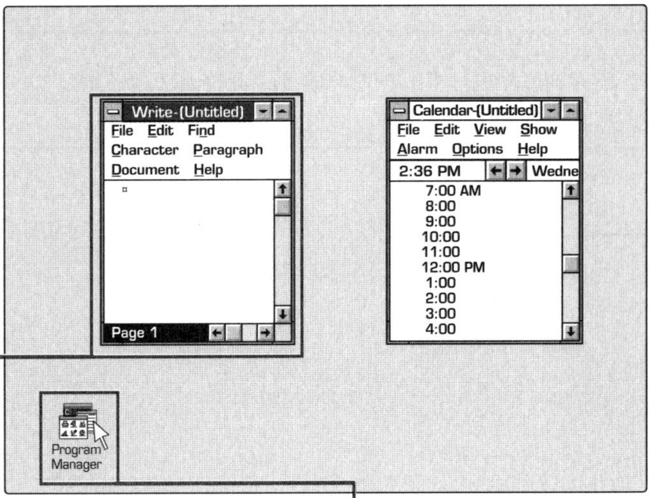

4 Resize and move the application window (example: **Write**) as shown above.

*Note: The **Calendar** window is hidden behind the **Program Manager** window.*

5 Reduce the **Program Manager** window to an icon by clicking its **Minimize** button.

*Note: All application windows can be reduced to icons by clicking their **Minimize** buttons.*

■ Both applications are running, however, only the window you are working in is active (example: **Write**).

Note: The current (or active) application is indicated by a dark title bar.

■ The **Program Manager** window can be opened by double clicking its icon.

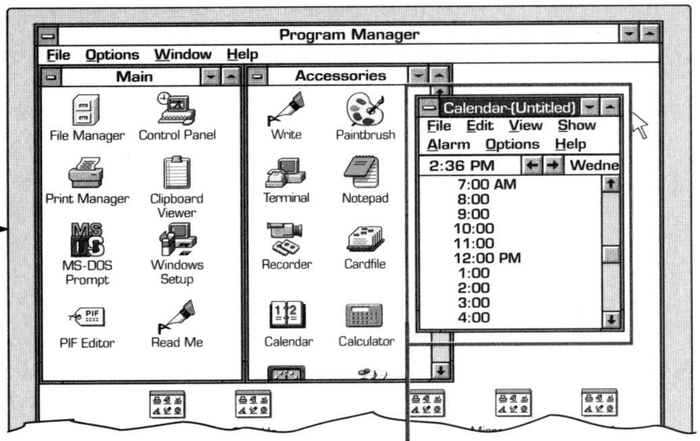

2 Press **Alt+Esc** until the next application (example: **Calendar**) you want to switch to becomes active.

Note: You can only add or edit information in the active application window.

*Note: If more than three applications are open, continue pressing **Alt+Esc** to switch through the remaining applications.*

or

*Hold down **Alt** and press **Tab** until the name of the desired application (example: **Calendar**) appears.*

*Release **Alt** and the application (example: **Calendar**) becomes active.*

USING THE TASK LIST

Switch Between Applications

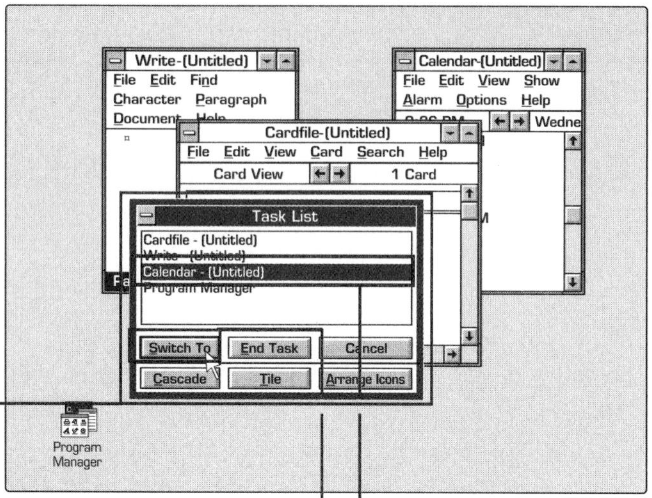

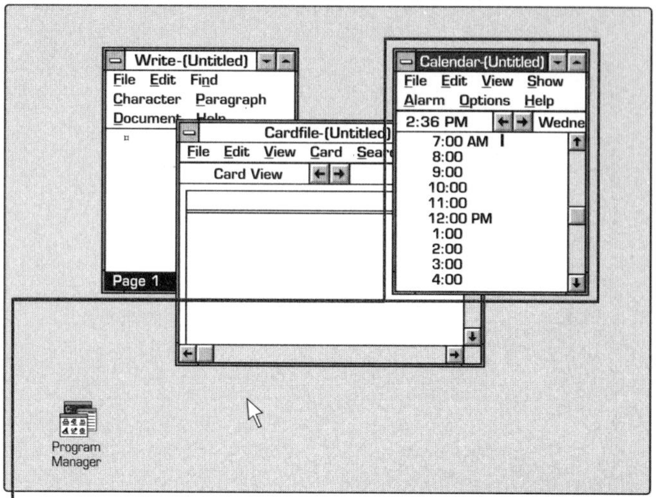

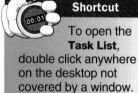

■ For this example, start the **Calendar**, **Write**, and **Cardfile** applications by double clicking their icons. Then minimize the **Program Manager** window by clicking its minimize button.

1 Press **Ctrl+Esc** and the **Task List** dialog box appears.

2 Click the application (example: **Calendar**) you would like to switch to.

3 Click the **Switch To** button, or press **Alt+S**.

■ The selected window (example: **Calendar**) moves to the foreground and becomes the active window.

*Note: To restore the **Program Manager** to a window, double click its icon.*

Shortcut

To open the **Task List**, double click anywhere on the desktop not covered by a window.

Tile or Cascade Application Windows

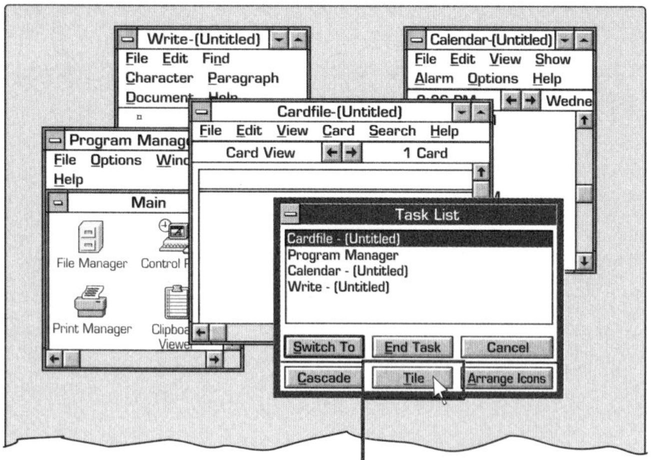

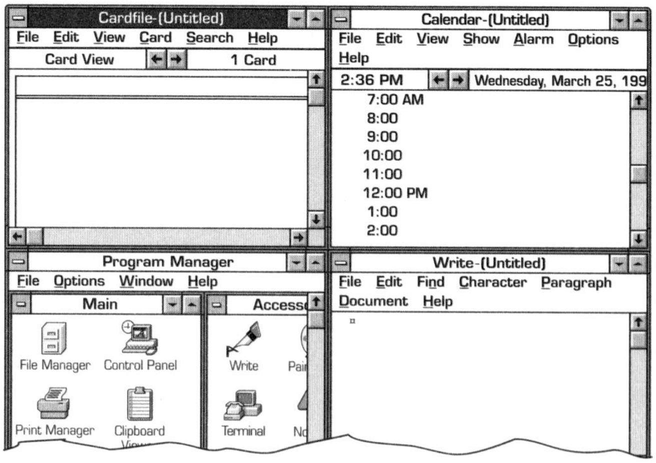

1 Press **Ctrl+Esc** and the **Task List** dialog box appears.

2 Click the **Tile** button, or press **Alt+T**.

■ The applications are tiled on the desktop.

*Note: Clicking the **Cascade** button displays all windows overlapped with their title bars showing.*

Arrange Application Icons

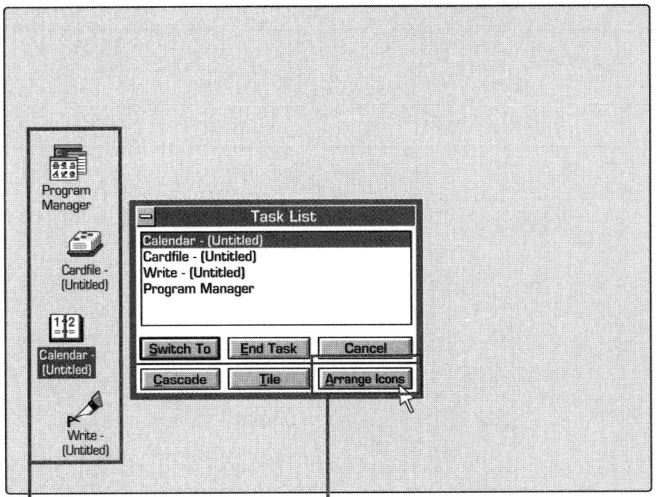

■ For this example, reduce all applications to icons by clicking their **Minimize** buttons. Then drag the icons to the locations shown above.

1 Press **Ctrl+Esc** and the **Task List** dialog box appears.

2 Click the **Arrange Icons** button, or press **Alt+A**.

■ The application icons are arranged in order along the bottom of the desktop.

Note: To restore an icon to a window, double click the icon.

End Task or Close an Application

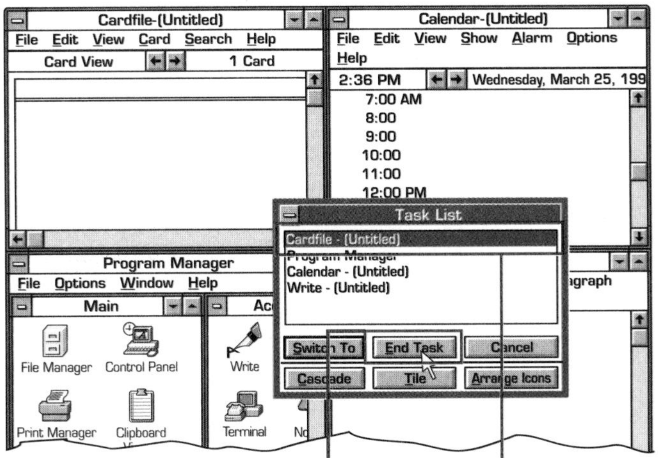

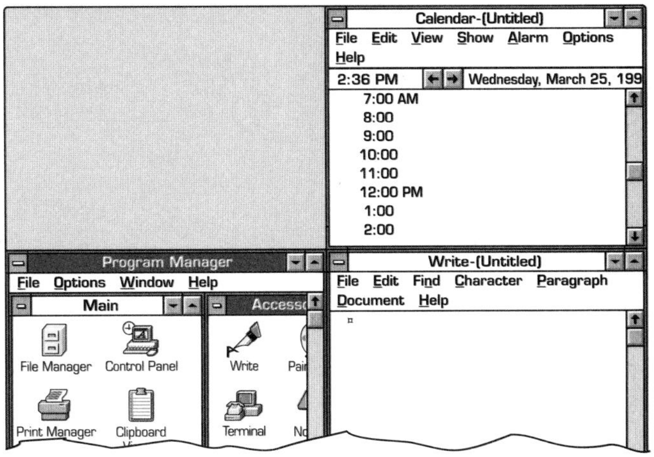

1 Press **Ctrl+Esc** and the **Task List** dialog box appears.

2 Click the application (example: **Cardfile**) you want to close.

3 Click the **End Task** button, or press **Alt+E**.

■ The application (example: **Cardfile**) is closed.

*Note: If you select an application which is minimized on the desktop, the **Task List** will still close it.*

STARTUP ON A SPECIFIC APPLICATION

Move an Application to the Startup Window

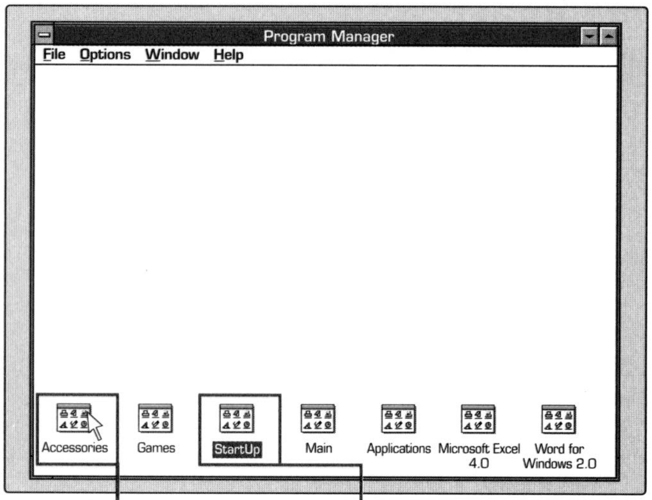

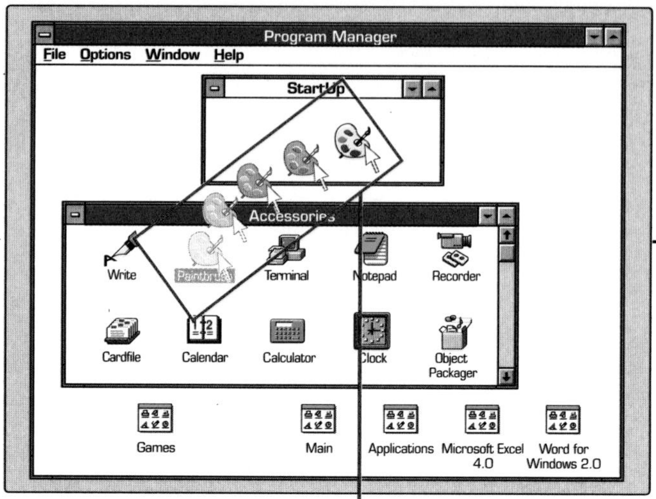

One or more applications can be automatically started when you open Windows.

If you always use the same program(s) after launching Windows, this can be a very convenient feature.

1. Double click the **Startup** Group window to open it.
2. Double click the Group window (example: **Accessories**) which contains the application you want to automatically start when Windows is opened.
3. Resize the windows as shown above.
4. Move the mouse over the desired Program item icon (example: **Paintbrush**). Click and hold down the left button as you drag the icon into the **Startup** Group window.

Start an Application when you Open Windows

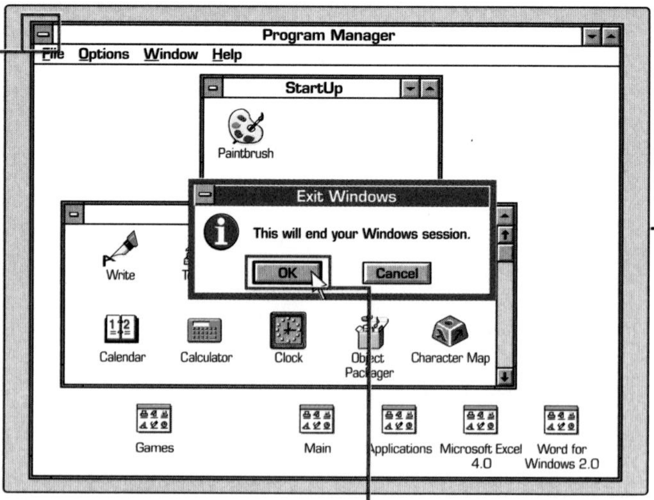

1. To exit Windows, double click the **Program Manager**'s Control menu box and the **Exit Windows** dialog box appears.
2. Click the **OK** button.

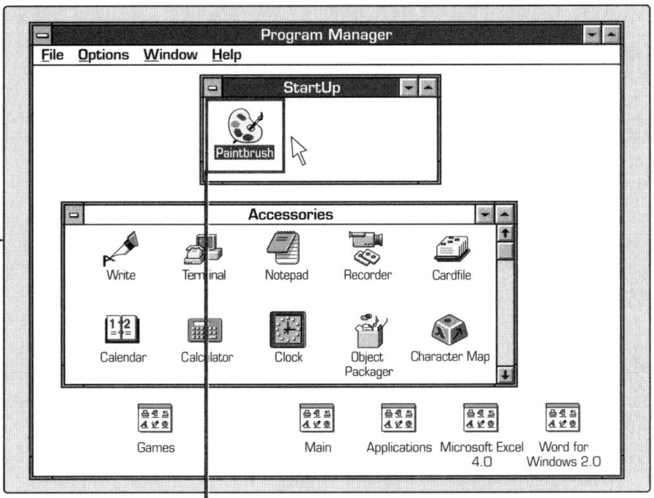

5 Release the button and the icon (example: **Paintbrush**) stays at its new position.

*Note: Multiple program item icons can be dragged into the **Startup** Group window.*

COPY OR MOVE A PROGRAM ITEM ICON

To **copy** a Program item icon from one Group window to another, hold down **Ctrl** and drag the icon between the windows. Release the button and then **Ctrl**.

To **move** a Program item icon from one Group window to another, drag the icon between the windows.

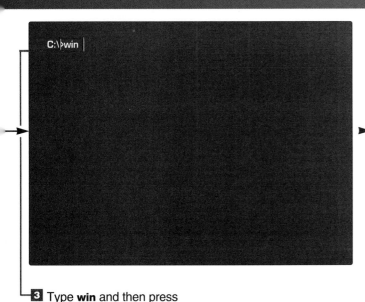

3 Type **win** and then press **Enter** to start **Windows**.

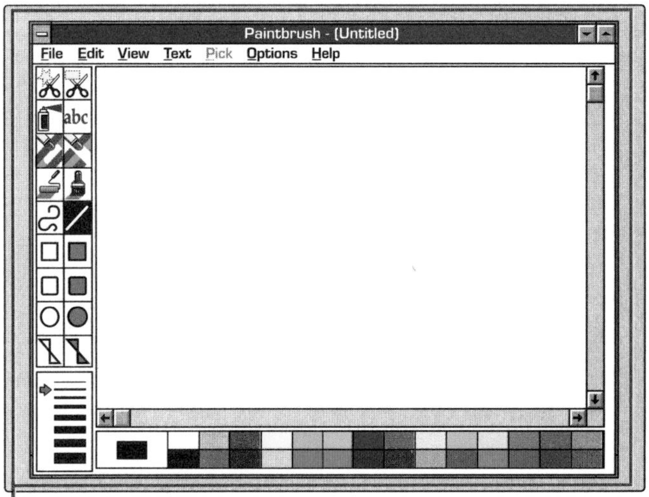

■ The application (example: **Paintbrush**) is automatically opened.

Note: To close an application, double click its Control menu box ▭.

WINDOWS BASICS • MANAGING YOUR PROGRAMS • MANAGING YOUR DIRECTORIES • CREATING A FILE • OBJECT LINKING AND EMBEDDING • MANAGING YOUR FILES • MANAGING YOUR DISKS • HELP

FILES AND DIRECTORIES

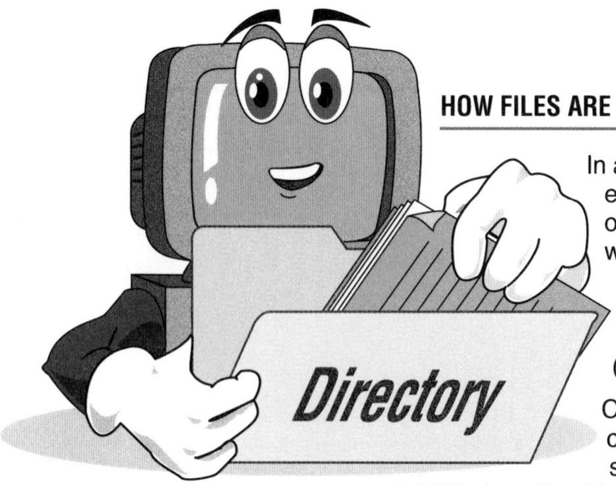

HOW FILES ARE SPECIFIED

In an efficient and productive office environment, people create, edit, review and organize paper documents (example: letters, worksheets, reports, etc.). These documents are stored in folders, which in turn are placed in cabinets. To retrieve a specific document, you must identify it by location (cabinet and folder) and then by name.

Computers work the same way. After creating a document, it must be named and saved. During the save process, you must tell Windows the drive (cabinet) and directory (folder) the file is to reside in.

Windows lets you create a multilevel directory filing system to store and retrieve your programs and data files. The first level of this directory structure is called the root directory. From this directory other subdirectories can be created. A typical multilevel filing system is illustrated on the next page.

Note: The terms "directory" and "subdirectory" are used interchangeably. The "root directory" is the only "directory" that cannot be called a "subdirectory".

File Specification

A file is specified by describing its drive, path and name (filename and extension).

C: \DATA\EXLDATA\ INCOME1Q .XLS

DRIVE

Tells Windows the drive the file is in.

PATH

Tells Windows the path through the directory structure to get to the file location.

FILENAME

The filename can contain up to 8 characters.

EXTENSION

The extension can contain up to 3 characters. In some cases, it is omitted.

Note: The first backslash (\) specifies the path to the root directory. Subsequent backslashes (\) are used to separate directories and the filename.

THE FOLLOWING CHARACTERS ARE ALLOWED:

- The letters A to Z, upper or lower case
- The digits 0 through 9
- The underscore (_) and hyphen (-) characters
- The filename cannot contain a . (period) or blank spaces

Using Directories to Organize your Files

Directories can contain files and/or paths to other directories (example: the root directory has paths to four subdirectories).

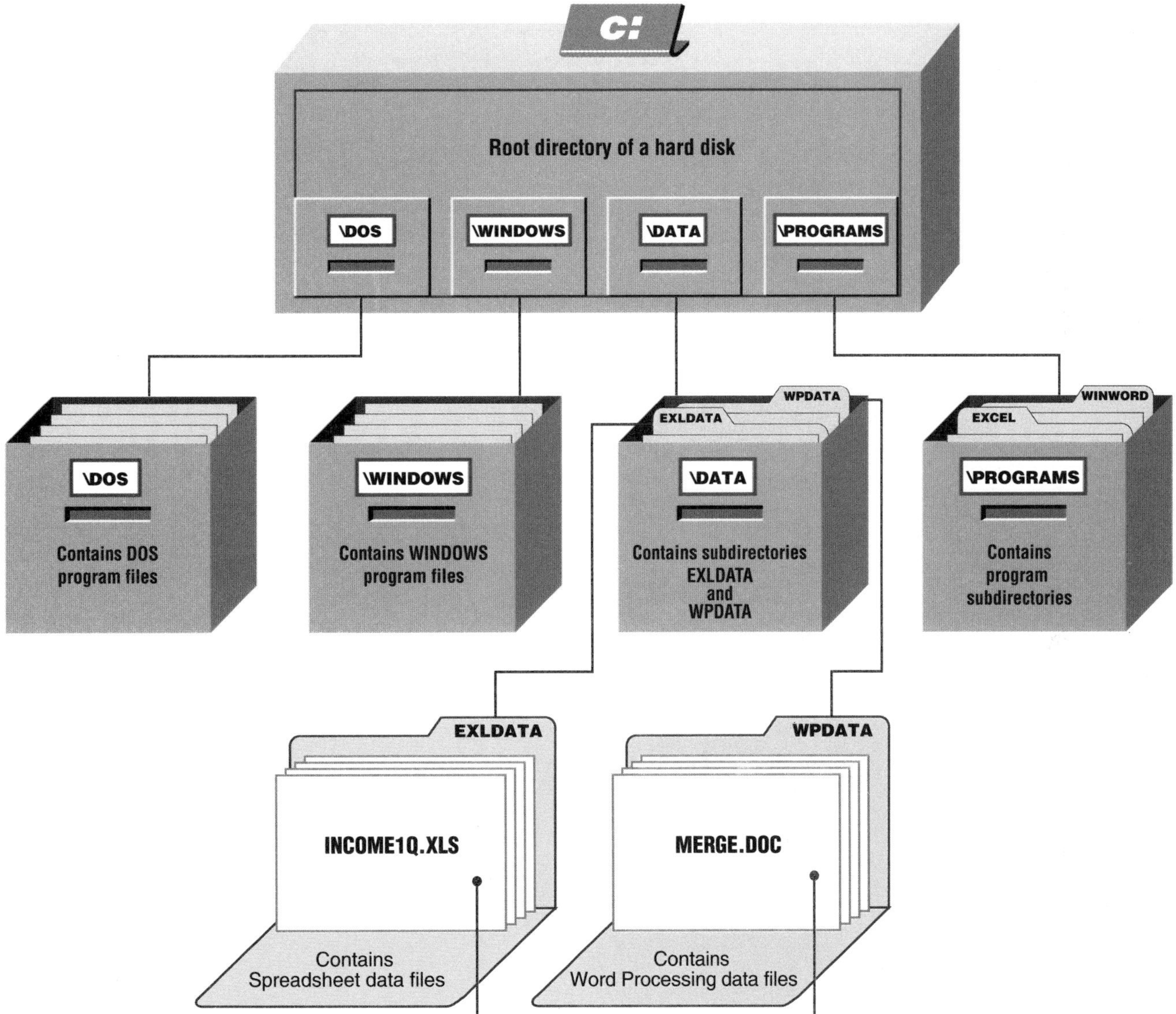

The file specification for this data file is:

C:\DATA\EXLDATA\INCOME1Q.XLS

The file specification for this data file is:

C:\DATA\WPDATA\MERGE.DOC

OPEN THE FILE MANAGER

The File Manager helps you create, organize and manage your files and directories.

1 To open the **File Manager**, double click its icon.

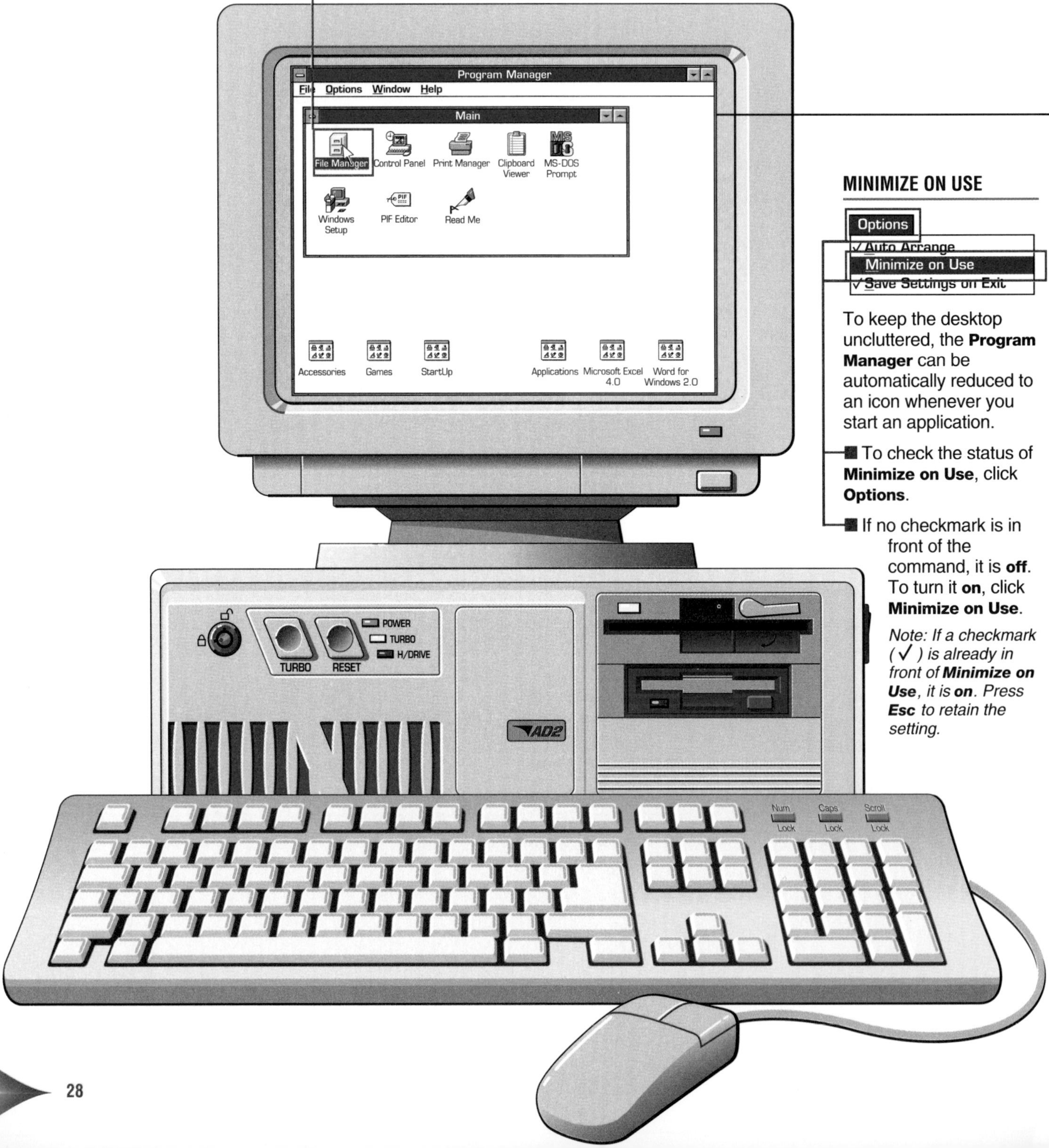

MINIMIZE ON USE

To keep the desktop uncluttered, the **Program Manager** can be automatically reduced to an icon whenever you start an application.

■ To check the status of **Minimize on Use**, click **Options**.

■ If no checkmark is in front of the command, it is **off**. To turn it **on**, click **Minimize on Use**.

*Note: If a checkmark (✓) is already in front of **Minimize on Use**, it is **on**. Press **Esc** to retain the setting.*

DISK DRIVE ICONS

Each floppy or hard drive on the computer is represented by an icon and drive letter.

a – represents disk drive A

b – represents disk drive B

c – represents hard drive C

The outlined icon (example: **drive c**) is the current drive.

DIRECTORY PATH

The directory path describes the path through the directory structure to get to the current directory. The current path is **C:**.

VOLUME LABEL

You can assign a name to each drive on the computer. The volume label name (example: **HARDDRIVE**) appears within the [ ] brackets. Naming the drives is optional.

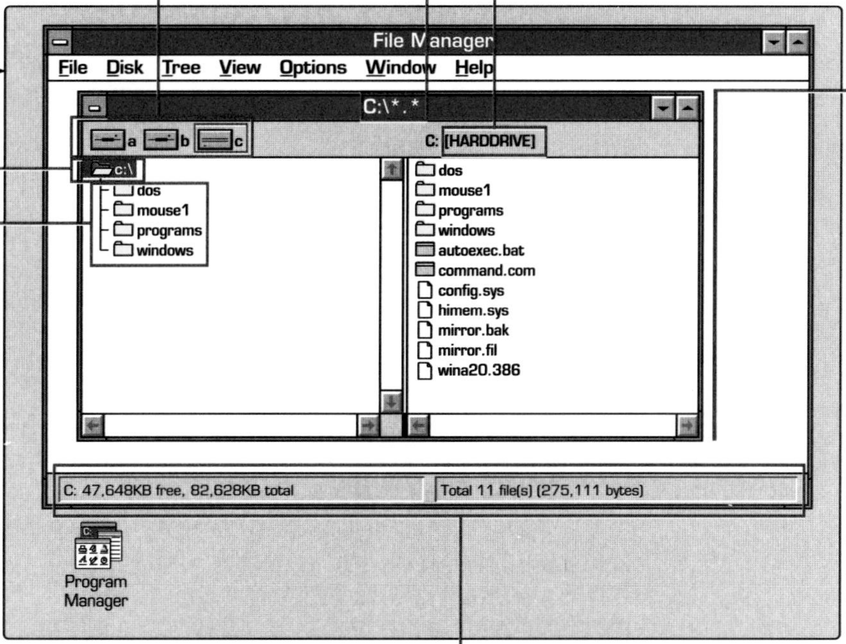

This window visually displays the organization of all directories on the current drive. It also displays the files in the current directory.

DIRECTORY ICONS

Each directory is represented by a folder. The directory folders are sorted alphabetically in ascending order.

CURRENT DIRECTORY

File Manager commands only work on the current directory. The current directory is the highlighted folder.

STATUS BAR

The status bar displays the number of available bytes, as well as the total number of bytes on the current drive. The status bar also displays the number of files in the current directory, and the total number of bytes they contain. A byte represents one character.

CHANGE SCREEN FONT

Change Screen Font (Example 1)

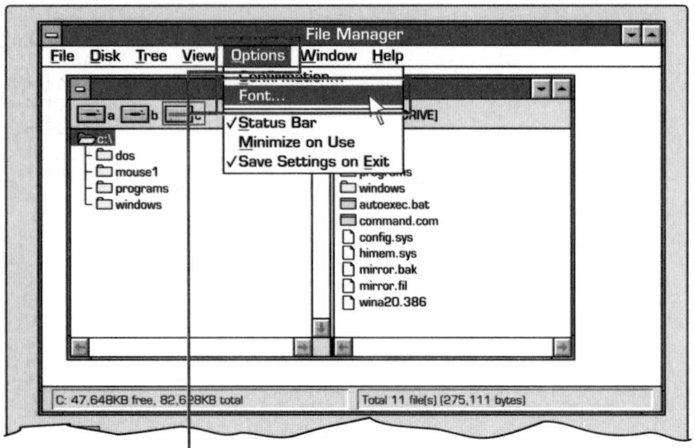

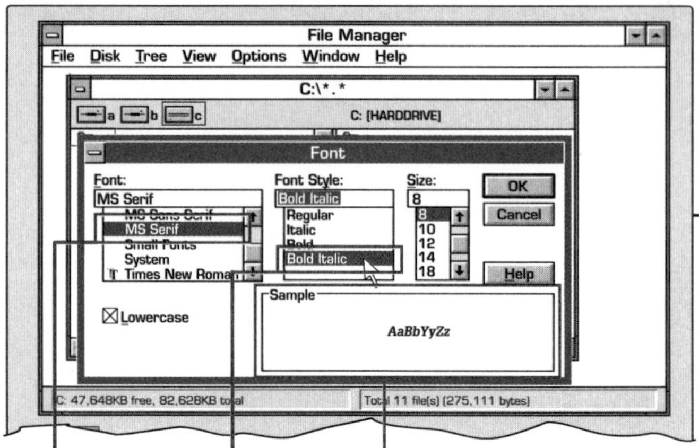

A font specifies the design and size of displayed characters. Depending on your personal preference, a wide variety of display choices are available to you.

1 Click **Options** and its menu appears.

2 Click **Font** and the **Font** dialog box appears on the next screen.

3 Click the desired font (example: **MS Serif**).

Note: Click the up ⬆ or down ⬇ scroll arrow to view more fonts.

4 Click the desired font style (example: **Bold Italic**).

■ A sample of the chosen font appears in the **Sample** box.

Change Screen Font (Example 2)

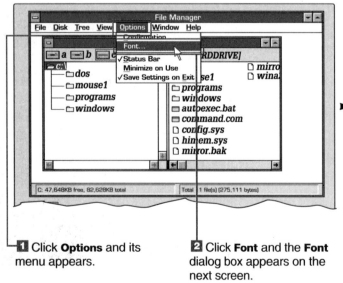

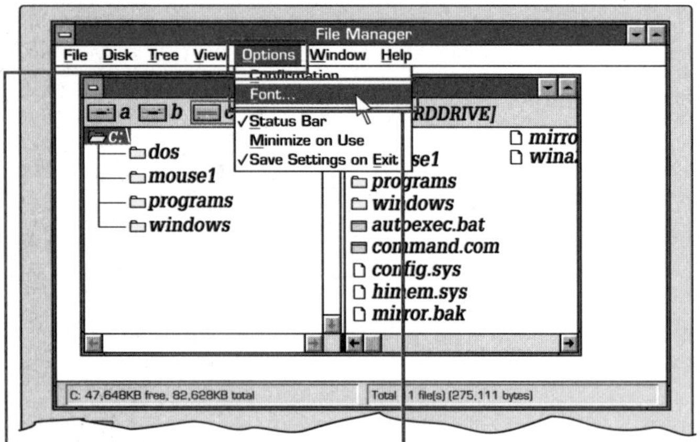

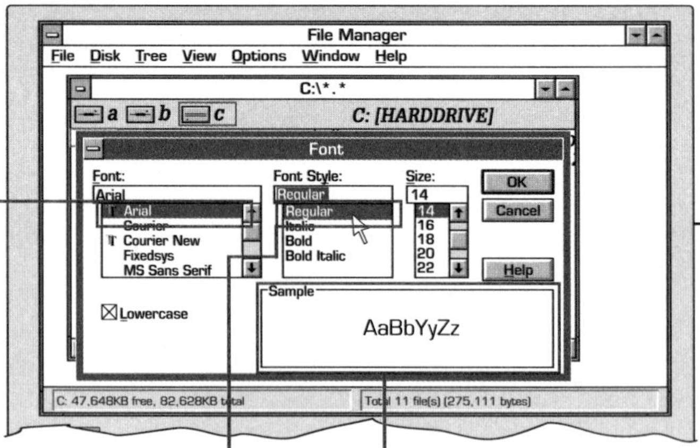

1 Click **Options** and its menu appears.

2 Click **Font** and the **Font** dialog box appears on the next screen.

3 Click the desired font (example: **Arial**).

Note: Click the up ⬆ or down ⬇ scroll arrow to view more fonts.

4 Click the desired font style (example: **Regular**).

■ A sample of the chosen font appears in the **Sample** box.

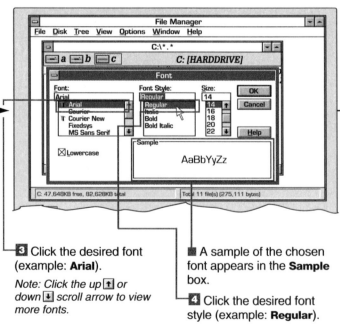

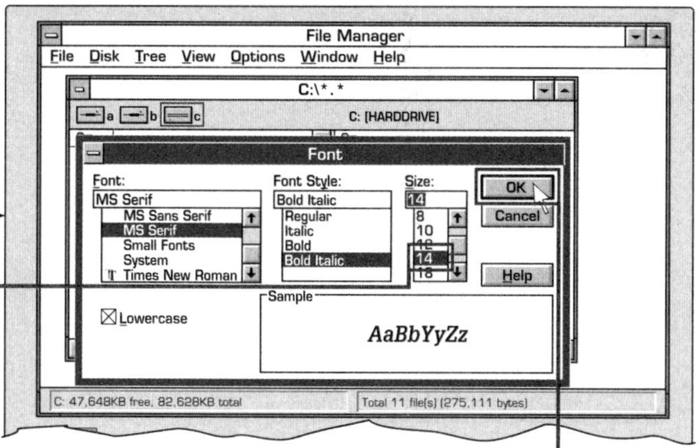

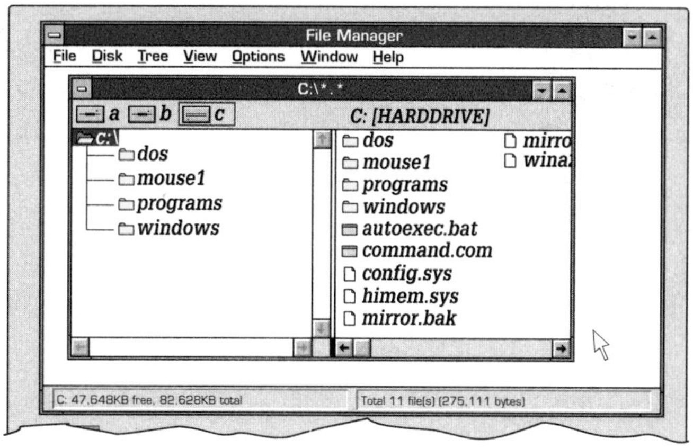

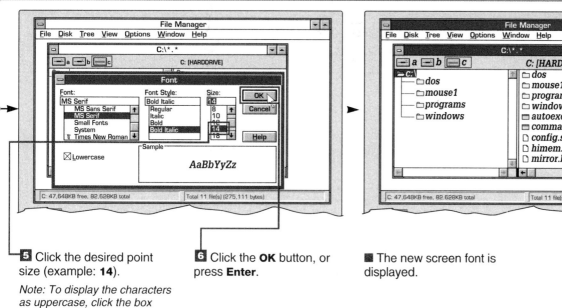

5 Click the desired point size (example: **14**).

Note: To display the characters as uppercase, click the box beside ***Lowercase*** *to turn it* ***off*** *and ☒ becomes ☐. To turn it* ***on****, click the box again.*

6 Click the **OK** button, or press **Enter**.

■ The new screen font is displayed.

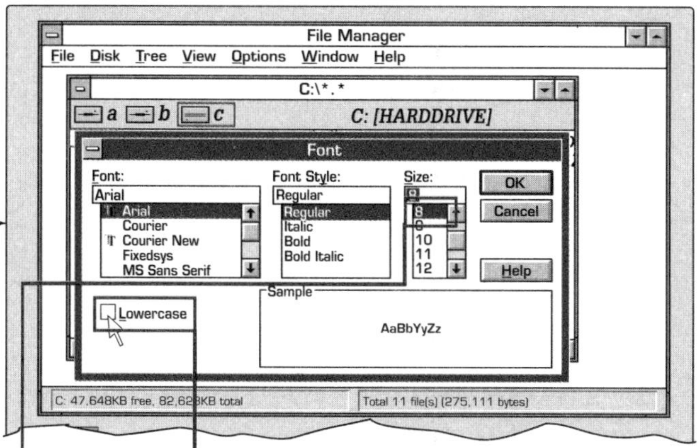

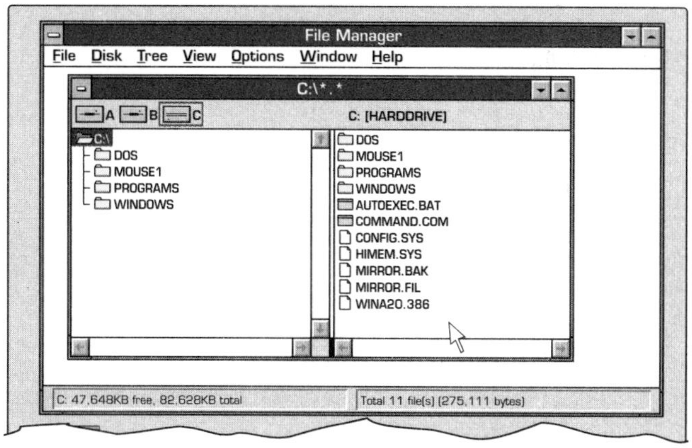

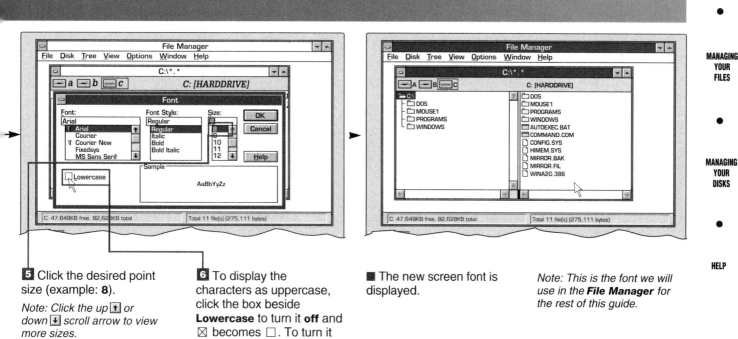

5 Click the desired point size (example: **8**).

Note: Click the up ⇧ or down ⇩ scroll arrow to view more sizes.

6 To display the characters as uppercase, click the box beside **Lowercase** to turn it **off** and ☒ becomes ☐. To turn it **on**, click the box again.

7 Press **Enter**.

■ The new screen font is displayed.

Note: This is the font we will use in the ***File Manager*** *for the rest of this guide.*

CHANGE DISK DRIVES | CHANGE DIRECTORIES | INDICATE EXPANDABLE BRANCHES

A B C Change Disk Drives

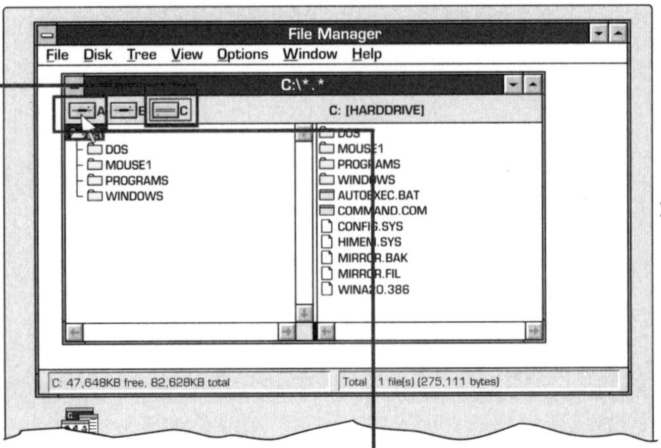

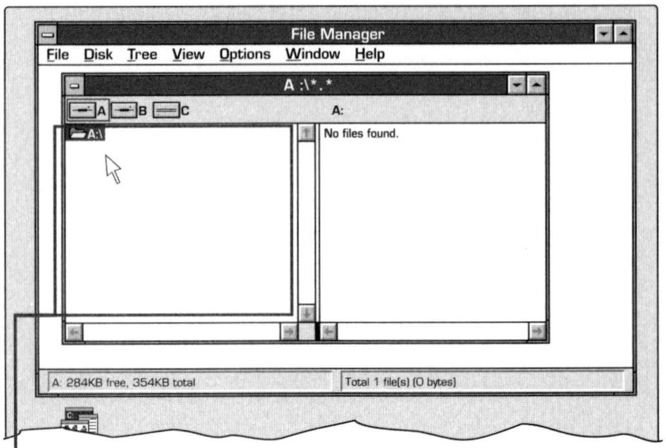

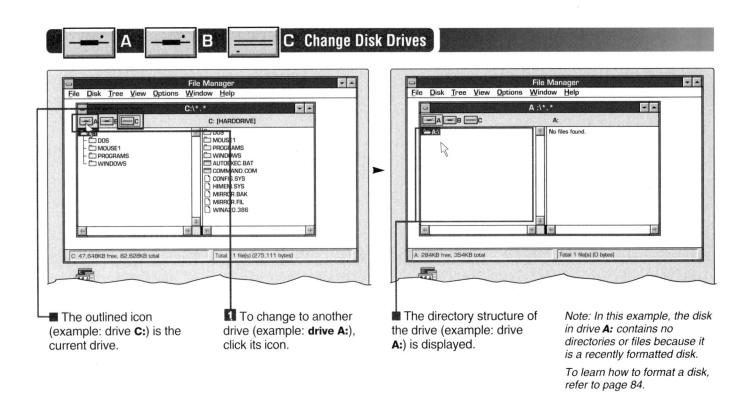

■ The outlined icon (example: drive **C:**) is the current drive.

1 To change to another drive (example: **drive A:**), click its icon.

■ The directory structure of the drive (example: drive **A:**) is displayed.

Note: In this example, the disk in drive ***A:*** *contains no directories or files because it is a recently formatted disk.*

To learn how to format a disk, refer to page 84.

Change Directories

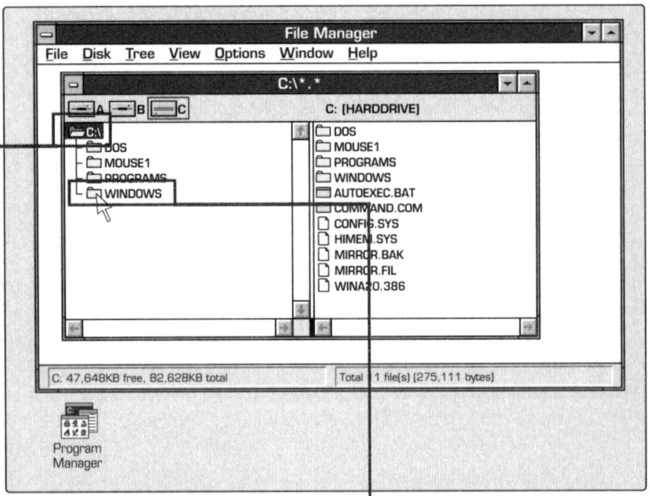

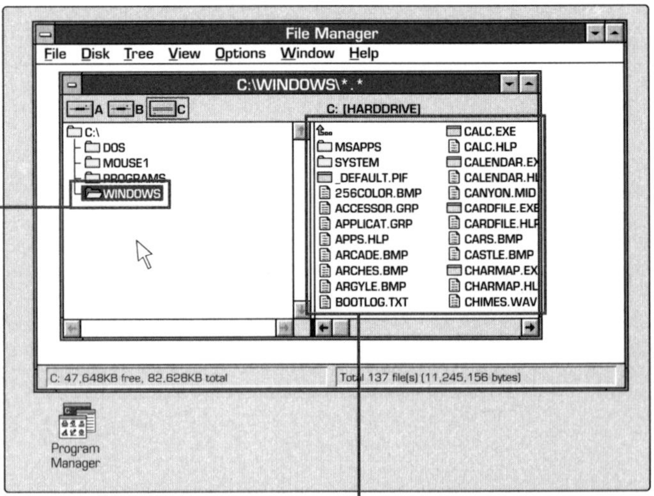

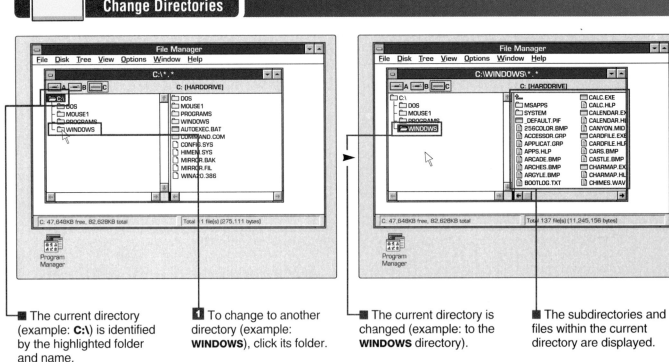

■ The current directory (example: **C:**) is identified by the highlighted folder and name.

1 To change to another directory (example: **WINDOWS**), click its folder.

■ The current directory is changed (example: to the **WINDOWS** directory).

■ The subdirectories and files within the current directory are displayed.

Indicate Expandable Branches

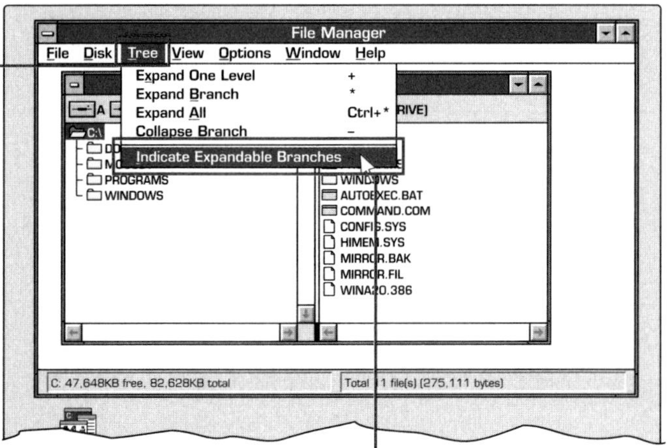

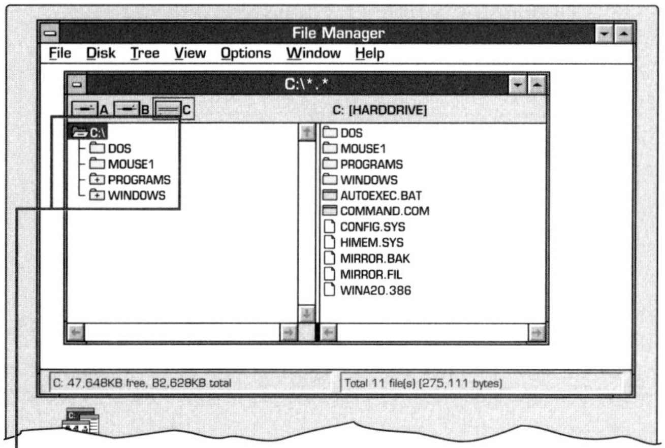

1 To turn on **Indicate Expandable Branches**, click **Tree** to open its menu.

■ If no checkmark (✓) is in front of **Indicate Expandable Branches**, it is **off**.

2 To turn it **on**, click **Indicate Expandable Branches**.

*Note: When **Indicate Expandable Branches** is **on**, the **File Manager** takes longer to display a large directory tree.*

■ Expandable branches are indicated.

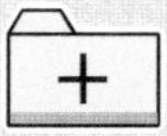

A plus sign (+) within a folder indicates that the directory contains one or more subdirectories.

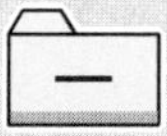

A minus sign (-) within a folder indicates that the directory is already expanded.

No sign within a folder indicates that the directory has no subdirectories.

KEYBOARD SHORTCUTS

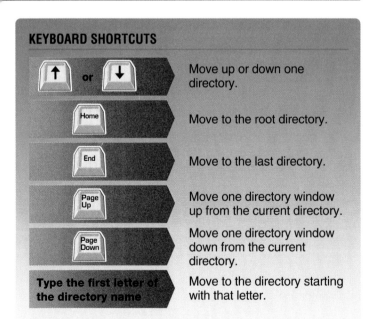

↑ or ↓	Move up or down one directory.
Home	Move to the root directory.
End	Move to the last directory.
Page Up	Move one directory window up from the current directory.
Page Down	Move one directory window down from the current directory.
Type the first letter of the directory name	Move to the directory starting with that letter.

*Note: To use the numeric keypad's arrows (PgUp, PgDn, Home and End keys), **NumLock** must be **off**.*

*If the **NumLock** status light is **on**, press **NumLock** to turn it **off**.*

CREATE DIRECTORIES

All examples in this guide are based on the directory structure illustrated below:

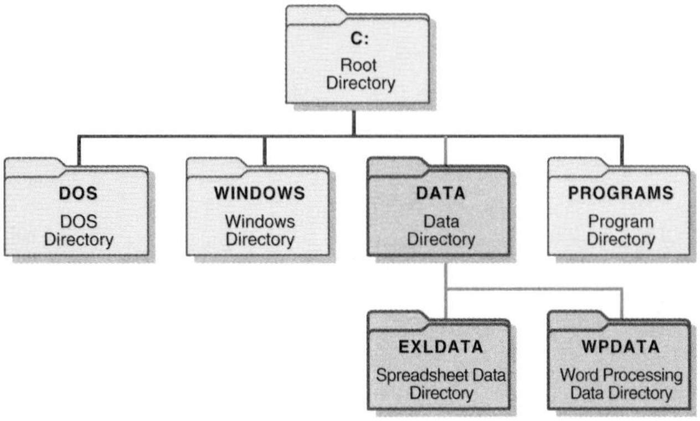

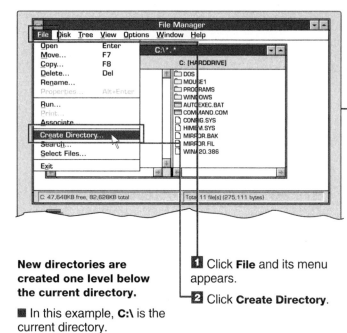

Create the Data Directory

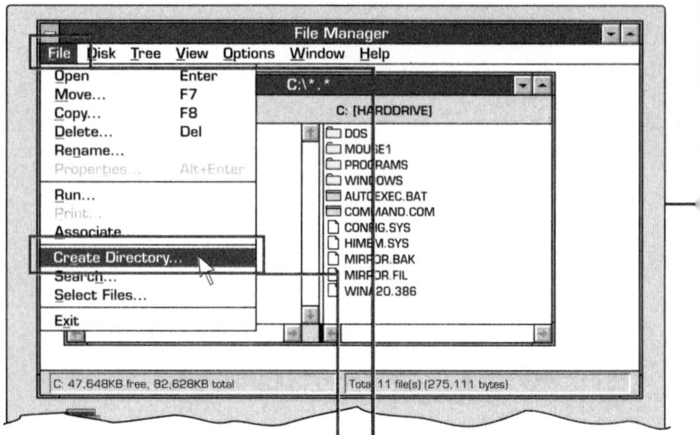

New directories are created one level below the current directory.

■ In this example, **C:** is the current directory.

1 Click **File** and its menu appears.

2 Click **Create Directory**.

Create the EXLDATA and WPDATA Directories

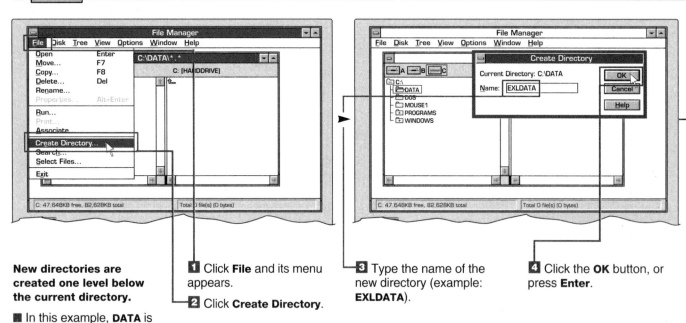

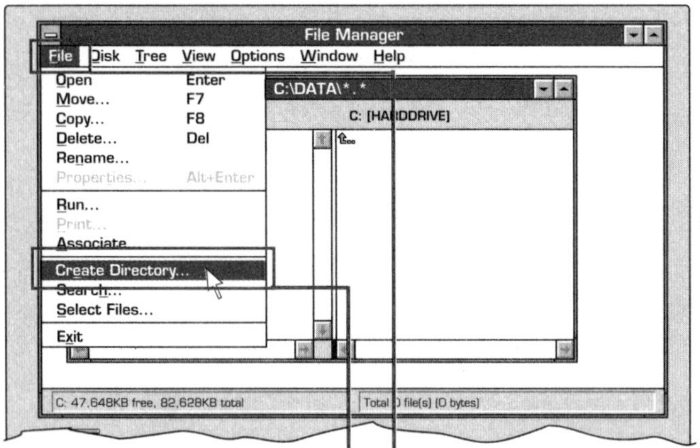

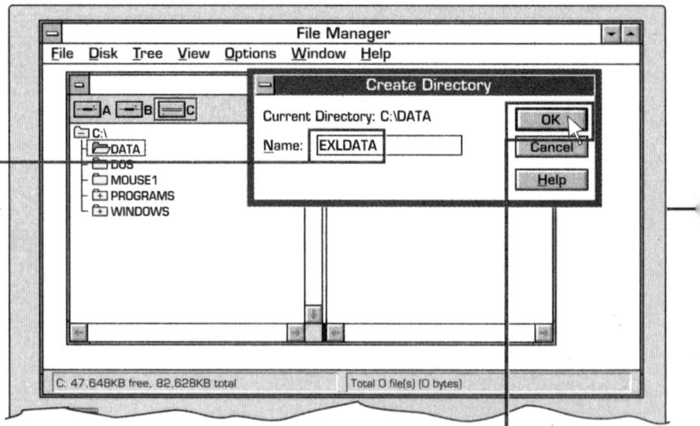

New directories are created one level below the current directory.

■ In this example, **DATA** is the current directory.

1 Click **File** and its menu appears.

2 Click **Create Directory**.

3 Type the name of the new directory (example: **EXLDATA**).

4 Click the **OK** button, or press **Enter**.

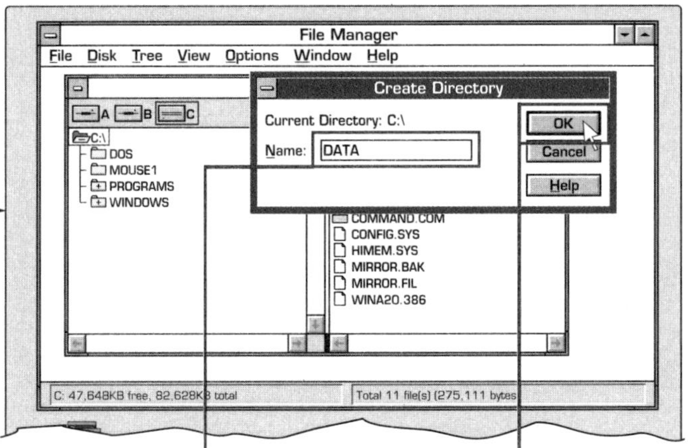

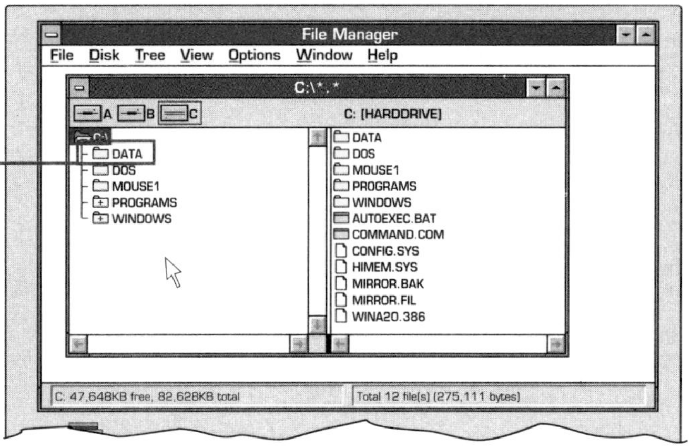

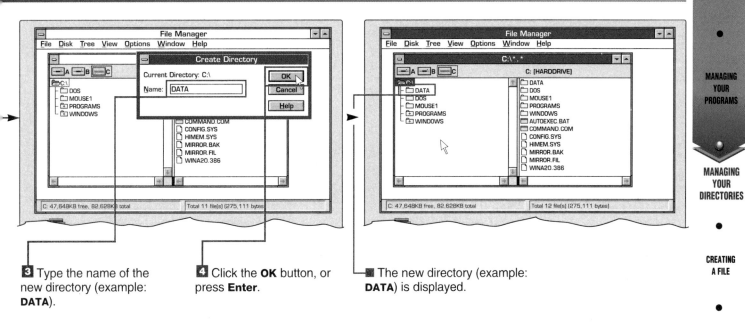

3 Type the name of the new directory (example: **DATA**).

4 Click the **OK** button, or press **Enter**.

■ The new directory (example: **DATA**) is displayed.

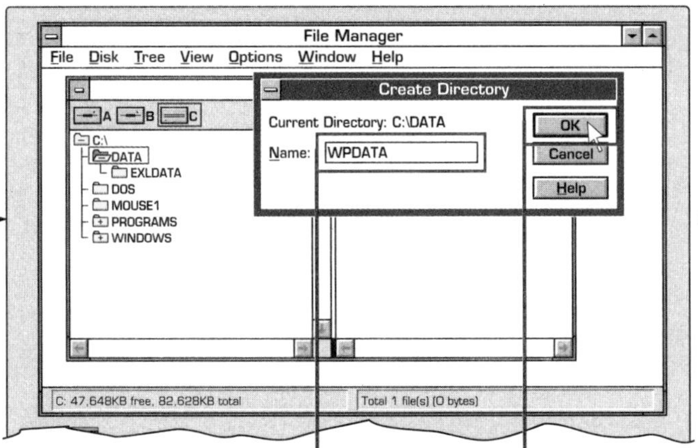

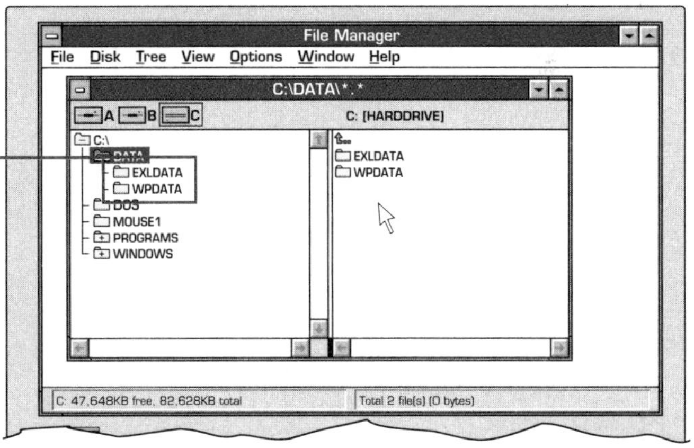

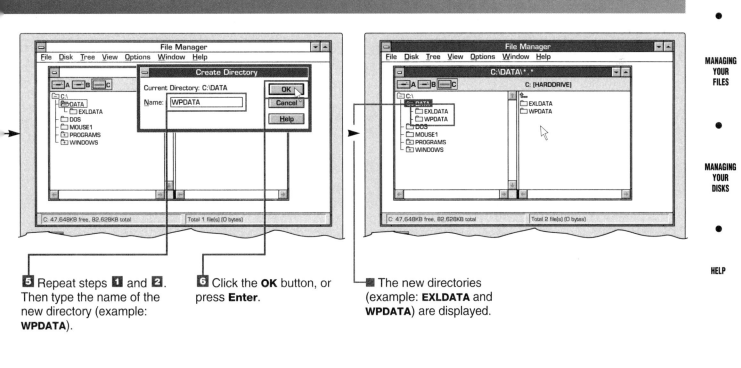

5 Repeat steps **1** and **2**. Then type the name of the new directory (example: **WPDATA**).

6 Click the **OK** button, or press **Enter**.

■ The new directories (example: **EXLDATA** and **WPDATA**) are displayed.

EXPAND OR COLLAPSE DIRECTORY LEVELS

Collapse an Entire Branch

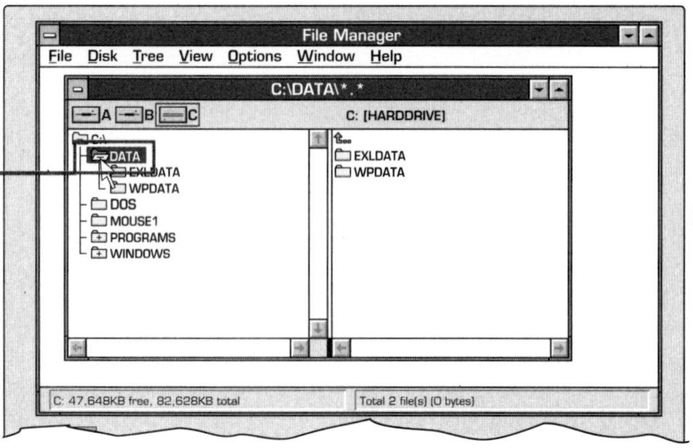

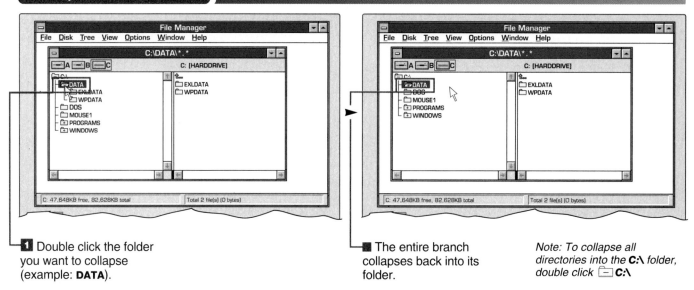

1 Double click the folder you want to collapse (example: **DATA**).

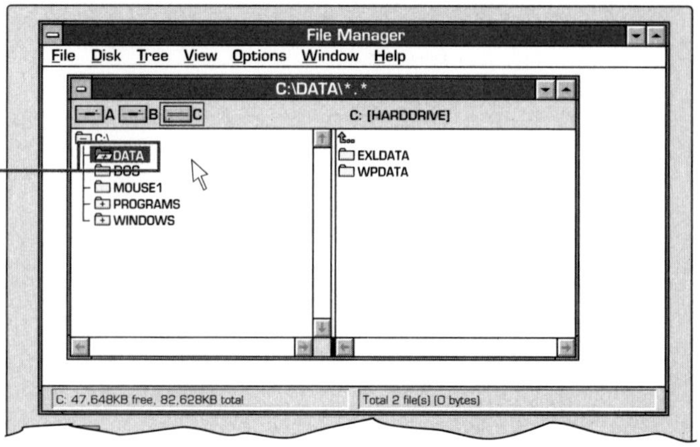

■ The entire branch collapses back into its folder.

Note: To collapse all directories into the **C:** *folder, double click* **C:**

Expand One Level of a Directory

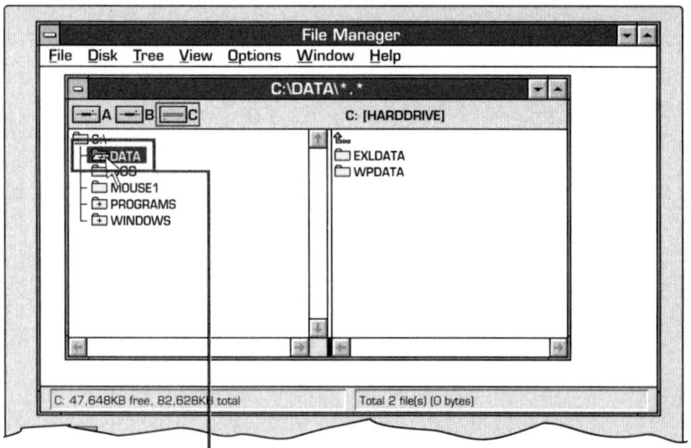

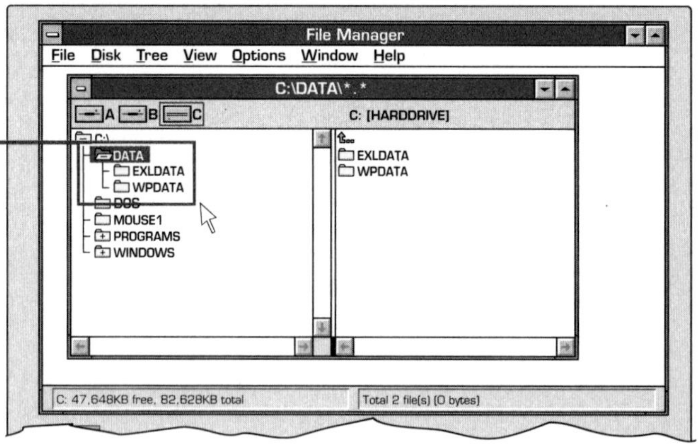

The (+) sign within a folder indicates that the directory contains one or more subdirectories.

Note: To display plus (+) and minus (-) signs within folders, refer to page 33.

1 Double click the folder of the directory you want to expand (example: **DATA**).

■ The folder is expanded to display its subdirectories (example: **EXLDATA** and **WPDATA**).

Note: The (-) sign within a folder indicates that the directory is already expanded.

Expand an Entire Branch

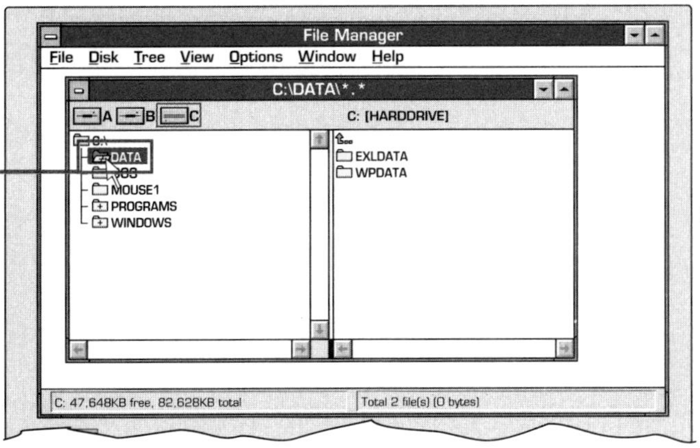

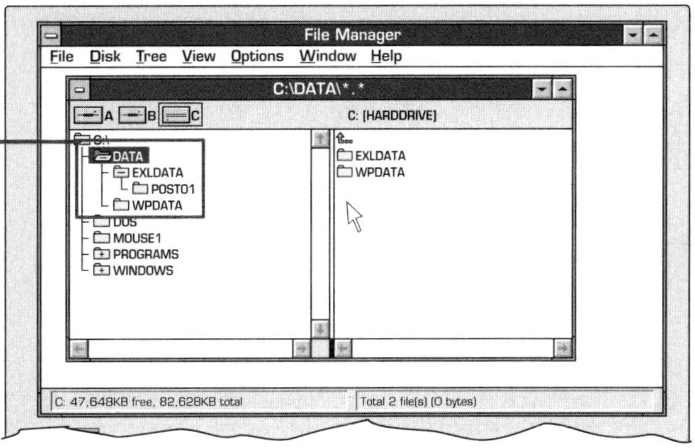

1 Select the directory you want to expand (example: **DATA**).

2 Press * (asterisk) and the entire branch of subdirectories under the selected folder is displayed.

Note: The subdirectory ***POST01*** *was created the same way as the* ***EXLDATA*** *and* ***WPDATA*** *subdirectories. Refer to page 34.*

Expand All Branches

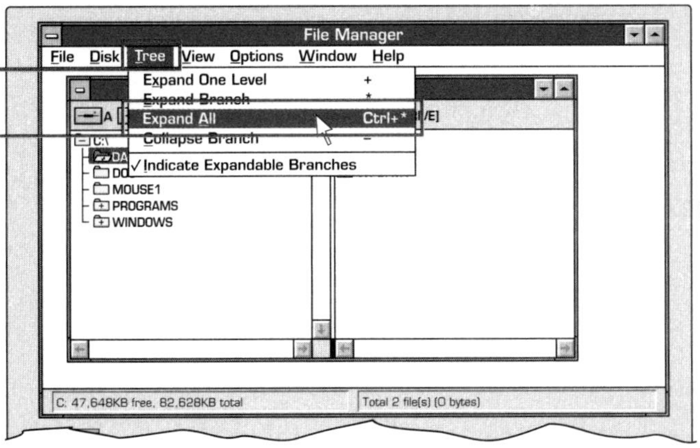

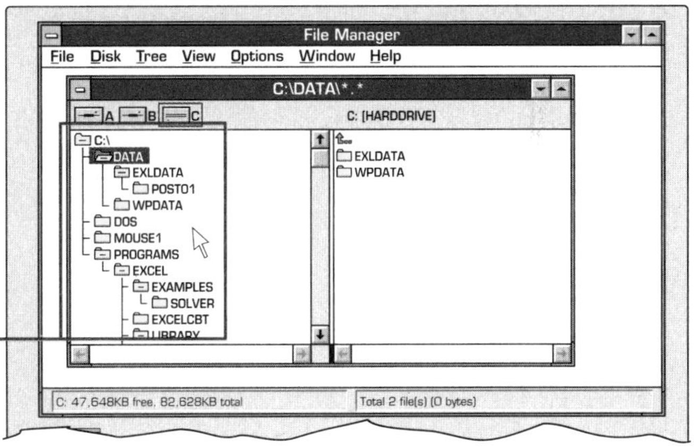

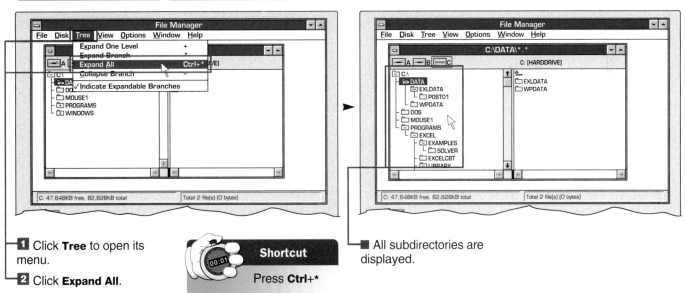

1 Click **Tree** to open its menu.

2 Click **Expand All**.

Shortcut

Press **Ctrl+***

■ All subdirectories are displayed.

MOVE OR COPY DIRECTORIES

Move a Directory within the Same Drive

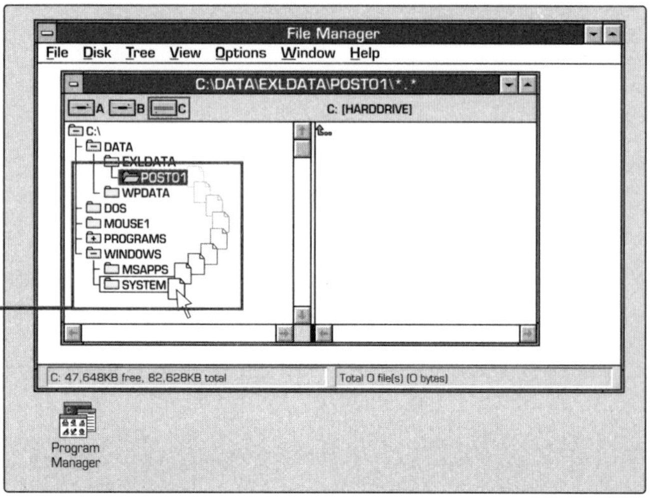

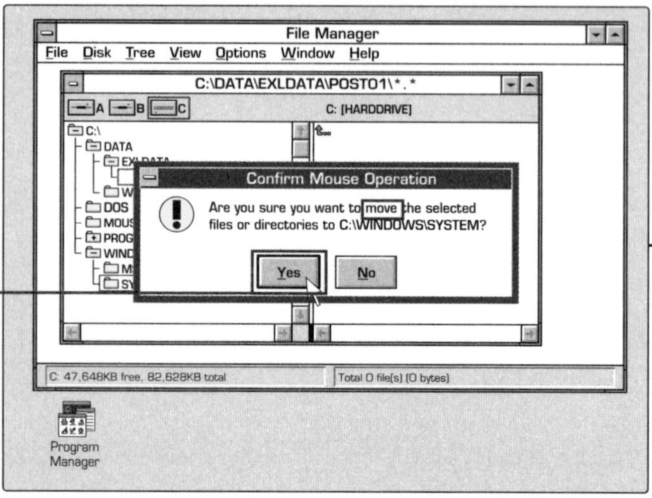

1 Drag the directory you want to move (example: **POST01**) to a new location.

2 When a rectangle appears around the destination directory (example: SYSTEM), release the mouse button.

3 To move the directory, click the **Yes** button.

*Note: To cancel the move, click the **No** button.*

Moving a directory can cause a problem if your autoexec.bat file contains a path command to that directory. Check with a system specialist before using this feature.

Copy Directories within the Same Drive

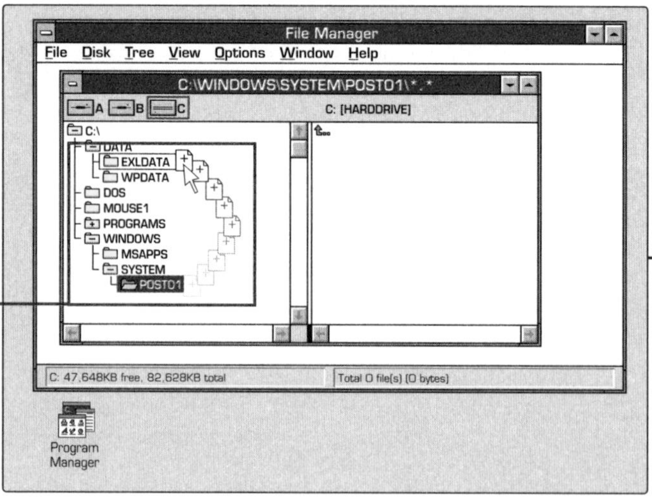

1 Hold down **Ctrl** while you drag the directory you want to copy (example: **POST01**) to a new location.

2 When a rectangle appears around the destination directory (example: EXLDATA), release the mouse button, then release **Ctrl**.

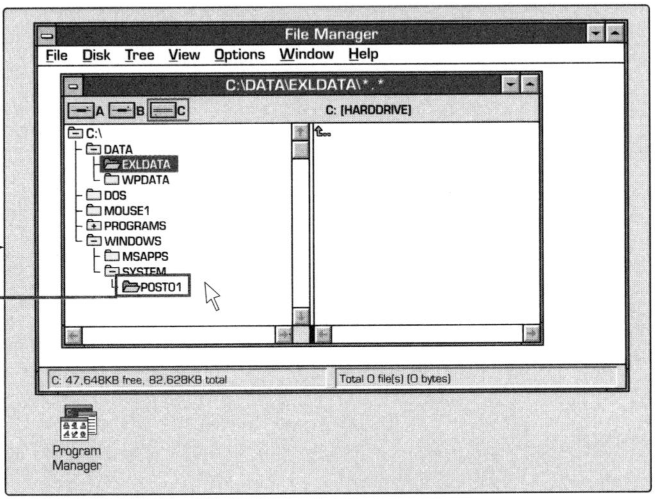

■ The directory (example: **POST01**) is moved.

Note: If the moved directory contained files, they would be moved at the same time.

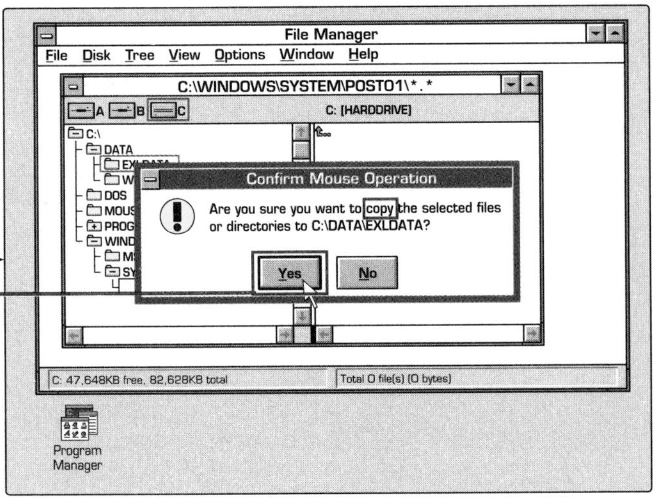

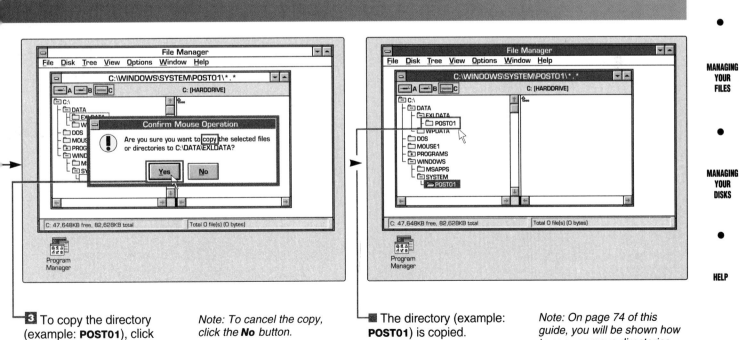

3 To copy the directory (example: **POST01**), click the **Yes** button.

*Note: To cancel the copy, click the **No** button.*

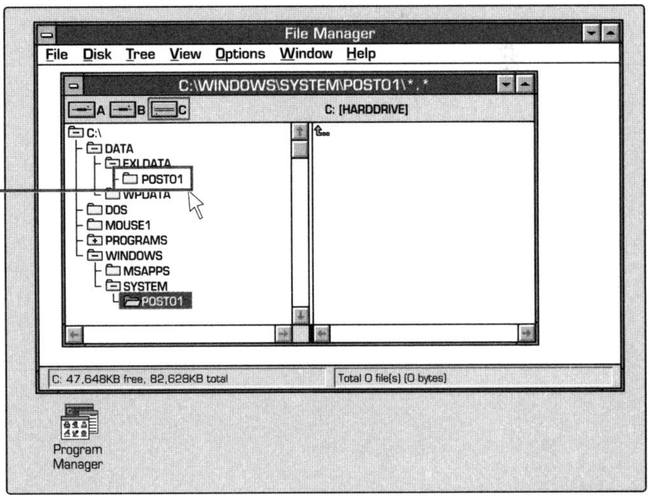

■ The directory (example: **POST01**) is copied.

Note: If the copied directory contained files, they would be copied at the same time.

Note: On page 74 of this guide, you will be shown how to copy or move directories to a different drive.

DELETE A DIRECTORY

Delete a Directory

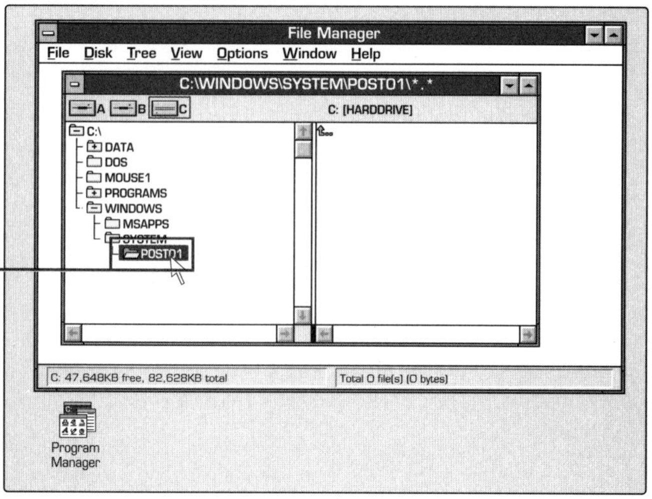

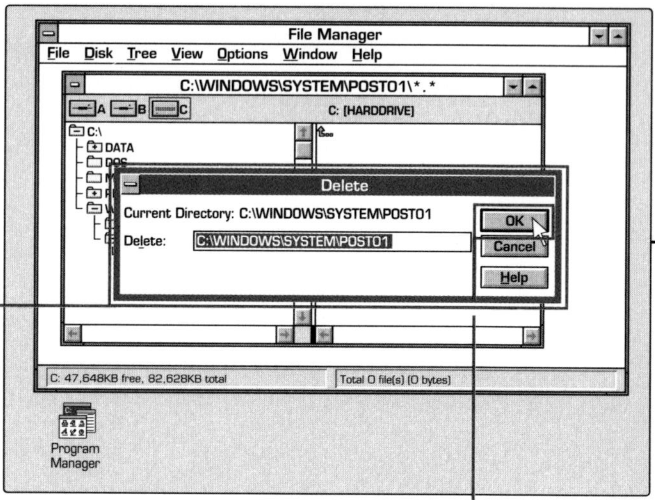

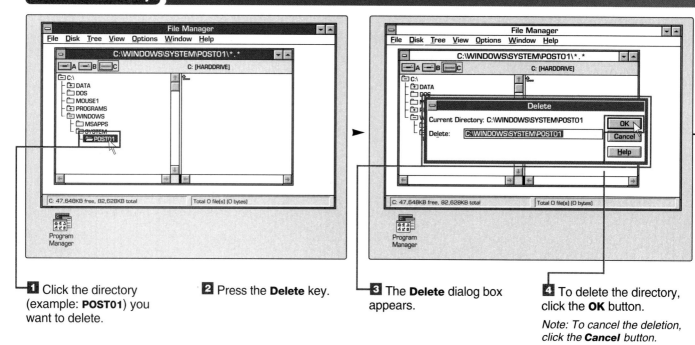

1 Click the directory (example: **POST01**) you want to delete.

2 Press the **Delete** key.

3 The **Delete** dialog box appears.

4 To delete the directory, click the **OK** button.

*Note: To cancel the deletion, click the **Cancel** button.*

CONFIRMATION STATUS

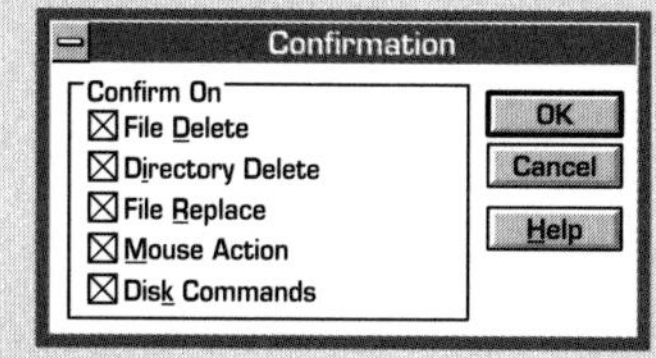

*Note: We recommend you keep all Confirmation options **on**.*

1 To check the Confirmation status, click **Options**, then click **Confirmation**.

If all Confirmation options are on, each time you delete files and directories, replace files, use the mouse when copying or moving files, or use disk commands (example: Format Disk), a Confirmation dialog box appears.

■ An empty box ☐ means a Confirmation option is **off**.

■ A box containing a cross ☒ means a Confirmation option is **on**.

2 To toggle between **on** and **off**, click the box.

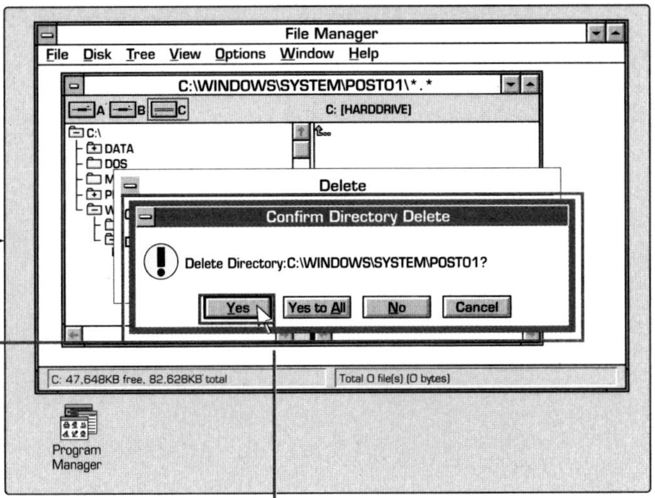

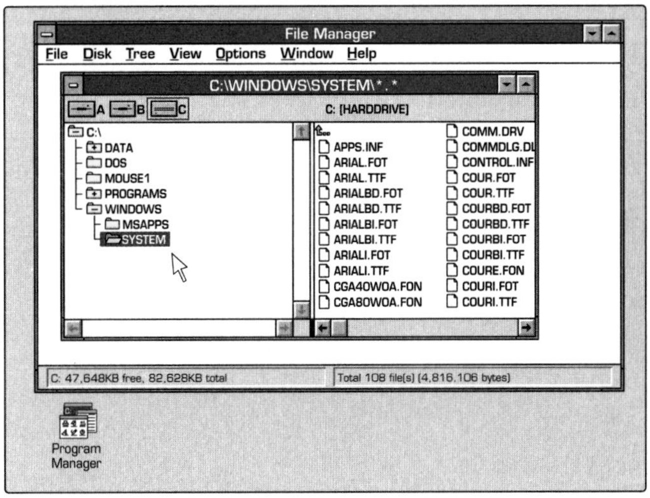

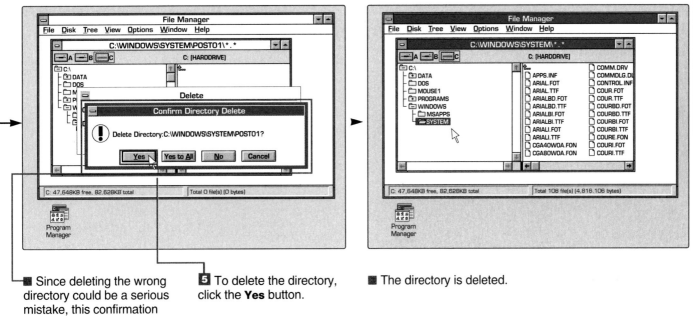

■ Since deleting the wrong directory could be a serious mistake, this confirmation request offers you a final chance to change your mind.

5 To delete the directory, click the **Yes** button.

■ The directory is deleted.

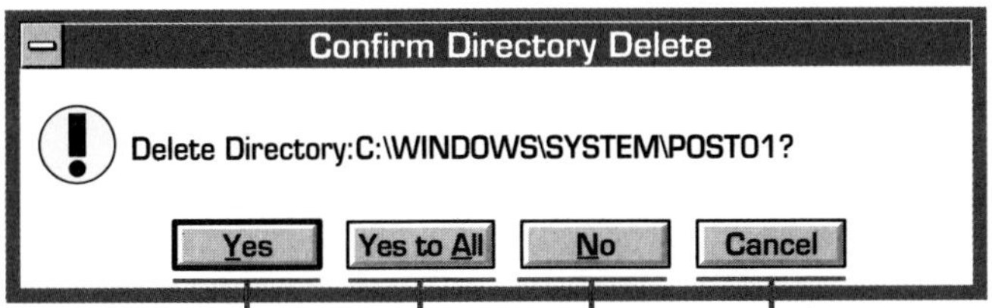

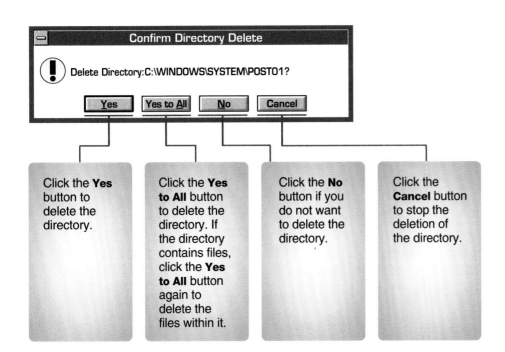

Click the **Yes** button to delete the directory.

Click the **Yes to All** button to delete the directory. If the directory contains files, click the **Yes to All** button again to delete the files within it.

Click the **No** button if you do not want to delete the directory.

Click the **Cancel** button to stop the deletion of the directory.

START AN APPLICATION

1 Double click the Group icon (example: **Accessories**) that contains the application you want to start.

2 Double click the application (example: **Write**) you want to start.

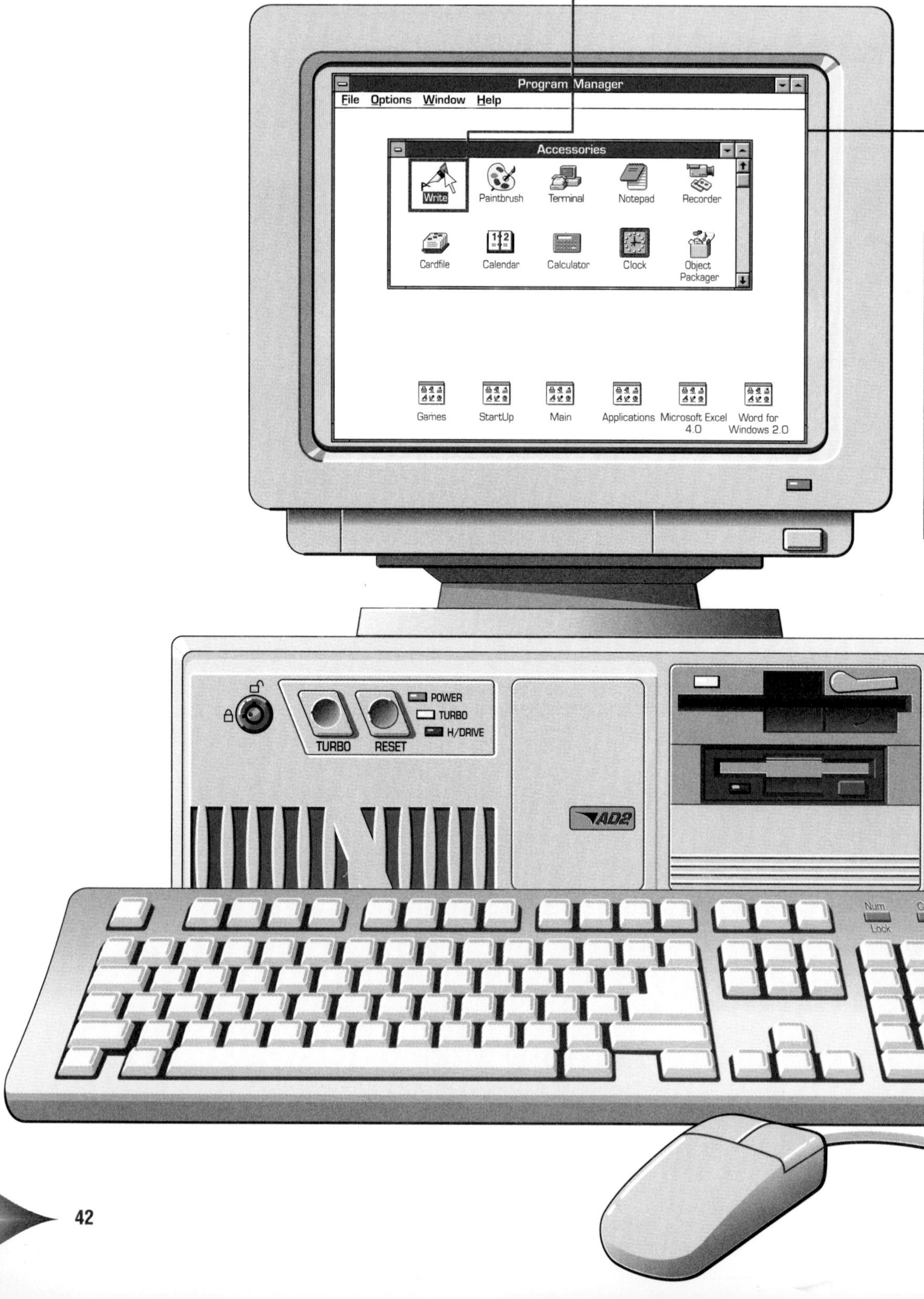

MINIMIZE ON USE

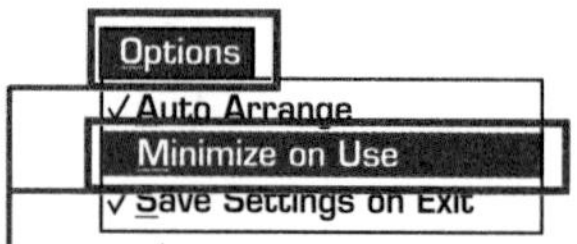

To keep the desktop uncluttered, the **Program Manager** can be automatically reduced to an icon whenever you start an application.

■ To check the status of **Minimize on Use**, click **Options**.

■ If no checkmark is in front of the command, it is **off**. To turn it **on**, click **Minimize on Use**.

*Note: If a checkmark (✓) is already in front of **Minimize on Use**, it is **on**. Press **Esc** to retain the setting.*

Most applications are used to create files. Typical files are letters, memos, worksheets, databases and graphic illustrations.

■ In this example, text was typed in the **Write** window.

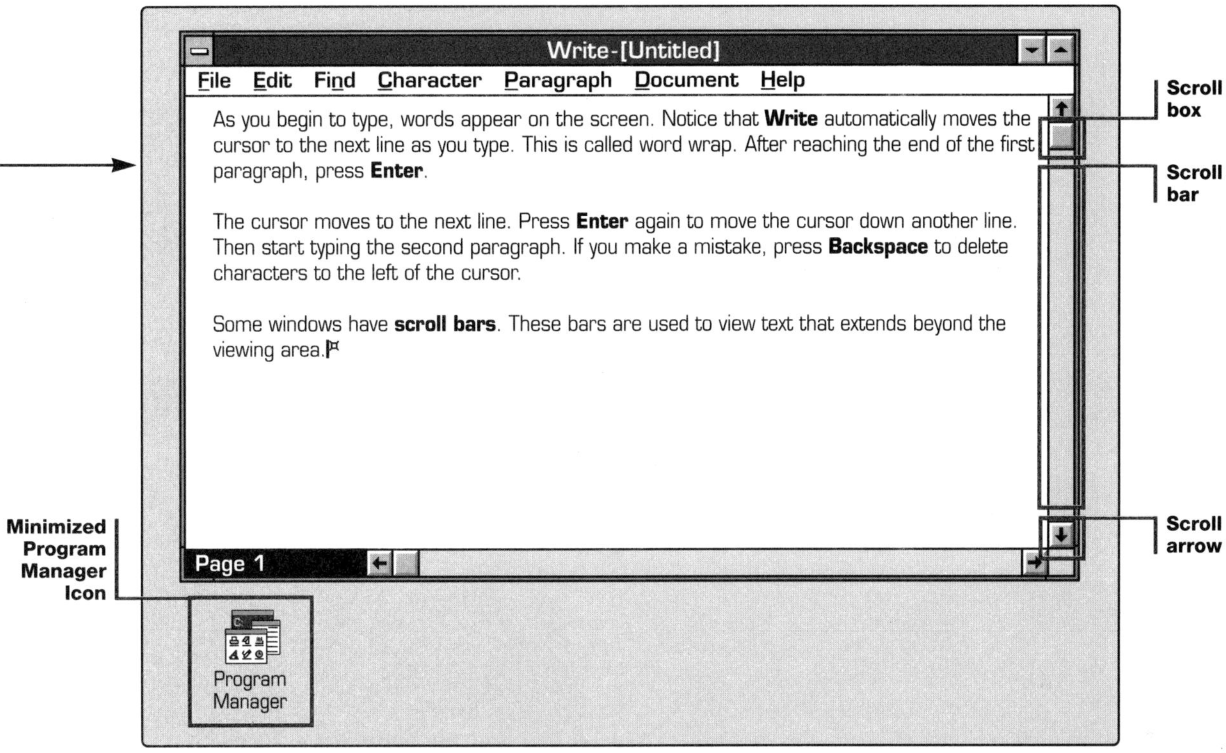
Write - [Untitled]
File Edit Find Character Paragraph Document Help
As you begin to type, words appear on the screen. Notice that Write automatically moves the cursor to the next line as you type. This is called word wrap. After reaching the end of the first paragraph, press Enter.
The cursor moves to the next line. Press Enter again to move the cursor down another line. Then start typing the second paragraph. If you make a mistake, press Backspace to delete characters to the left of the cursor.
Some windows have scroll bars. These bars are used to view text that extends beyond the viewing area.
Page 1
Program Manager
Scroll box
Scroll bar
Scroll arrow
Minimized Program Manager Icon

SCROLLING THROUGH A DOCUMENT

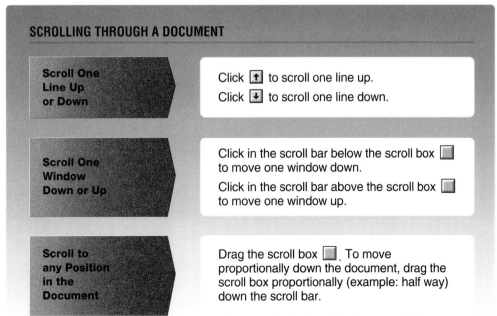

Scroll One Line Up or Down

Click ↑ to scroll one line up.

Click ↓ to scroll one line down.

Scroll One Window Down or Up

Click in the scroll bar below the scroll box ▢ to move one window down.

Click in the scroll bar above the scroll box ▢ to move one window up.

Scroll to any Position in the Document

Drag the scroll box ▢. To move proportionally down the document, drag the scroll box proportionally (example: half way) down the scroll bar.

Changing Text using a TrueType Font

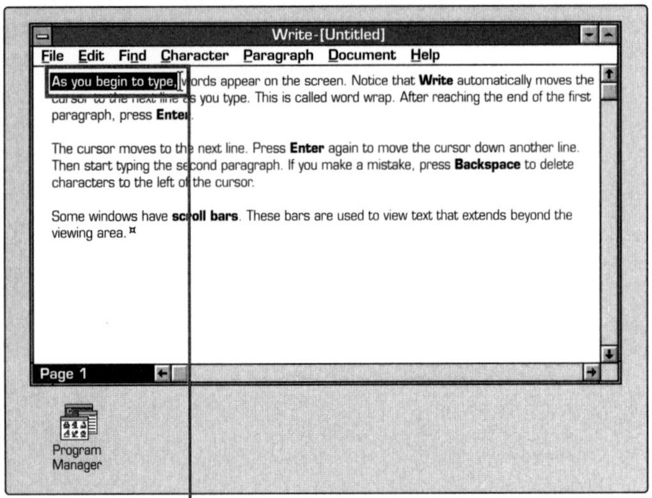
Write - [Untitled]
File Edit Find Character Paragraph Document Help
As you begin to type, words appear on the screen. Notice that Write automatically moves the cursor to the next line as you type. This is called word wrap. After reaching the end of the first paragraph, press Enter.
The cursor moves to the next line. Press Enter again to move the cursor down another line. Then start typing the second paragraph. If you make a mistake, press Backspace to delete characters to the left of the cursor.
Some windows have scroll bars. These bars are used to view text that extends beyond the viewing area.
Page 1
Program Manager

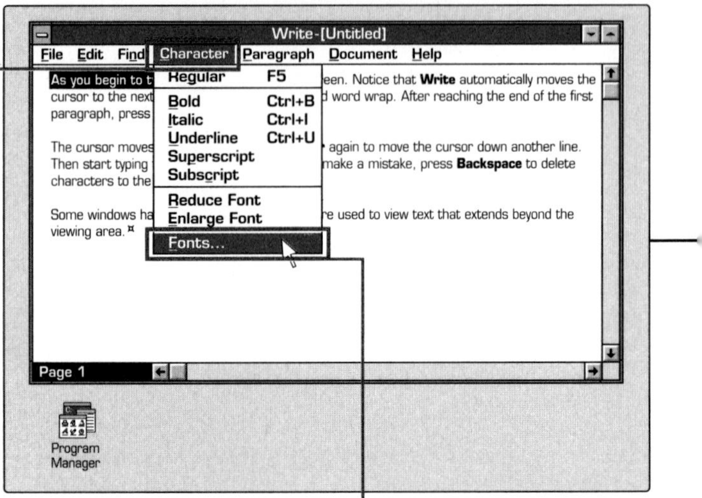
Write - [Untitled]
File Edit Find Character Paragraph Document Help
Regular F5
Bold Ctrl+B
Italic Ctrl+I
Underline Ctrl+U
Superscript
Subscript
Reduce Font
Enlarge Font
Fonts...
Page 1
Program Manager

Windows 3.1 includes several TrueType fonts. These fonts are scalable (can be scaled to any size). Furthermore, with TrueType fonts, what you see on the screen is identical to what you print on paper.

1 Move the mouse over the first character of the text you want to select and it changes to I.

2 Click and hold down the left button as you drag the mouse over the words you want to select. Then release the mouse button.

3 Click **Character** and its menu appears.

4 Click **Fonts** and the **Font** dialog box appears on the next screen.

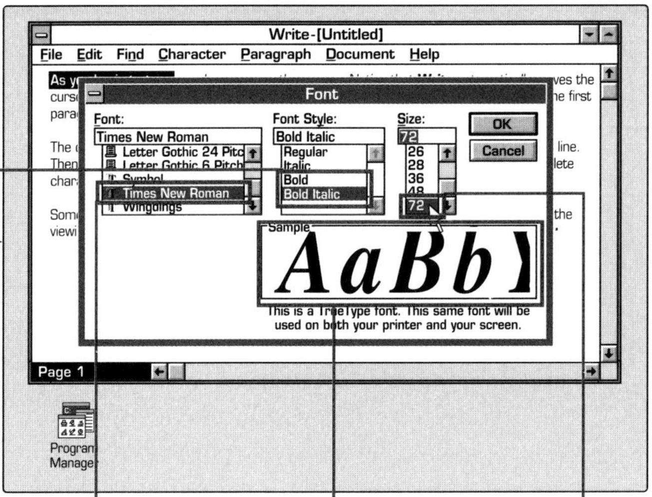

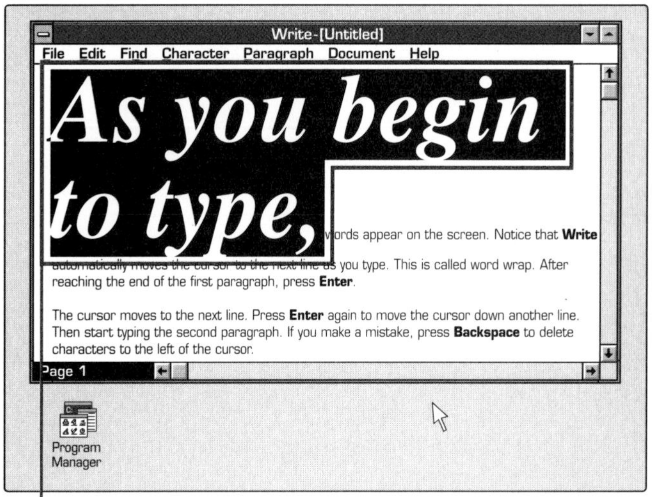

5 Click the desired font (example: **Times New Roman**).

6 Click the desired font type (example: **Bold Italic**).

7 Click the desired point size (example: **72**).

Note: 36 points is 1/2 an inch.

■ The **Sample** box displays a sample of the selected font.

8 Press **Enter**.

■ The new font appears.

Note: If you require a wider selection of fonts, other TrueType fonts can be purchased and installed in Windows 3.1.

SCROLLING THROUGH OPTIONS

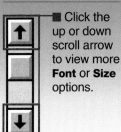

■ Click the up or down scroll arrow to view more **Font** or **Size** options.

TRUETYPE FONTS versus PRINTER FONTS

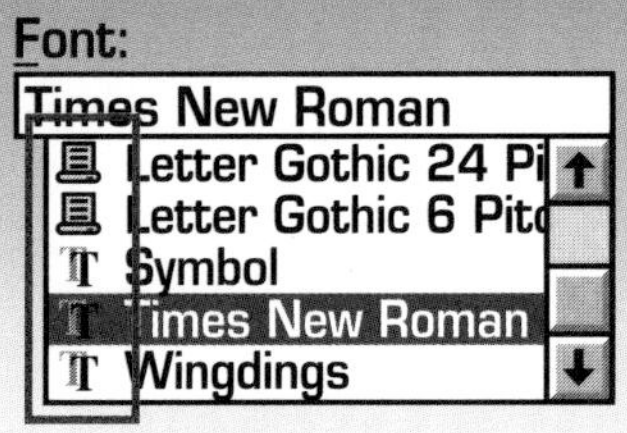

This tells you that the font is a printer font. What you see on the screen may not be identical to what you print on paper.

This tells you that the font is a TrueType font.

TO SELECT A SIZE NOT SHOWN IN THE SIZE BOX

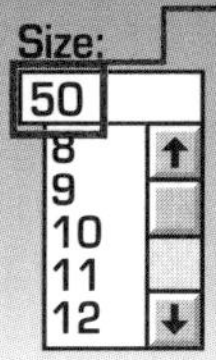

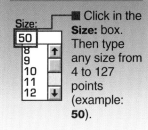

■ Click in the **Size:** box. Then type any size from 4 to 127 points (example: **50**).

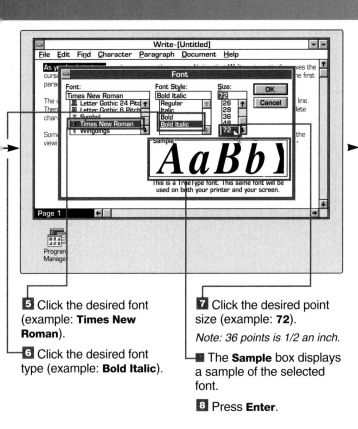

SAVE A FILE

Save a File

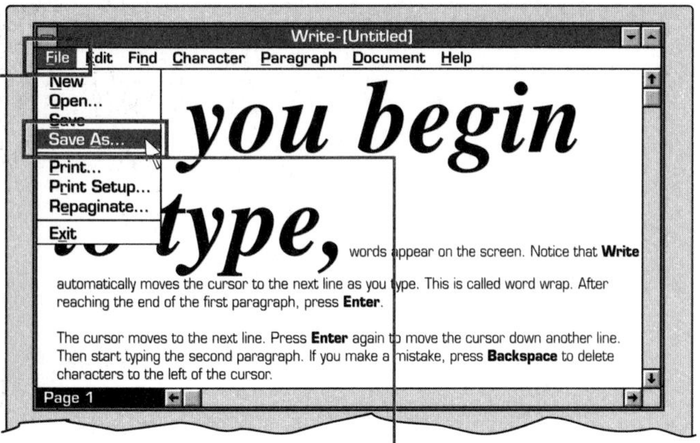

A document must be saved before leaving an application if it is required for future use.

1 Click **File** and its menu appears.

Note: A file is a document that you have named and saved to a disk.

2 Click **Save As** and the **Save As** dialog box appears.

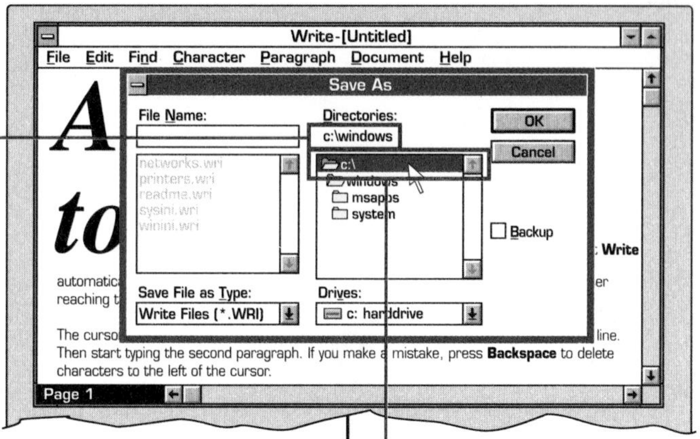

■ The contents of the current directory (example: **c:\windows**) are displayed.

3 Double click the directory (example: **c:**) you want to change to.

In this example, we are saving a document to the **wpdata** directory. To change the current directory from the **windows** directory to the **wpdata** directory, you must follow the path illustrated:

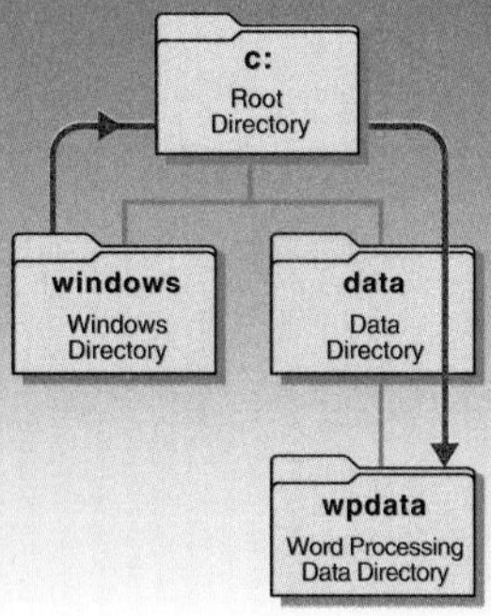

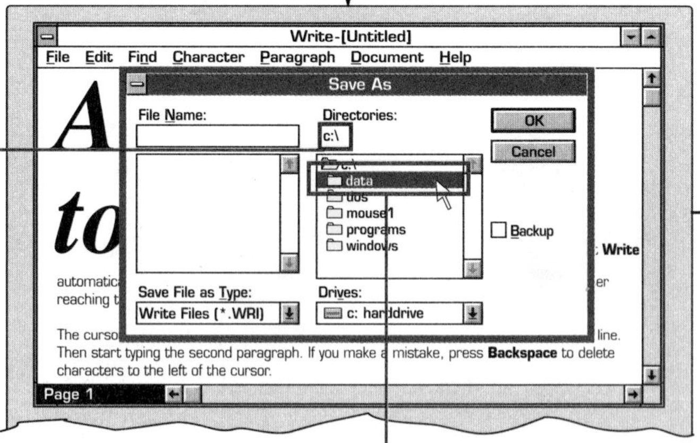

■ The contents of the current directory (example: **c:**) are displayed.

4 Double click the directory (example: **data**) you want to change to.

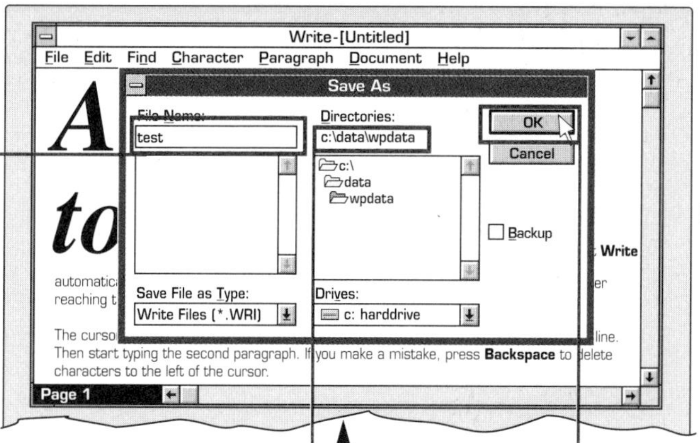

■ The contents of the current directory (example: **c:\data\wpdata**) are displayed.

6 Click in the **File Name** box, then type a name (example: **test**) for your document.

7 Click the **OK** button.

Shortcut

To replace steps 3 to 7, type the file specification (example: **c:\data\wpdata\test**) in the **File Name** box. Then press **Enter**.

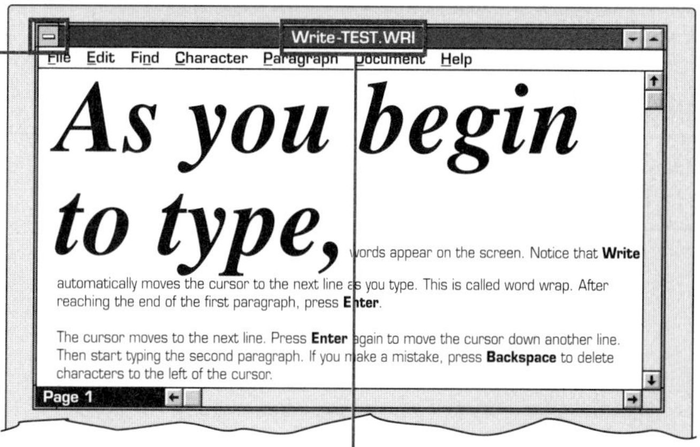

■ The file (example: **TEST.WRI**) is saved.

8 To exit an application, double click its Control menu box.

*Note: If an extension is not specified, many applications automatically add an extension (example: **.WRI** for **Write**).*

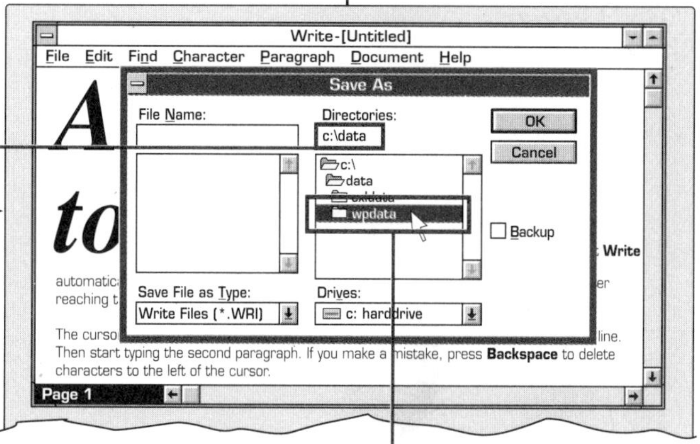

■ The contents of the current directory (example: **c:\data**) are displayed.

5 Double click the directory (example: **wpdata**) you want to change to.

SAVE FUTURE CHANGES TO THE FILE

1 Click **File** to open its menu.

2 Click **Save**.

The file will replace the previously saved file.

Note: You should save regularly to prevent losing work due to power failure or hardware malfunctions.

Open an Existing File

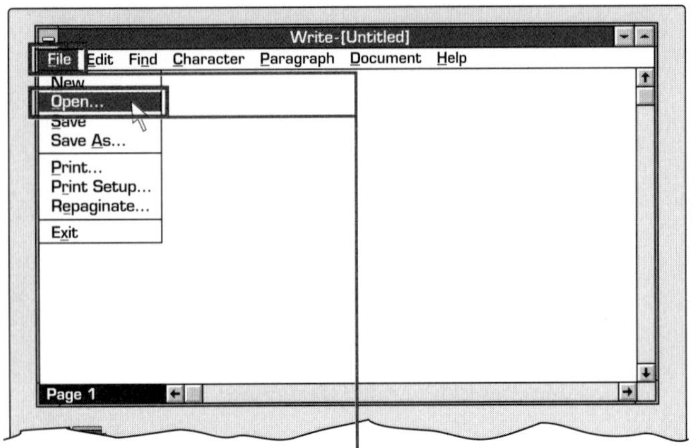

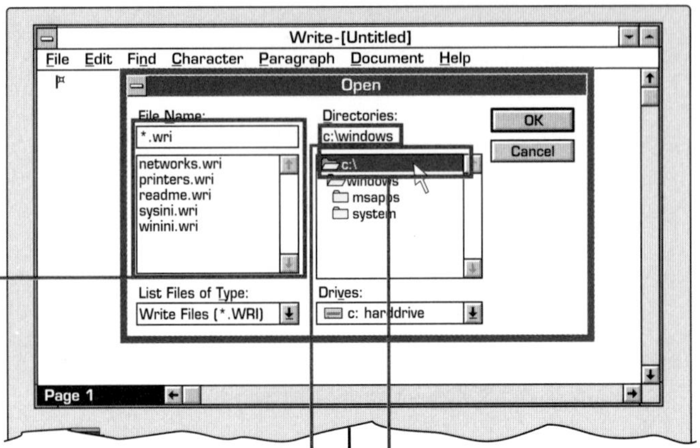

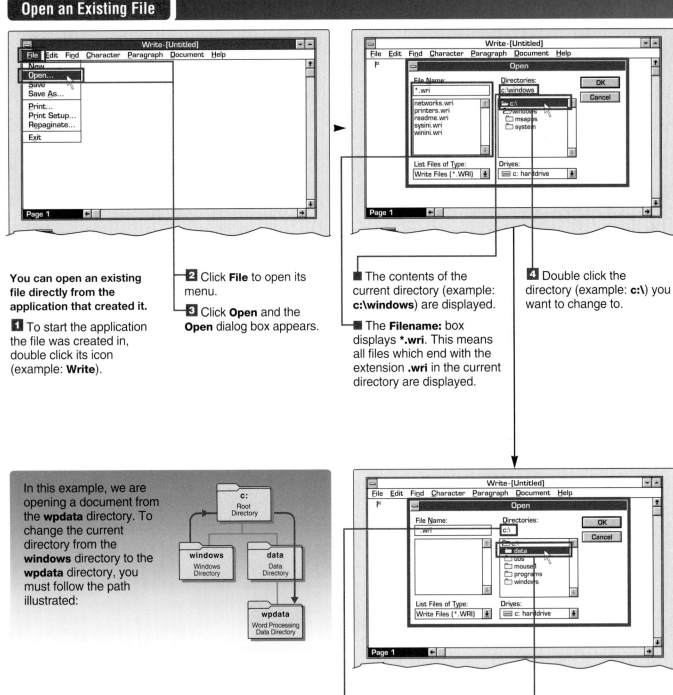

You can open an existing file directly from the application that created it.

1 To start the application the file was created in, double click its icon (example: **Write**).

2 Click **File** to open its menu.

3 Click **Open** and the **Open** dialog box appears.

■ The contents of the current directory (example: **c:\windows**) are displayed.

■ The **Filename:** box displays ***.wri**. This means all files which end with the extension **.wri** in the current directory are displayed.

4 Double click the directory (example: **c:**) you want to change to.

In this example, we are opening a document from the **wpdata** directory. To change the current directory from the **windows** directory to the **wpdata** directory, you must follow the path illustrated:

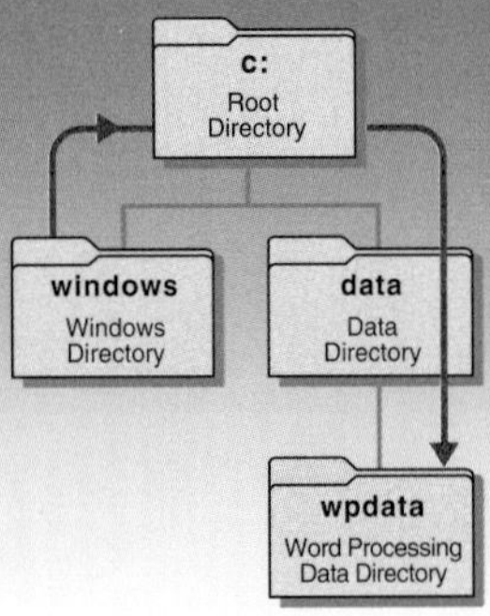

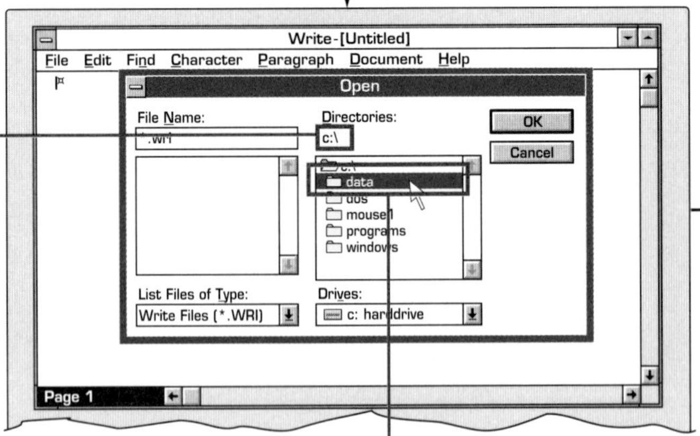

■ The contents of the current directory (example: **c:**) are displayed.

5 Double click the directory (example: **data**) you want to change to.

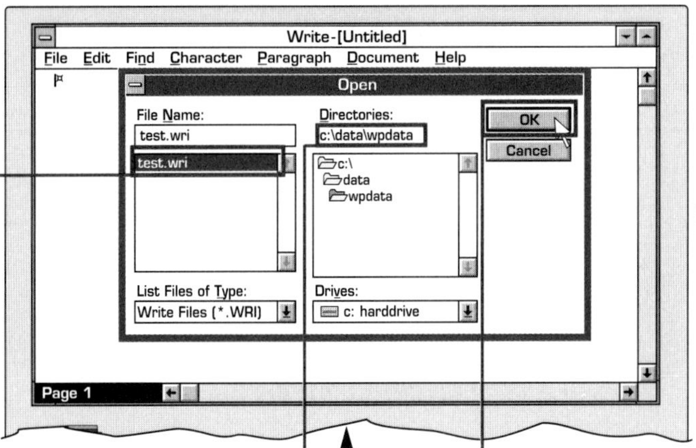

■ The contents of the current directory (example: **c:\data\wpdata**) are displayed.

7 Click the file (example: **test.wri**) you want to open.

8 Click the **OK** button.

Shortcut

To replace steps 4 to 8, type the file specification (example: **c:\data\wpdata\test.wri**) in the **File Name** box. Then press **Enter**.

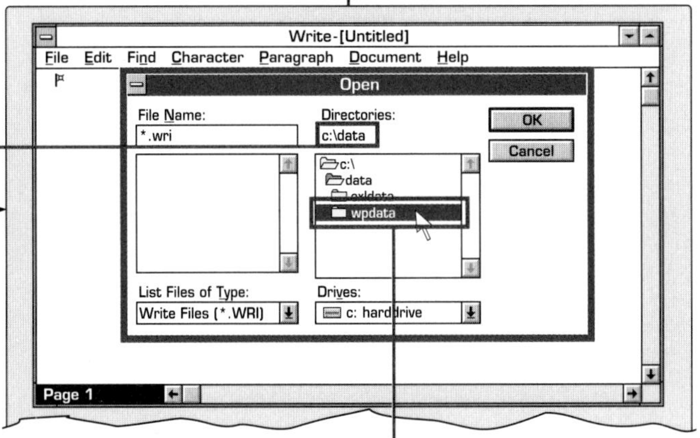

■ The contents of the current directory (example: **c:\data**) are displayed.

6 Double click the directory (example: **wpdata**) you want to change to.

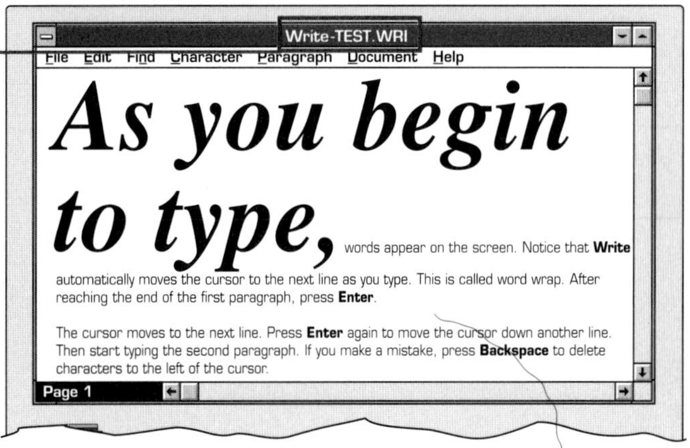
Write-TEST.WRI
File Edit Find Character Paragraph Document Help
As you begin to type, words appear on the screen. Notice that Write automatically moves the cursor to the next line as you type. This is called word wrap. After reaching the end of the first paragraph, press Enter.
The cursor moves to the next line. Press Enter again to move the cursor down another line. Then start typing the second paragraph. If you make a mistake, press Backspace to delete characters to the left of the cursor.
Page 1

■ The file (example: **TEST.WRI**) is opened.

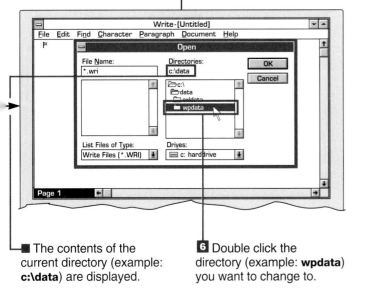

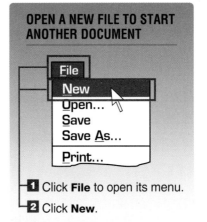

OPEN A NEW FILE TO START ANOTHER DOCUMENT

1 Click **File** to open its menu.

2 Click **New**.

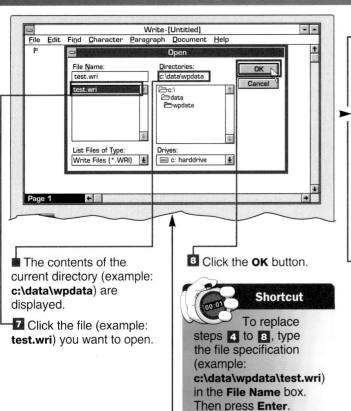

Print a File

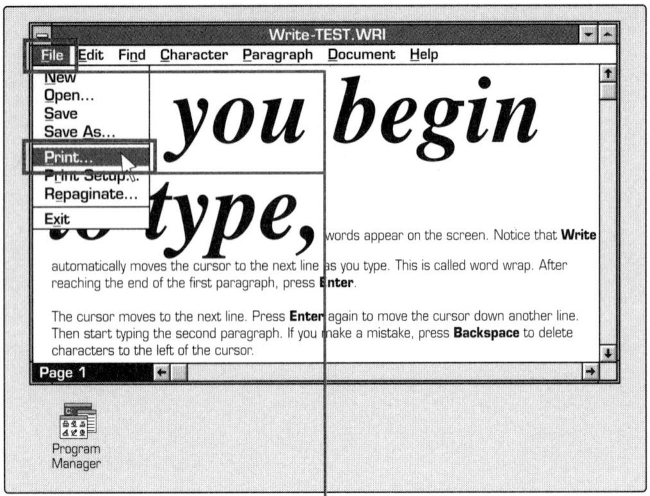

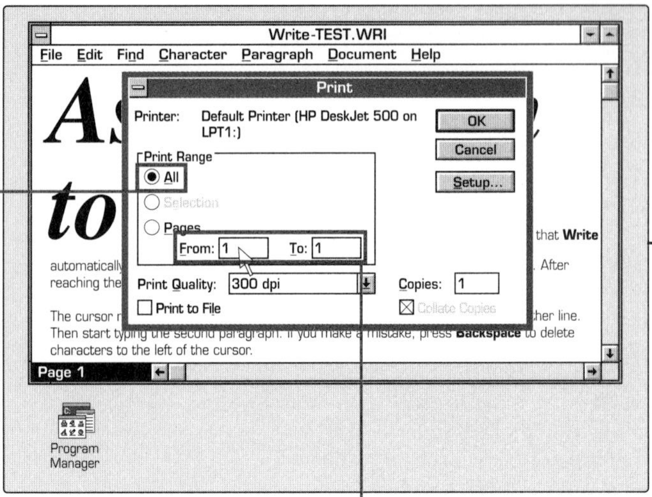

Most applications designed to work with Windows have a Print command in their File menu. Each application offers its own formatting features and options to optimize the printed document.

1 Click **File** to open its menu.

2 Click **Print** and the **Print** dialog box appears.

Print Range

■ **All** is the default setting. All the pages in the document will be printed.

3 To print specific pages, double click in the **From:** box and type the starting page number.

Then, double click in the **To:** box and type the last page number.

Note: To print a selection of text, select the text you want to print before step 1. *Then click the circle beside* ***Selection*** *and* ○ *becomes* ◉.

IMPORTANT

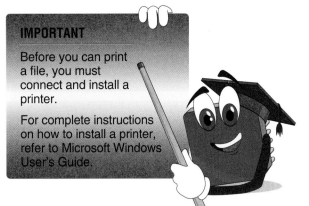

Before you can print a file, you must connect and install a printer.

For complete instructions on how to install a printer, refer to Microsoft Windows User's Guide.

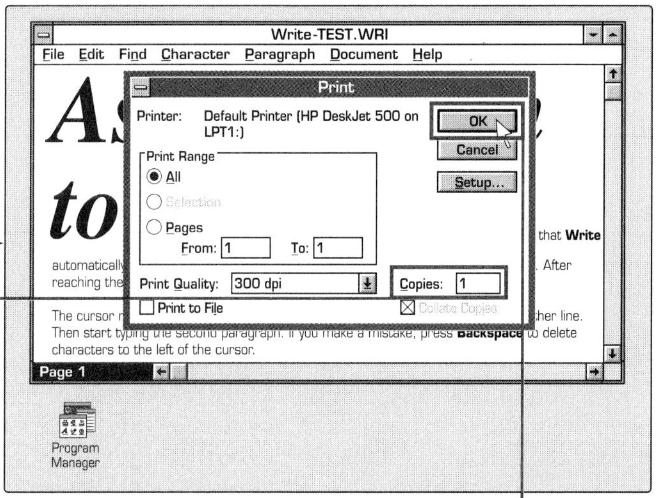

Number of Copies

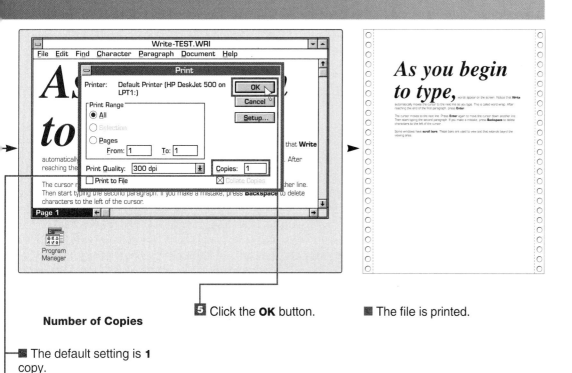

■ The default setting is **1** copy.

4 To print multiple copies, double click in the **Copies:** box and type the number of copies you want to print.

5 Click the **OK** button.

■ The file is printed.

PRACTICE FILES

Normally, files are created using application software (such as word processing, spreadsheet, graphic packages, etc.). The method below is used to create practice files for the examples that follow in this guide.

1 To create a practice file from the **Write** program, press **Alt**,**F**,**A**.

2 Type the new file specification and press **Enter**.

Examples: (refer to page 26)

■ Type **C:\DATA\WPDATA\MERGE.LET** and then press **Enter**. The file is copied to the C: drive \DATA\WPDATA directory and named MERGE.LET.

■ Type **C:\DATA\EXLDATA\INCOME1Q.XLS** and then press **Enter**. The file is copied to the C: drive \DATA\EXLDATA directory and named INCOME1Q.XLS.

EXIT AN APPLICATION

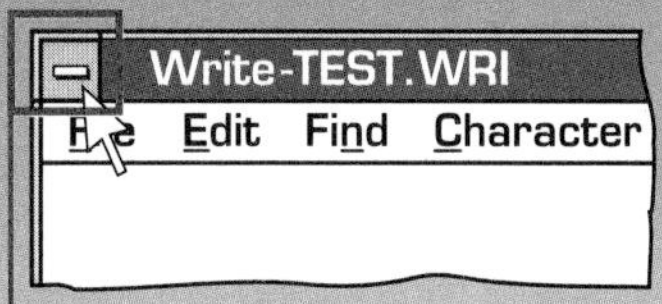

1 To exit any application, double click its **Control menu box**.

Note: If a change had been made to the application since the last time it was saved, a dialog box appears asking if you want to save the change before exiting the application.

PRINT A FILE

Start the Print Manager

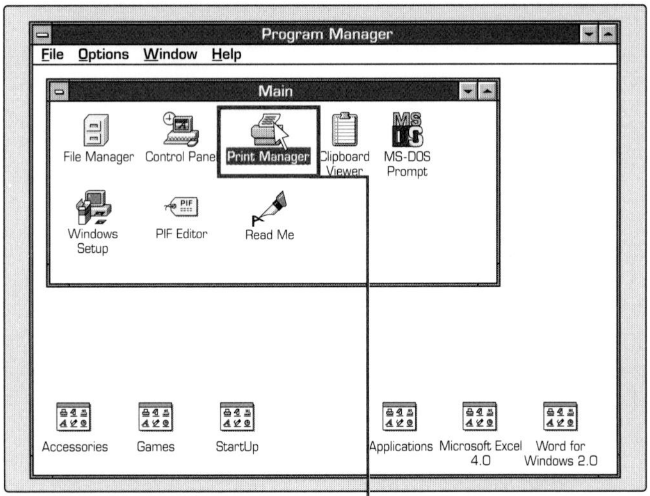

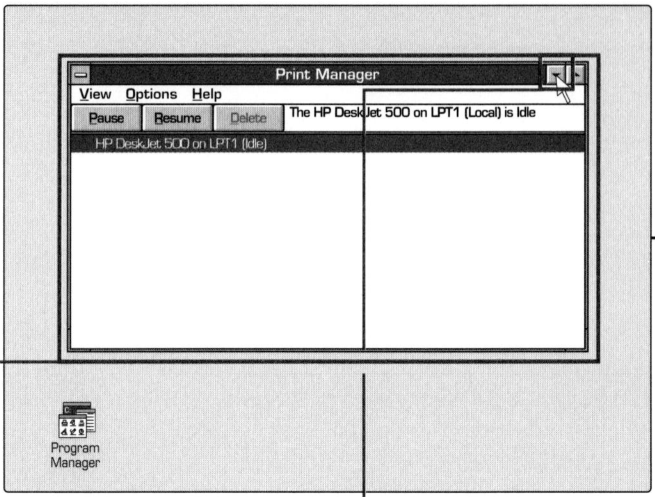

The Print Manager allows you to print a file directly from the File Manager. This means you can print a file without opening the application that created the file.

1 To start the **Print Manager**, double click its icon.

■ The **Print Manager** is started.

2 Click the **Print Manager**'s minimize button.

Print a File from the File Manager

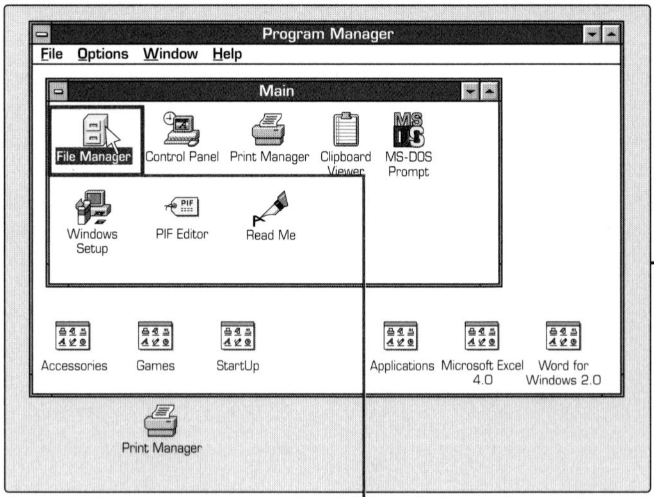

You can easily print a file using the Print Manager's drag-and-drop feature.

1 To start the **File Manager**, double click its icon.

■ The **Print Manager** is still running, but now appears as an icon on the desktop.

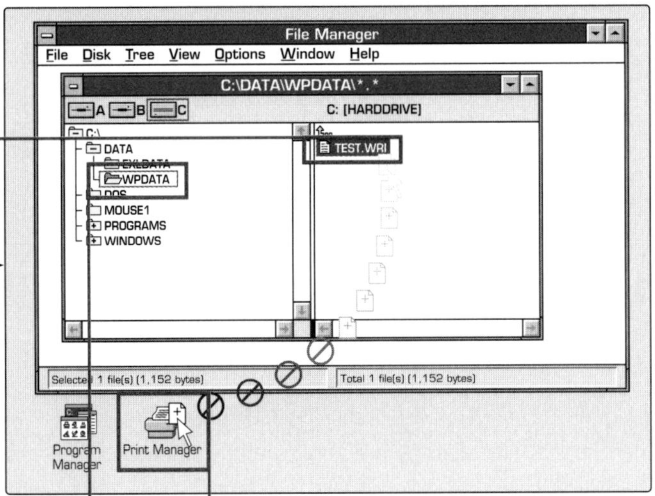

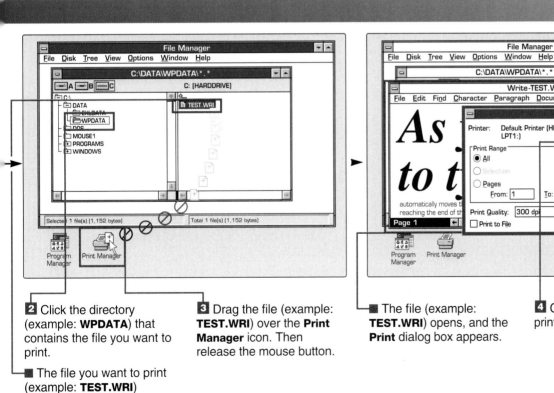

2 Click the directory (example: **WPDATA**) that contains the file you want to print.

■ The file you want to print (example: **TEST.WRI**) appears.

3 Drag the file (example: **TEST.WRI**) over the **Print Manager** icon. Then release the mouse button.

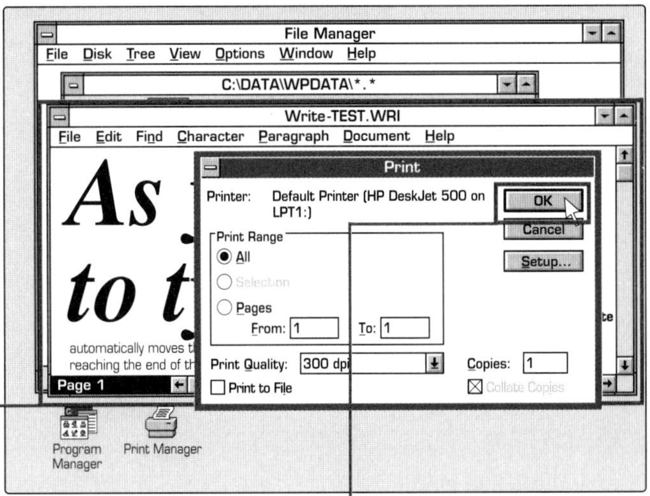

■ The file (example: **TEST.WRI**) opens, and the **Print** dialog box appears.

4 Click the **OK** button to print the file.

CREATE AN OBJECT

Object Linking and Embedding (OLE) is a new technology that allows applications to share information (objects) even if they have different data formats.

An object can be a line of text, chart, graphic or even a sound or video clip.

Objects are linked (using the Paste Link command) or embedded (using the Paste command) into documents. When you double click a linked or embedded object, the application which created the object is launched. This allows you to edit objects from within a document without having to return and open the applications which originally created them.

Create an Object

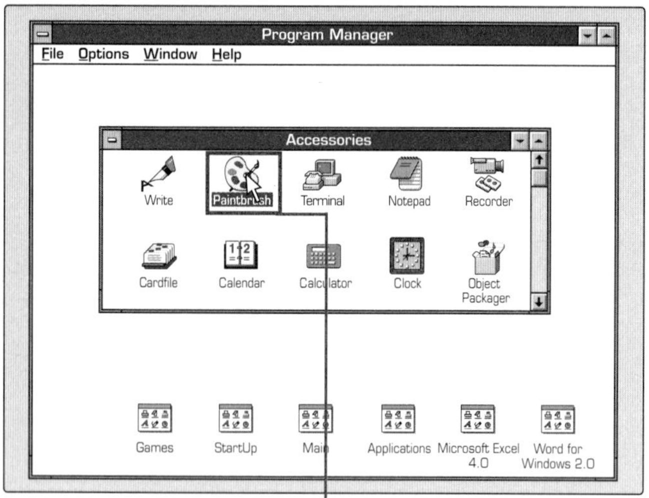

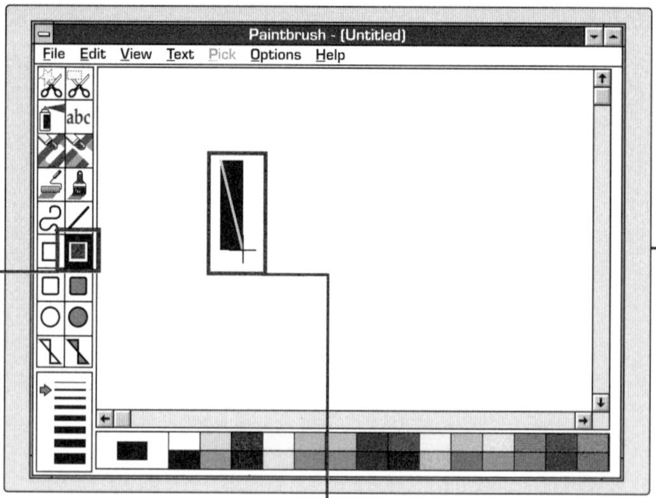

In the following example, an object is created using the Paintbrush application.

1 Open the **Accessories** Group window by double clicking its Group icon.

2 Start the **Paintbrush** application by double clicking its Program item icon.

3 Resize the **Paintbrush** window as shown above.

4 Click the desired drawing tool. For example, to draw a box, click the **Box** tool.

Note: The mouse ↖ changes to + when moved into the drawing area.

5 Move the cursor + to the position where you want to begin drawing the object.

6 Hold down the left button and drag the edges of the object to the desired size. Then release the button.

LINKING	EMBEDDING
The Paste Link command allows you to link an object from one application to another.	The Paste command allows you to embed a copy of the object in the destination document.
The destination document only stores a link to where the object is located.	This means all components of the document are contained in a single file.
Double clicking the linked object in the destination document launches the source application containing the object. Edits to this object are reflected in the source and all linked destination documents.	Double clicking the embedded object launches the source application containing the object. Edits to this object only change the information in the destination document, not the source document.
Linking is used if you want automatic updates to all linked documents and small destination files.	Embedding is used if you want document portability (all information in one file).

Over the next 6 pages we will:

- Create an object in the **Paintbrush** program.
- Link the object into the **Write** program.
- Edit the object from within the **Write** program.

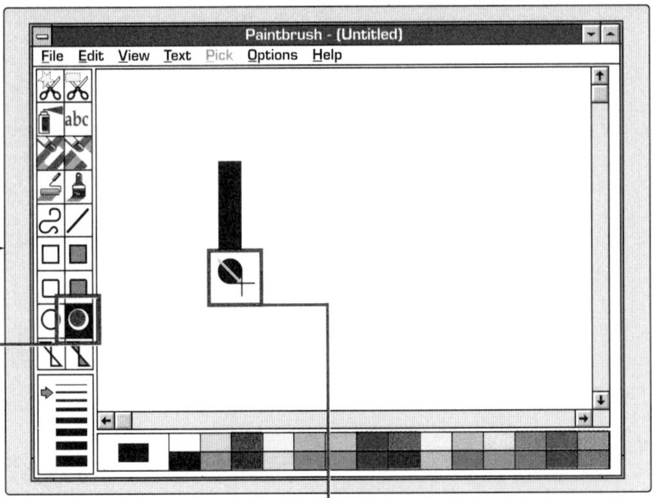

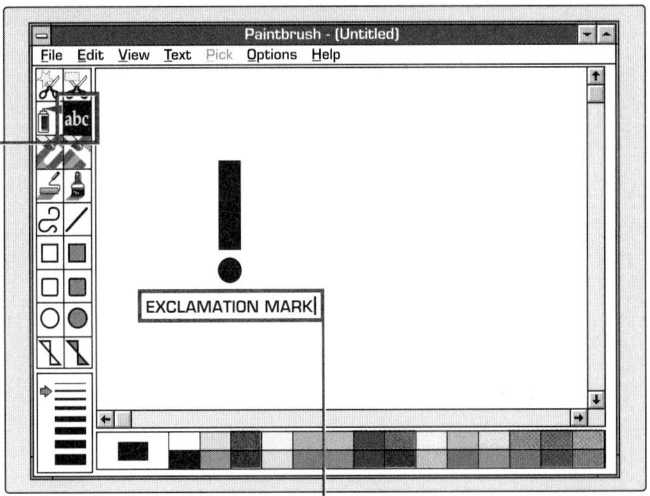

7 Click another drawing tool. For example, to draw an ellipse, click the **Ellipse** drawing tool.

Note: The mouse ↖ changes to + when moved into the drawing area.

8 Move the cursor + to the position where you want to begin drawing the object.

9 Hold down the left button and drag the edges of the object to the desired size. Then release the button.

10 Click another drawing tool. For example, to type text, click the **Text** tool.

Note: The mouse ↖ changes to I when moved into the drawing area.

11 Move the cursor I to the position where you want to type text. Then click the left button.

12 Type the text (example: **EXCLAMATION MARK**).

Save the Object

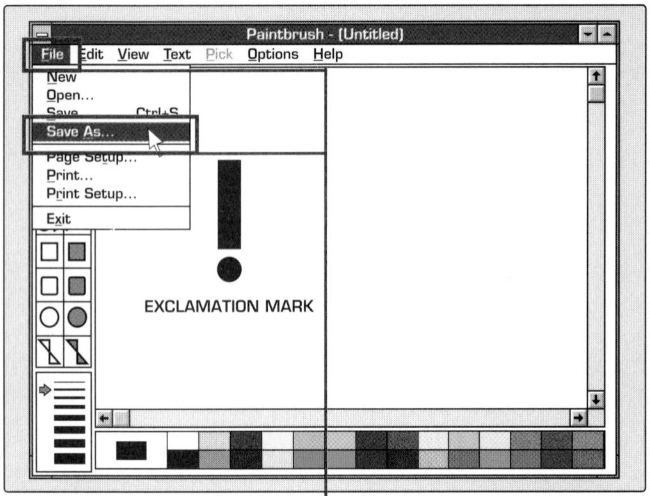

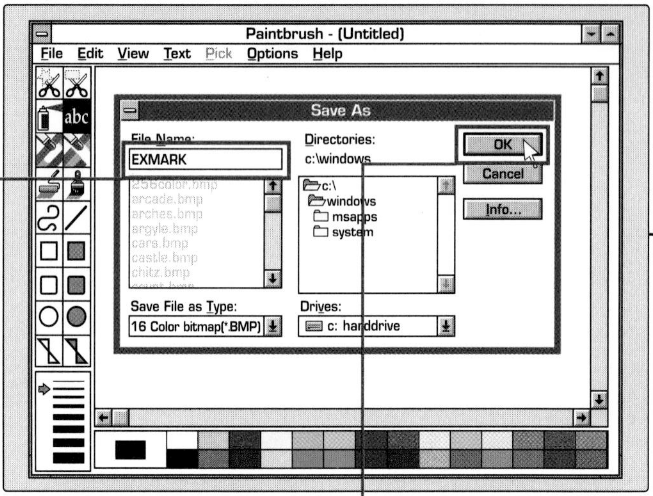

You cannot link an object into another application until it is saved to your hard disk.

In this example, the object created in Paintbrush will be saved.

1 Click **File** to open its menu.

2 Click **Save As** and the **Save As** dialog box appears.

3 Type a name (example: **EXMARK**) for your document.

4 Click the **OK** button.

Link the Object

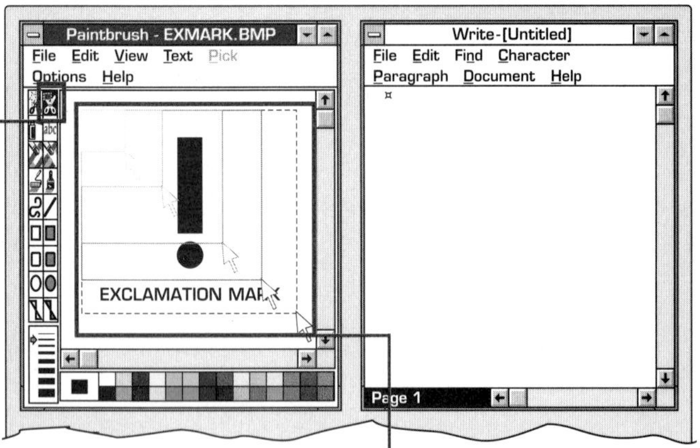

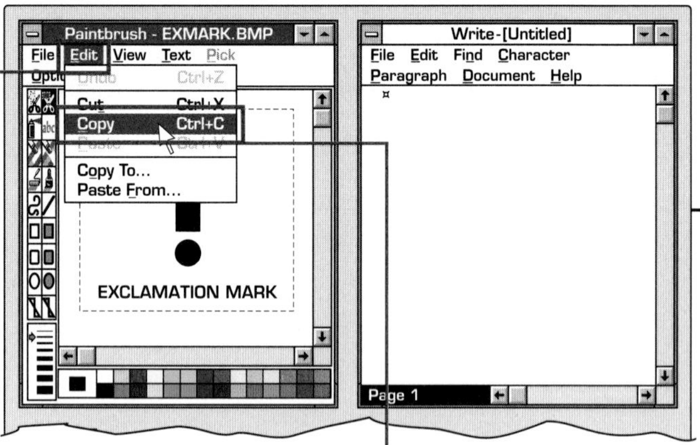

1 Start the application you want to link an object into. For example, start the **Write** program by double clicking its icon.

2 Resize and move the windows as shown above.

3 Click the **Pick** tool in the **Paintbrush** program.

4 Hold down the left button and drag until a box outlines the area you want to copy. Then release the mouse button.

Note: If you make a mistake drawing the box, click anywhere outside the drawing area and start again.

5 Click **Edit** to open its menu.

6 Click **Copy** to copy the selected object.

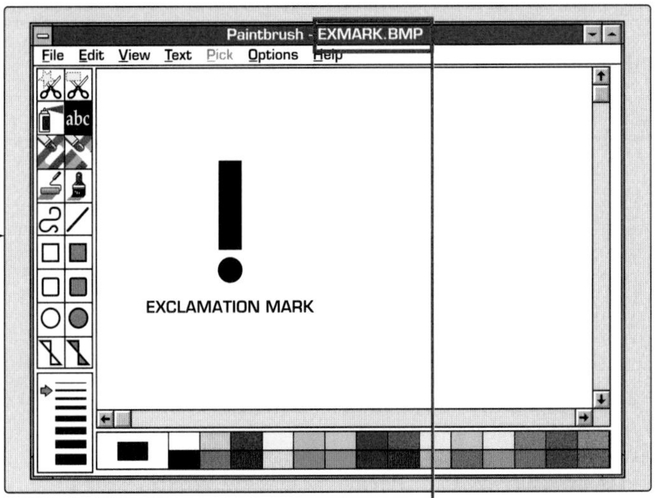

■ The file (example: **EXMARK**) is saved.

Note: The ***Paintbrush*** *program automatically adds the* ***.BMP*** *extension.*

TIP Windows applets (example: Write, Paintbrush, Cardfile) support OLE. Microsoft Excel and Word Version 2.0 also support OLE.

If you are not sure if the application you are working with supports OLE, check the application's User Manual.

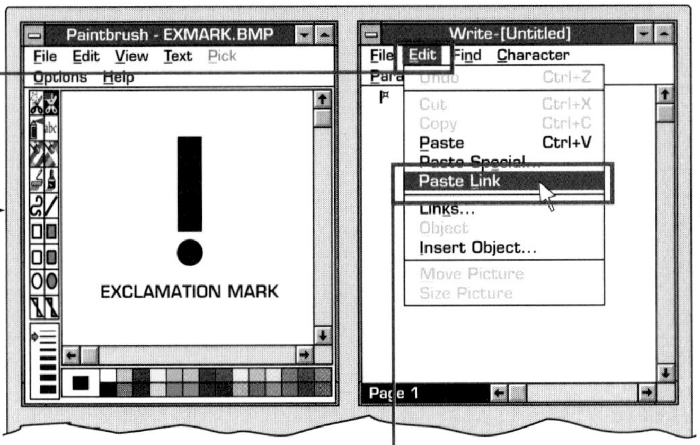

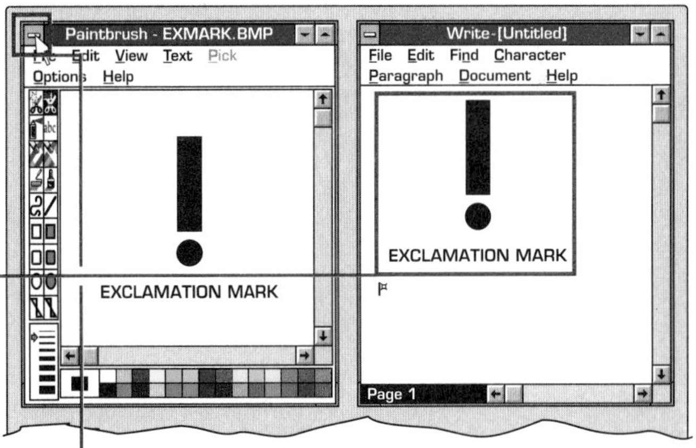

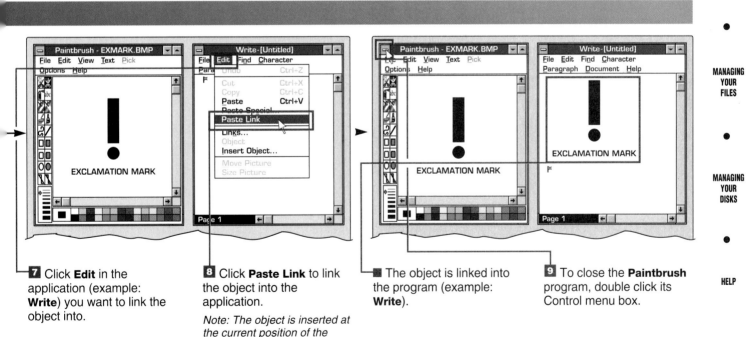

7 Click **Edit** in the application (example: **Write**) you want to link the object into.

8 Click **Paste Link** to link the object into the application.

Note: The object is inserted at the current position of the insertion point.

■ The object is linked into the program (example: **Write**).

9 To close the **Paintbrush** program, double click its Control menu box.

ACCESS THE LINKED OBJECT

EDIT THE LINKED OBJECT

Access the Linked Object

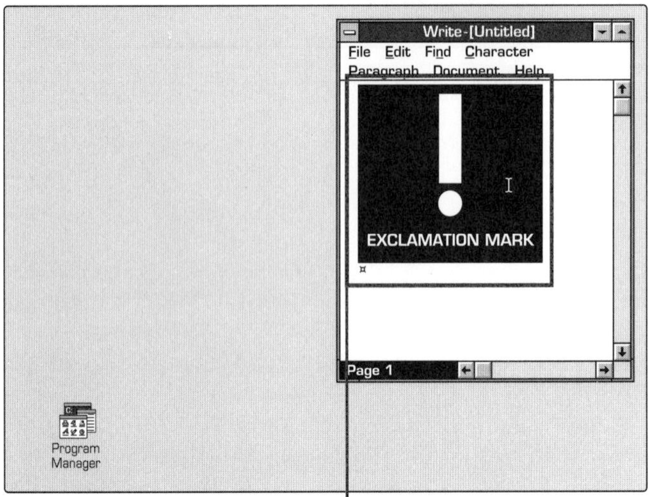

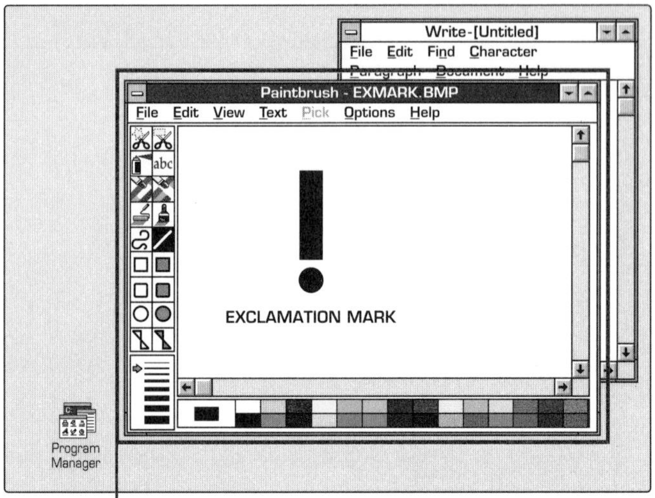

You can access the linked object without having to open the application which created it.

1 Double click anywhere in the object area.

■ The application (example: **Paintbrush**) which created the object opens, allowing you to quickly edit the object.

Edit the Linked Object

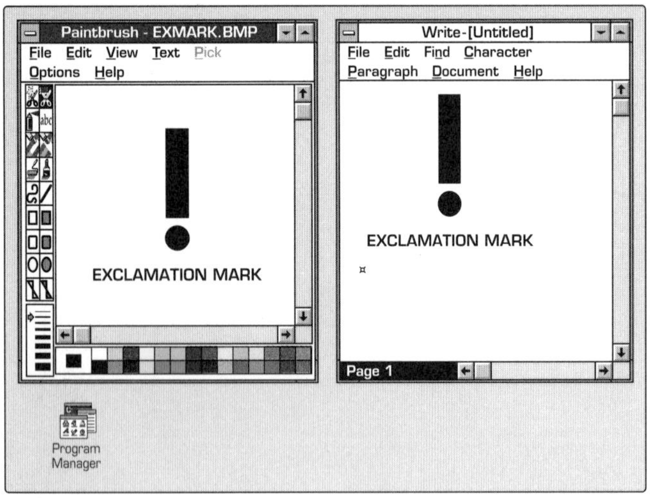

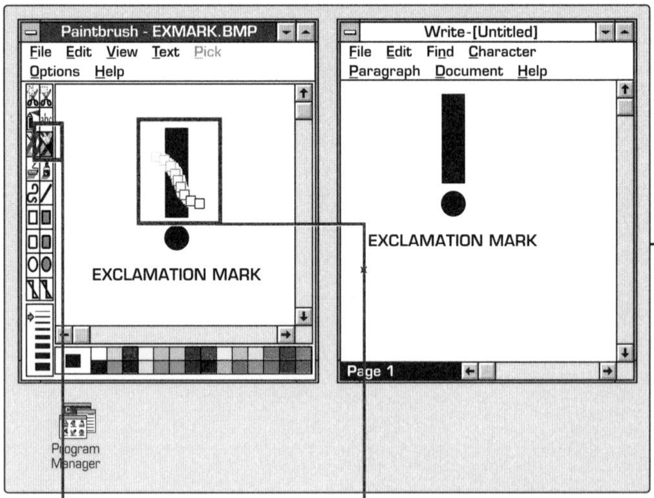

If you make changes to a linked object, the changes are automatically reflected in all applications containing the linked object.

1 Resize and move the **Write** and **Paintbrush** programs as shown above.

Note: The terms "application" and "program" are used interchangeably.

2 Click a drawing tool. For example, to use the eraser, click the **Eraser** tool.

Note: The mouse changes to ☐ when moved into the drawing area.

3 Hold down the left button and drag through the area you want to erase.

LINKING versus EMBEDDING

There is a slight difference between linking and embedding an object. When you **link** an object (using the **Paste Link** command), changes made to the object are reflected in **all** documents linked to it.

However, when you **embed** an object (using the **Paste** command), it is embedded directly into the destination document. This means changes made to that object are only reflected in the destination document.

DYNAMIC DATA EXCHANGE (DDE)

Many Windows applications support DDE, which is very similar to OLE. DDE, however, cannot embed objects within applications.

Using OLE, double clicking the object in the destination document opens up the source application containing the object. The object can then be edited.

To edit an object using DDE, both the source and destination documents must be open.

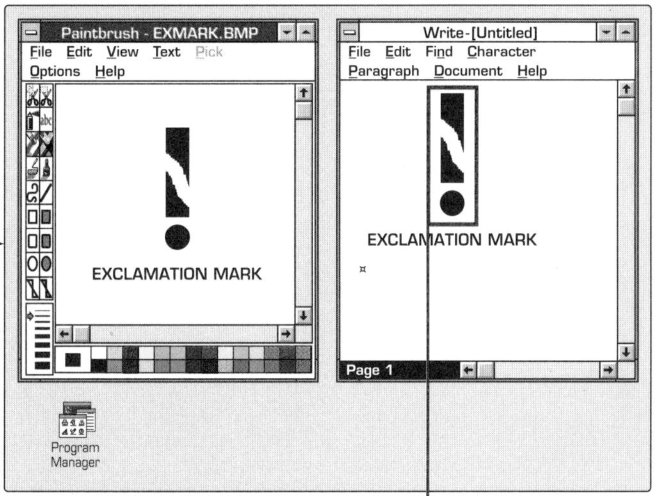

4 Release the mouse button and the linked object in the **Write** window automatically reflects the change.

Note: To close an application, double click its Control menu box ⊟.

SAVE CHANGES

1 To save changes made to the **Paintbrush** program, click **File** in the **Paintbrush** window. Then click **Save**.

2 To save the document created in the **Write** application, click anywhere in its window to make it current. Then save the document (refer to page 46 on saving files).

SPLIT A DIRECTORY WINDOW

TREE AND DIRECTORY VIEWS

Split a Directory Window

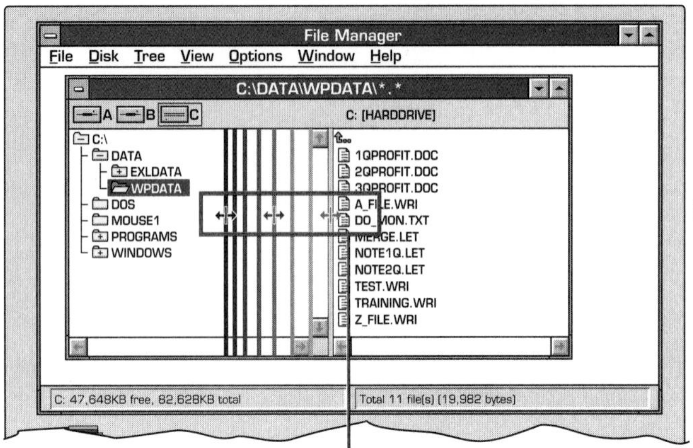

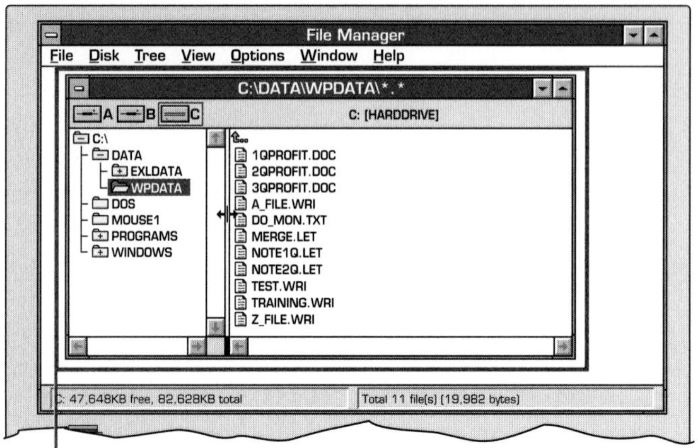

A directory window can be split to allow more viewing area of the directory tree or contents list.

1 Move the mouse over the line to the left of the file names and it changes to ↔.

2 Hold down the left mouse button and drag the vertical line to a new position.

3 Release the mouse button and the directory window is split at the position you specified.

Note: To create practice files, refer to page 51.

Tree and Directory Views

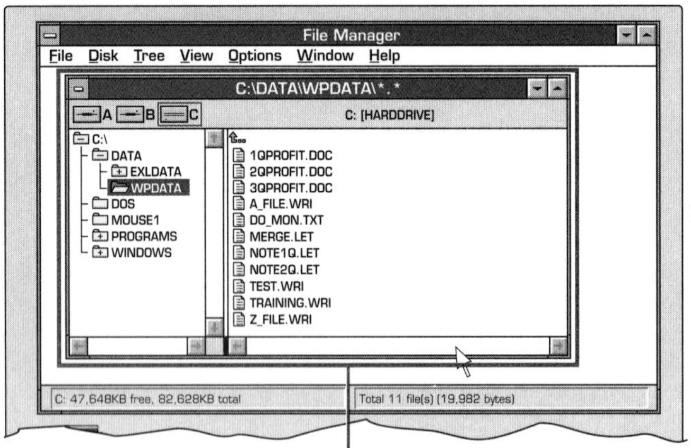

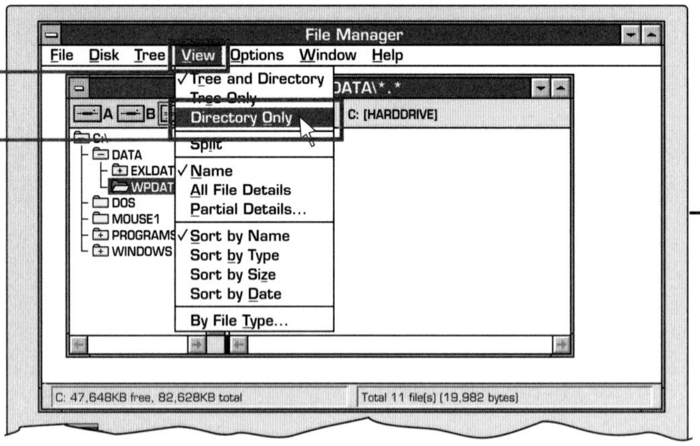

Within a directory window, you can display directories and files in three view formats.

Tree and Directory

■ This is the default setting. Both the directory tree and the contents of the current directory are displayed.

Directory only

1 To display only the contents of the current directory, click **View** to open its menu.

2 Click **Directory Only**.

EACH FILENAME HAS AN ICON BESIDE IT INDICATING ITS FILE TYPE

Directories.

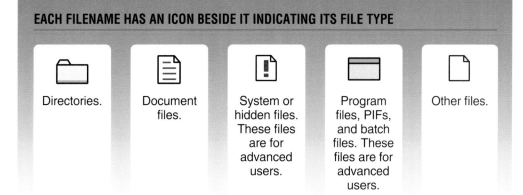

Document files.

System or hidden files. These files are for advanced users.

Program files, PIFs, and batch files. These files are for advanced users.

Other files.

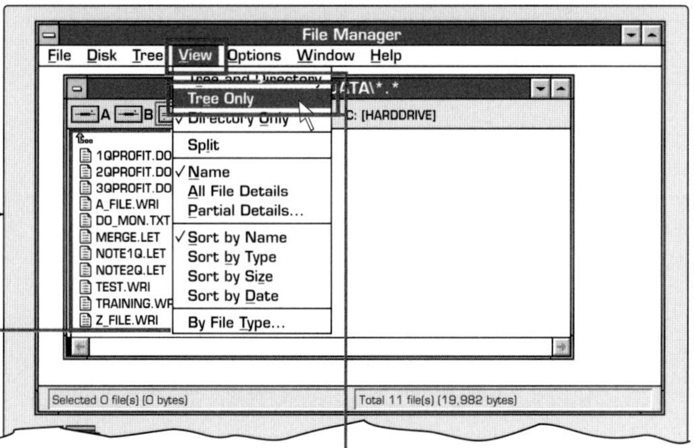

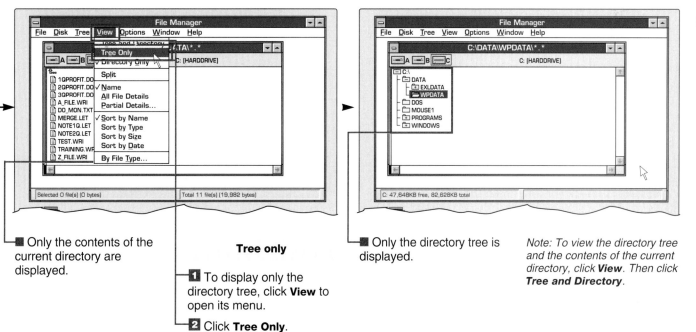

■ Only the contents of the current directory are displayed.

Tree only

1 To display only the directory tree, click **View** to open its menu.

2 Click **Tree Only**.

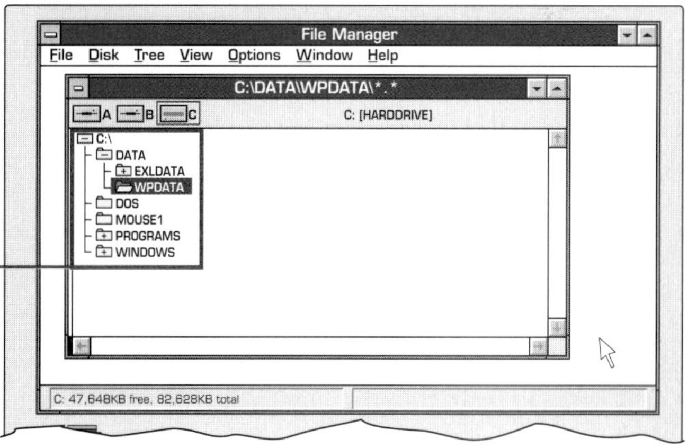

■ Only the directory tree is displayed.

Note: To view the directory tree and the contents of the current directory, click ***View****. Then click* ***Tree and Directory****.*

DISPLAY FILE INFORMATION

Change File Information Display

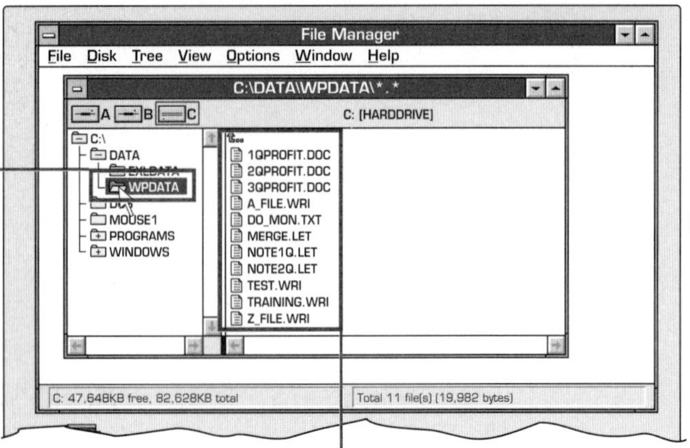

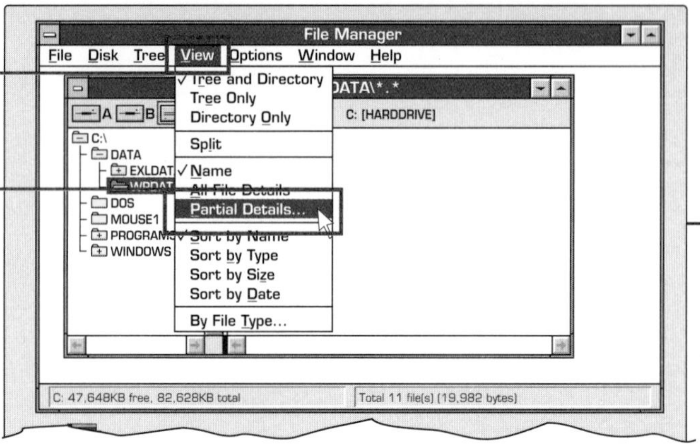

You can change the way file information is displayed in the File Manager.

1 Click the directory (example: **WPDATA**) you want to make current.

■ The contents of the selected directory are displayed.

*Note: This is the default setting. If your display is different, refer to **Display Only Filenames** on the next page.*

2 Click **View** to open its menu.

3 Click **Partial Details** and the **Partial Details** dialog box appears.

Shortcut

Press **Alt**,**V**,**P**

Display All File Details

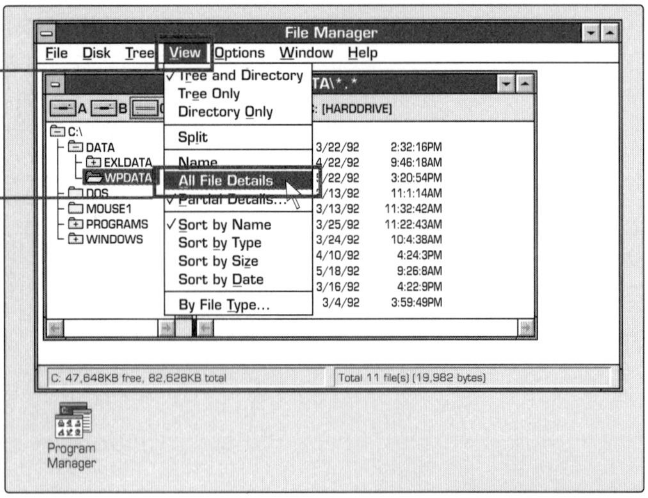

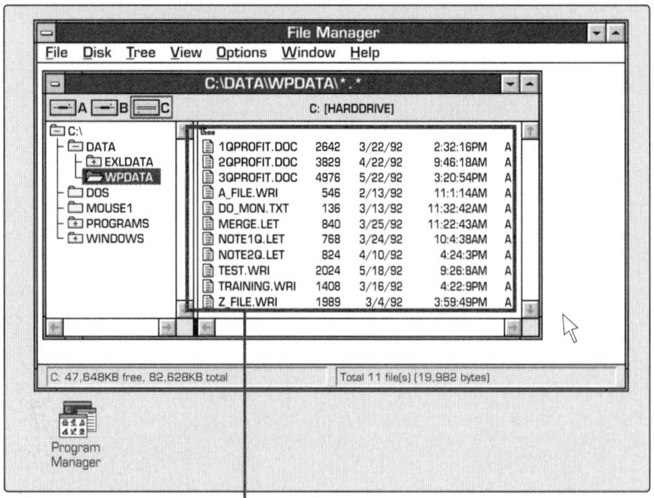

1 Click **View** to open its menu.

2 Click **All File Details**.

Shortcut

Press **Alt**,**V**,**A**

■ Complete file information is displayed including Size, Last Modification Date/Time and File Attribute status.

Note: File attributes are for advanced users. Refer to your Microsoft Windows User's Guide.

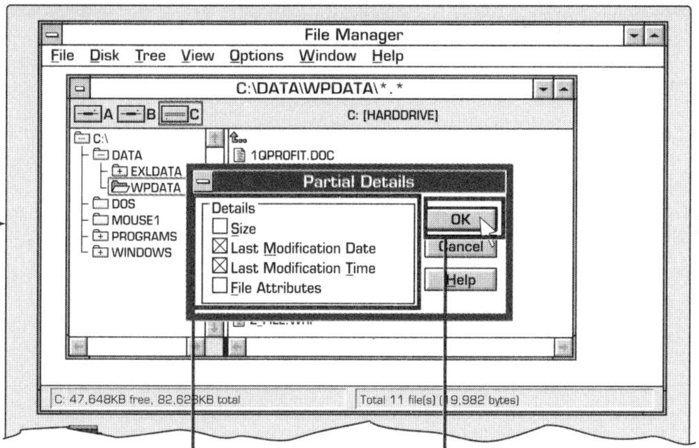

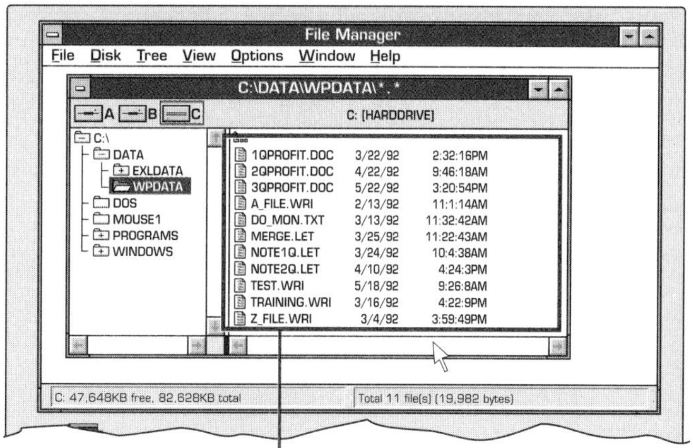

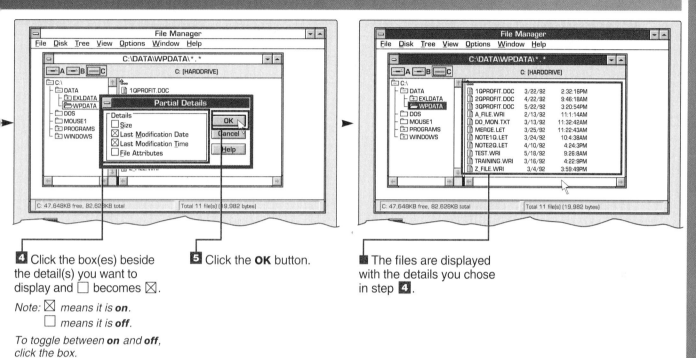

4 Click the box(es) beside the detail(s) you want to display and ☐ becomes ☒.

Note: ☒ *means it is* ***on****.*
☐ *means it is* ***off****.*

To toggle between ***on*** *and* ***off****, click the box.*

5 Click the **OK** button.

■ The files are displayed with the details you chose in step **4**.

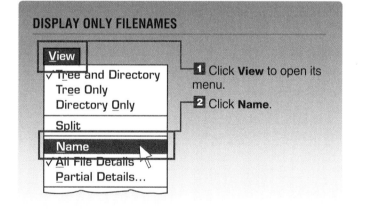

DISPLAY ONLY FILENAMES

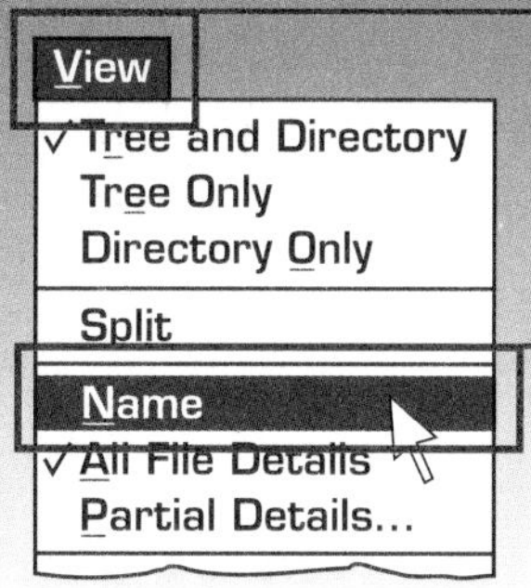

1 Click **View** to open its menu.

2 Click **Name**.

SORT FILES

Sort By Type

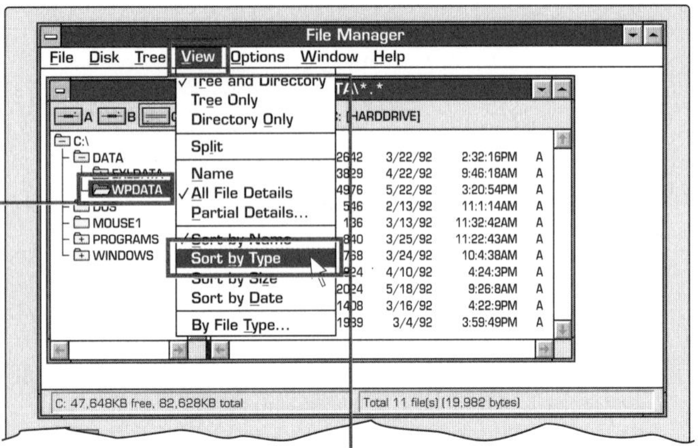

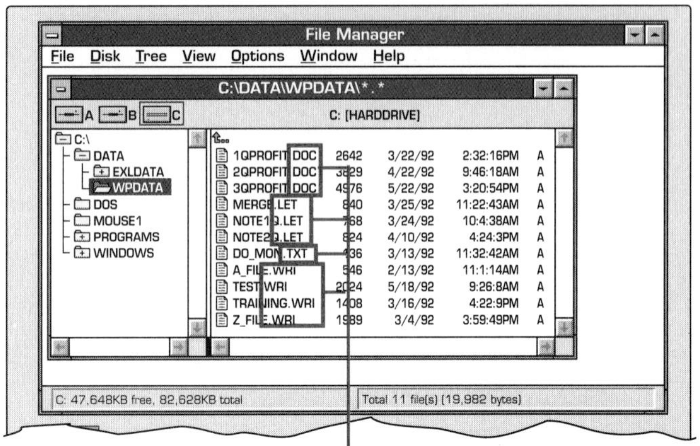

1 Click the folder (example: **WPDATA**) that contains the files you want to view sorted.

Note: To display all file details, refer to page 62.

2 Click **View**.

3 Click **Sort by Type**.

■ The files are sorted by file type (extension) in alphabetical order.

Shortcut

Press **Alt**,**V**,**B**

Sort By Size

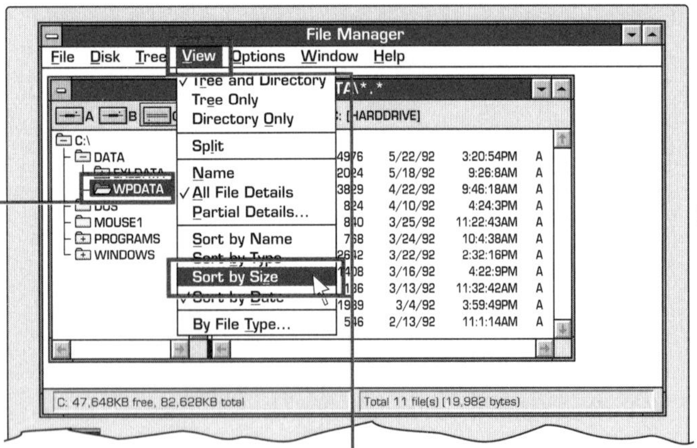

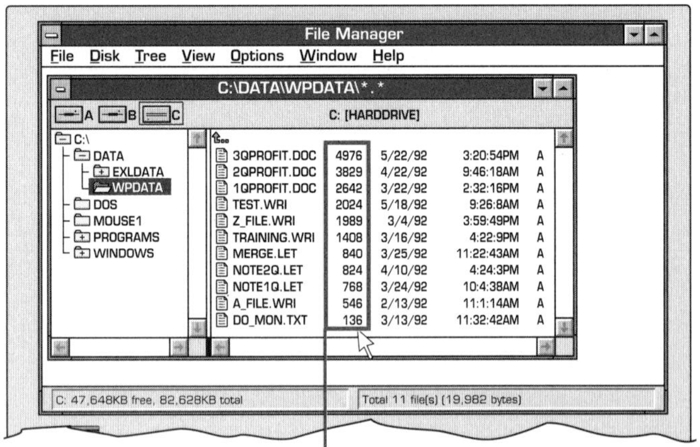

1 Click the folder (example: **WPDATA**) that contains the files you want to view sorted.

2 Click **View**.

3 Click **Sort by Size**.

■ The files are sorted by file size, starting with the largest.

Shortcut

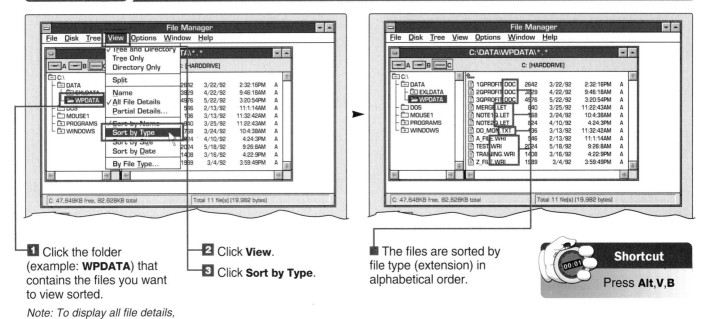

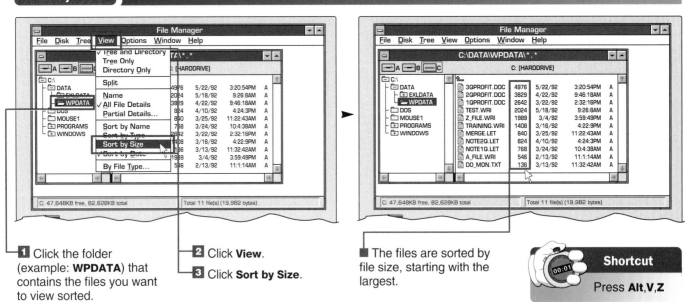

Press **Alt**,**V**,**Z**

Sort By Date

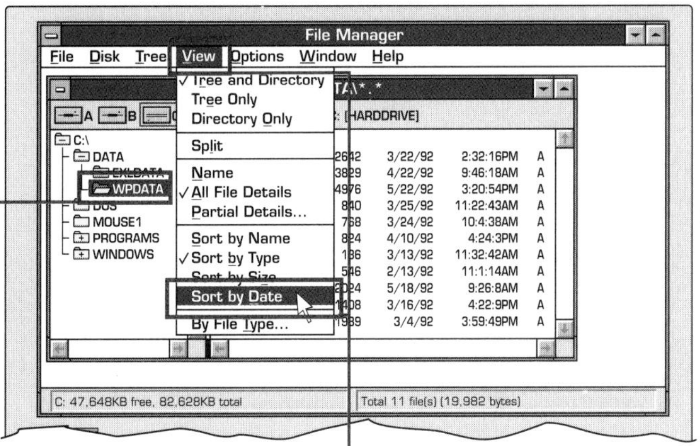

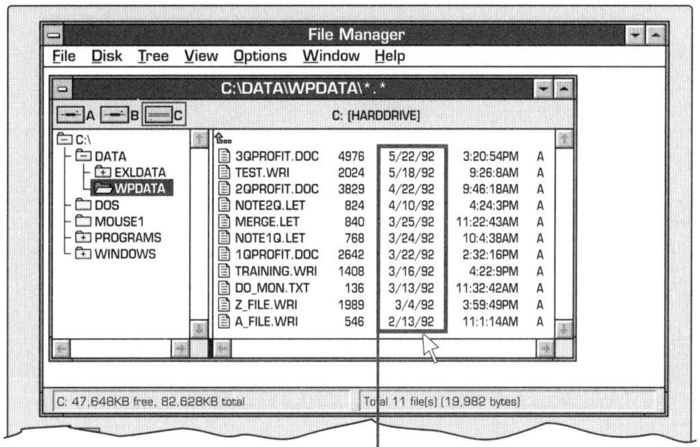

1 Click the folder (example: **WPDATA**) that contains the files you want to view sorted.

2 Click **View**.

3 Click **Sort by Date**.

■ The files are sorted by date, displaying the most recently modified files first.

Shortcut

Press **Alt**,**V**,**D**

Sort By Name

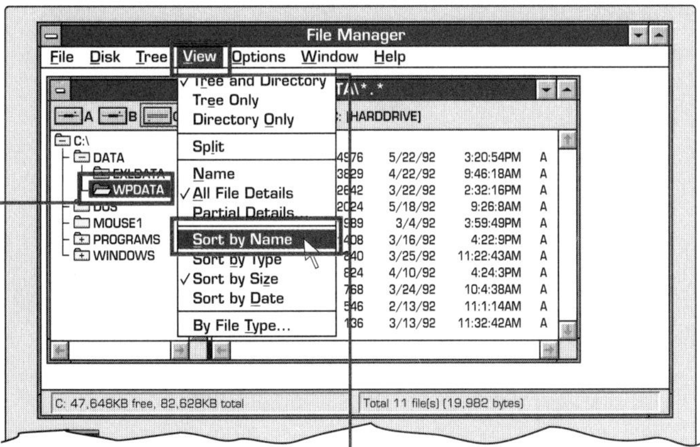

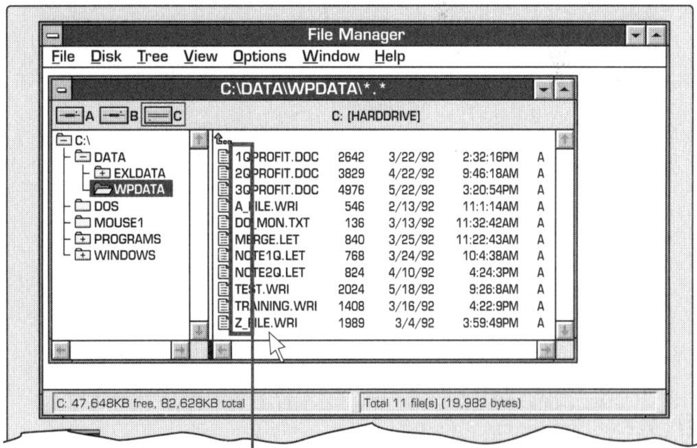

1 Click the folder (example: **WPDATA**) that contains the files you want to view sorted.

2 Click **View**.

3 Click **Sort by Name**.

■ The files are sorted by filename in alphabetical order.

*Note: To display only the file names, click **View**. Then click **Name**.*

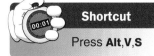

Shortcut

Press **Alt**,**V**,**S**

SEARCH FOR FILES

Search For Files

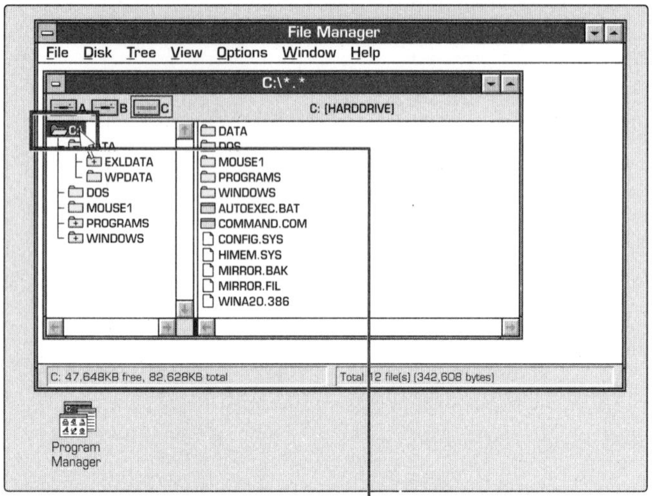

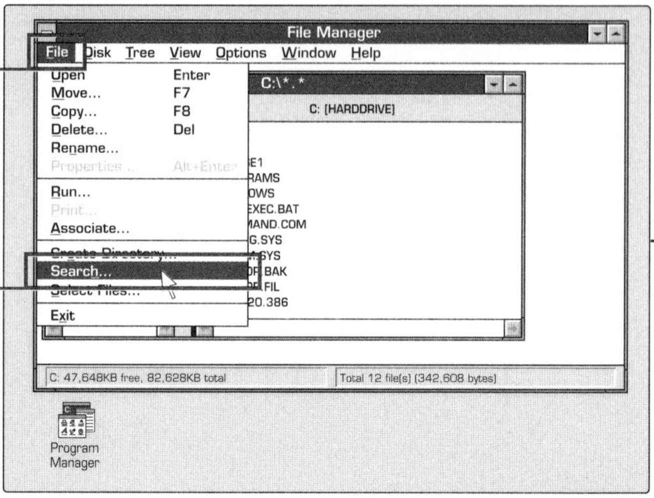

1 Open the **File Manager**.

2 Click the directory (example: **C:**) you want to search.

3 Click **File**.

4 Click **Search** and the **Search** dialog box appears.

Shortcut

Press **Alt**,**F**,**H**

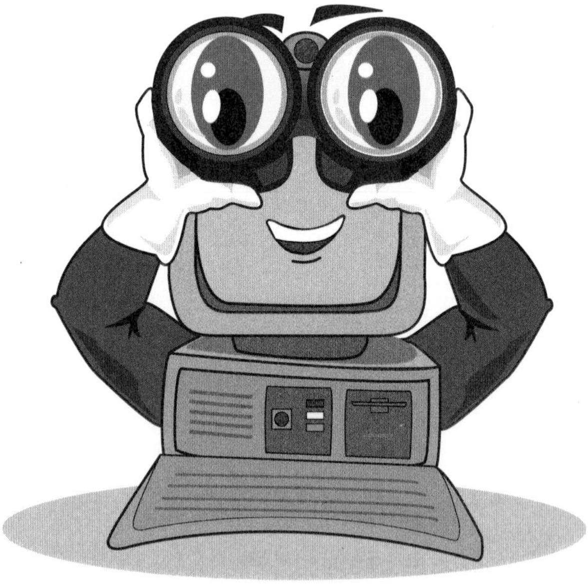

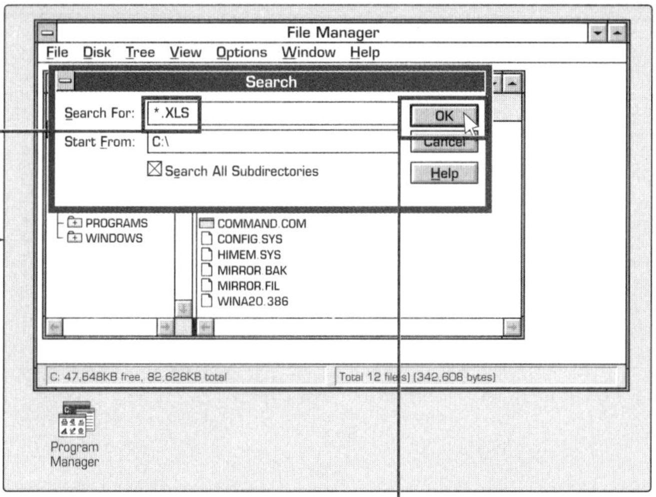

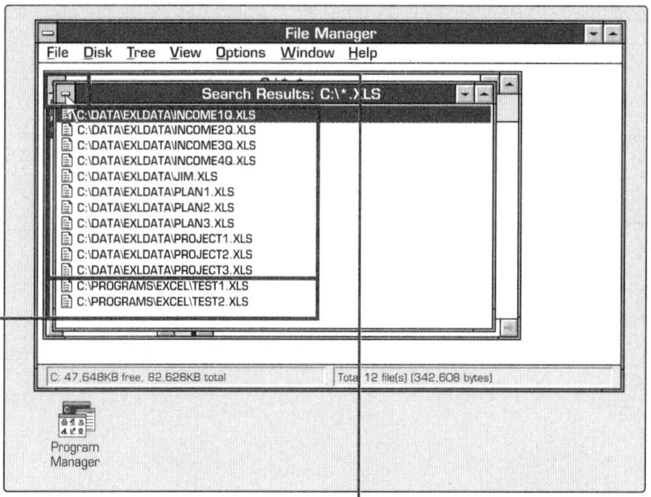

5 To search for all files with a specific extension, type ***.** and then the extension (example: ***.XLS**).

Note: To search for a specific file, type the name of the file (example: ***EXMARK.BMP****).*

Note: To search only the current directory, click the ***Search All Subdirectories*** *box to turn it* ***off*** *and ☒ becomes ☐. This speeds up the search process.*

6 Click the **OK** button.

■ The search is complete. In this example, the search found **11** files in the **C:\DATA\EXLDATA** directory and **2** files in the **C:\PROGRAMS\EXCEL** directory that satisfied the search criteria.

7 To close the **Search Results** window, double click its Control menu box.

Note: Files found in the ***Search Results*** *window can be moved or copied to other directories.*

WILDCARD CHARACTERS

When you use an * (asterisk) in the **Search For:** box, the * is interpreted to mean any number of characters (example: **LET*.*** searches for all files starting with **LET**).

When you use a **?** (question mark) in the **Search For:** box, the **?** is interpreted to mean any character in that position (example: **LETTER?.WK1** matches **LETTER1.WK1** and **LETTER2.WK1**).

SELECT FILES

Select a Group of Files in Sequence

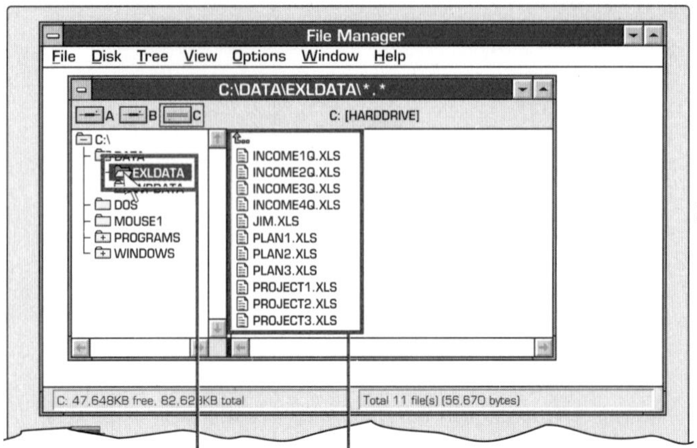

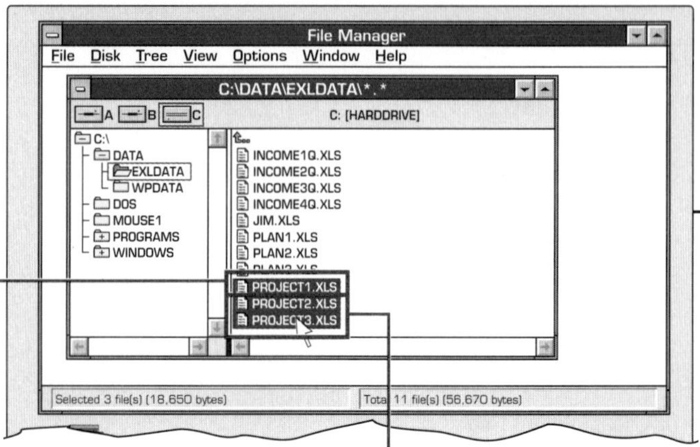

Multiple file selection is very useful for moving, copying or deleting groups of files.

The technique described on these two pages is for selecting files that do not extend beyond the directory window.

1 Click the directory (example: **EXLDATA**) that contains the files you want to select.

■ The files in the selected directory are displayed.

2 Click the first file in the group (example: **PROJECT1.XLS**) you want to select.

3 To select the group, hold down **Shift** and click the file at the end of the group (example: **PROJECT3.XLS**).

Select Two or More Files Randomly

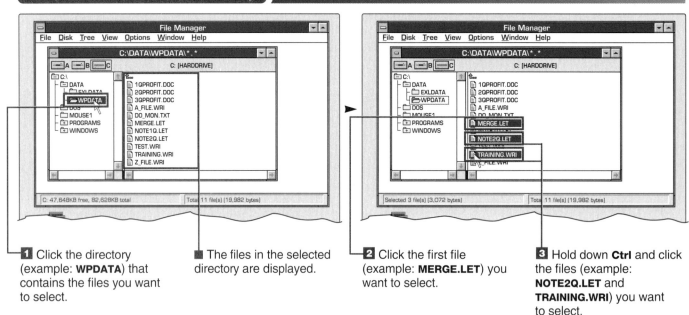

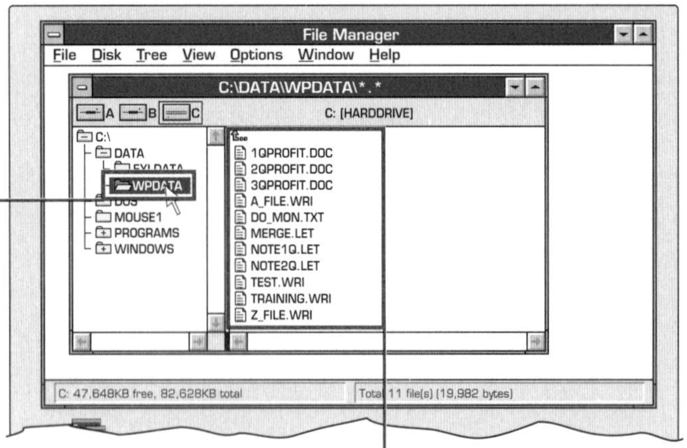

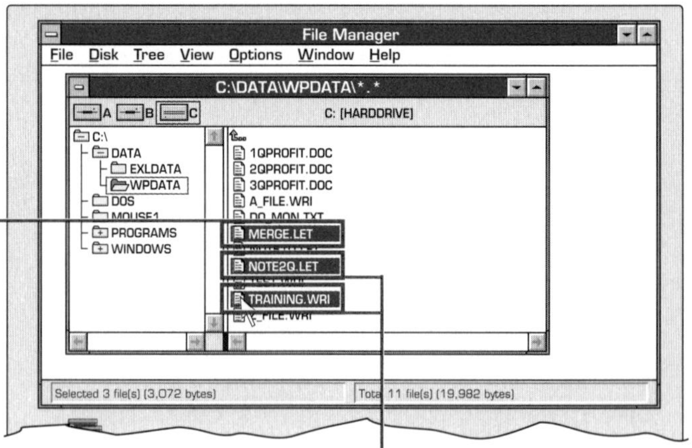

1 Click the directory (example: **WPDATA**) that contains the files you want to select.

■ The files in the selected directory are displayed.

2 Click the first file (example: **MERGE.LET**) you want to select.

3 Hold down **Ctrl** and click the files (example: **NOTE2Q.LET** and **TRAINING.WRI**) you want to select.

Select Multiple Groups of Files

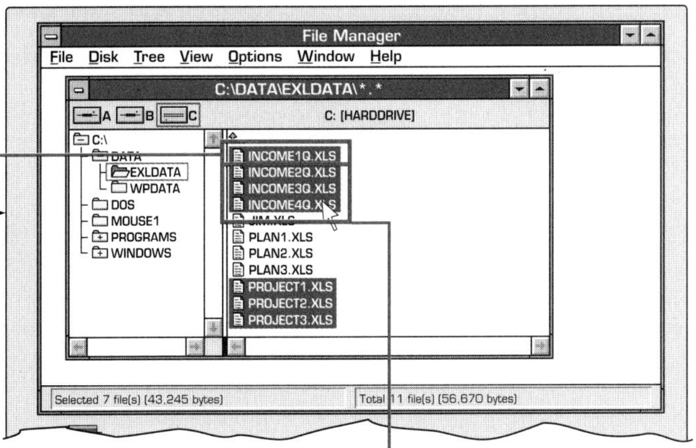

4 Hold down **Ctrl** and click the first file of the second group (example: **INCOME1Q.XLS**) you want to select.

5 To select the second group, hold down **Ctrl+Shift** and click the file at the end of the second group (example: **INCOME4Q.XLS**).

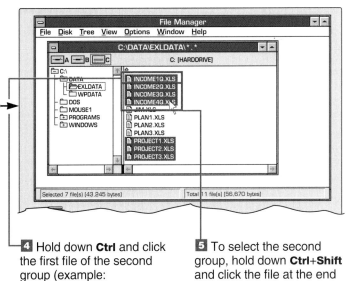

Note: To cancel any group of sequential or randomly selected files, click any file in the window.

Select All Files

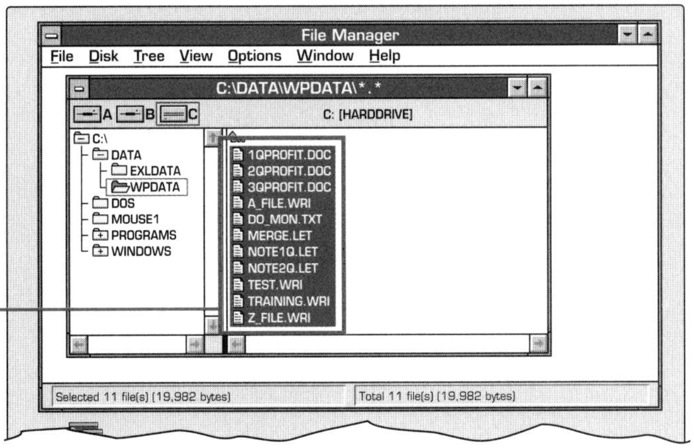

1 To select all files, press **Ctrl+/** (slash).

Deselect All Files

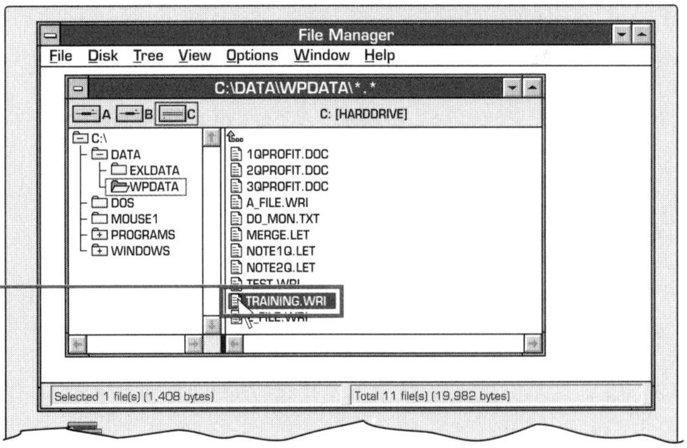

1 To deselect all files, click any file (example: **TRAINING.WRI**).

*Note: To deselect a single file, hold down **Ctrl** and click that file.*

SELECT FILES

Select Files Using the Wildcard Characters

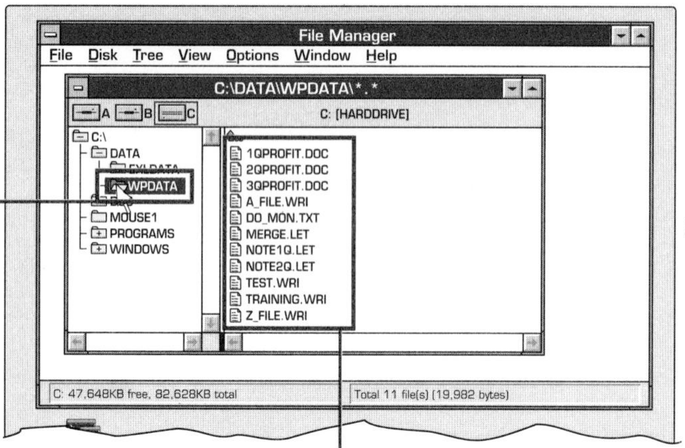

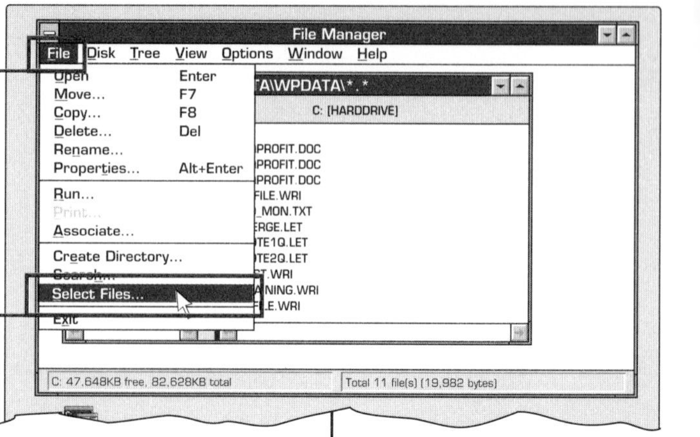

The technique described on these two pages is for selecting large numbers of files that extend beyond the directory window.

1 Click the directory (example: **WPDATA**) that contains the files you want to select.

■ The files in the selected directory are displayed.

Note: In this example, all files in the current directory are displayed in the directory window. However, this selection technique applies to all files in the current directory, even if they are not visible on the computer screen.

2 Click **File** to open its menu.

3 Click **Select Files** and the **Select Files** dialog box appears.

Shortcut

Press **Alt**,**F**,**S**

WILDCARD CHARACTERS

When you use an * (asterisk) in the **File(s)** box, the * is interpreted to mean any number of characters (example: **LET*.*** selects all files starting with **LET**).

When you use a **?** (question mark) in the **File(s)** box, the **?** is interpreted to mean any character in that position (example: **LETTER?.WK1** matches **LETTER1.WK1** and **LETTER2.WK1**).

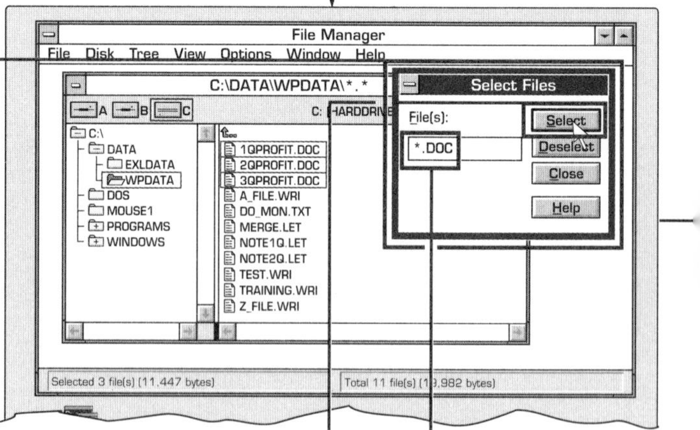

Select files

4 To view the files while selecting them, move the dialog box to the position shown on the above screen.

5 To select all files with the extension **DOC**, type ***.DOC**.

6 Click the **Select** button and the files with the **DOC** extension are selected.

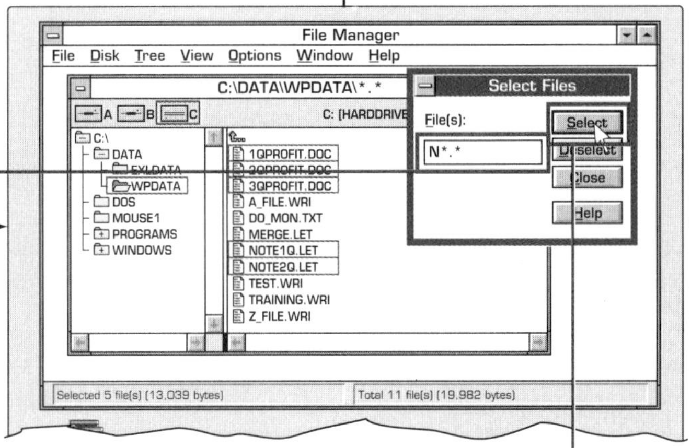

Select more files

7 Double click in the **File(s):** box to select it.

8 To select all files starting with **N**, type **N*.***

9 Click the **Select** button and the files starting with **N** are selected.

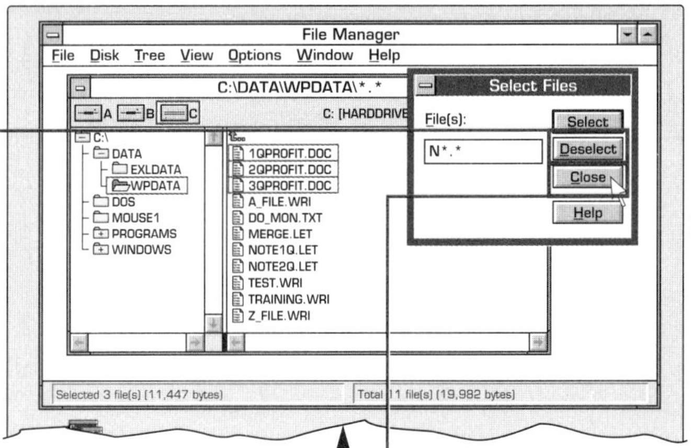

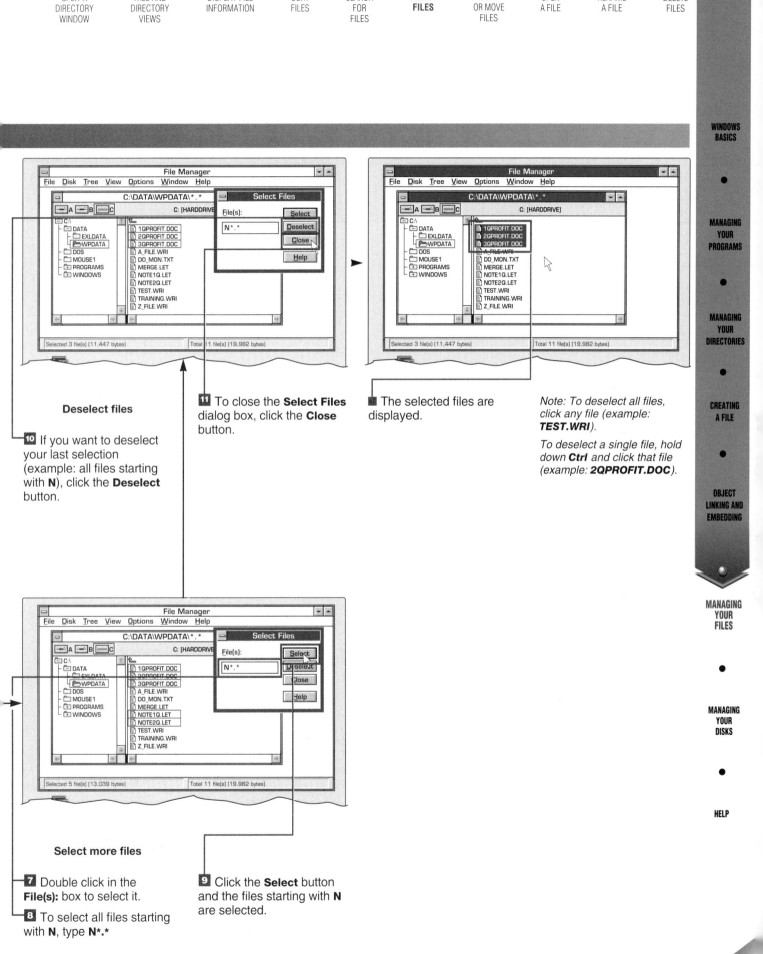

Deselect files

10 If you want to deselect your last selection (example: all files starting with **N**), click the **Deselect** button.

11 To close the **Select Files** dialog box, click the **Close** button.

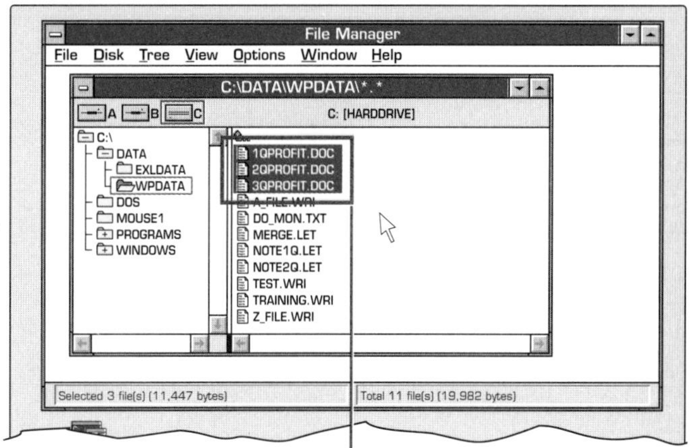

■ The selected files are displayed.

*Note: To deselect all files, click any file (example: **TEST.WRI**).*

*To deselect a single file, hold down **Ctrl** and click that file (example: **2QPROFIT.DOC**).*

COPY OR MOVE FILES

Copy Files to a Different Drive

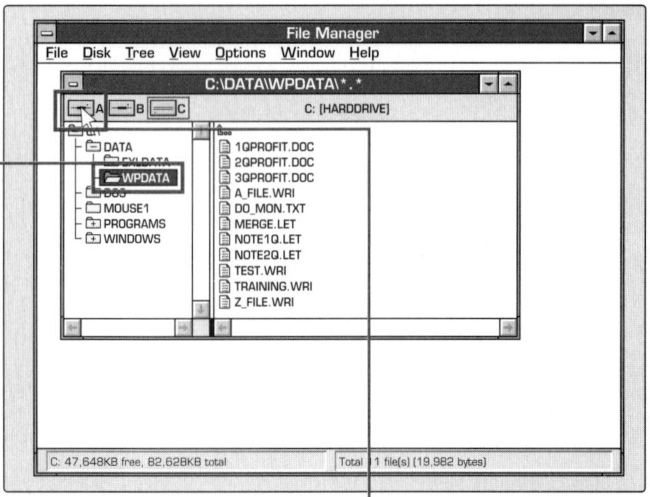

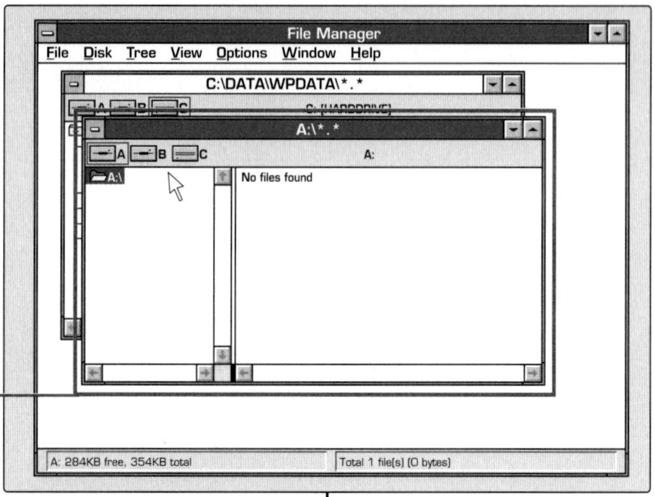

This is useful for backing up selected data files to a disk.

1 Click the directory (example: **WPDATA**) that contains the files you want to copy to a disk.

2 Double click the drive icon (example: **A:**) you want to copy the files to.

Note: Make sure you have a formatted disk in the drive you want to copy the files to.

■ A new directory window appears, displaying the contents of the current drive (example: drive **A:**).

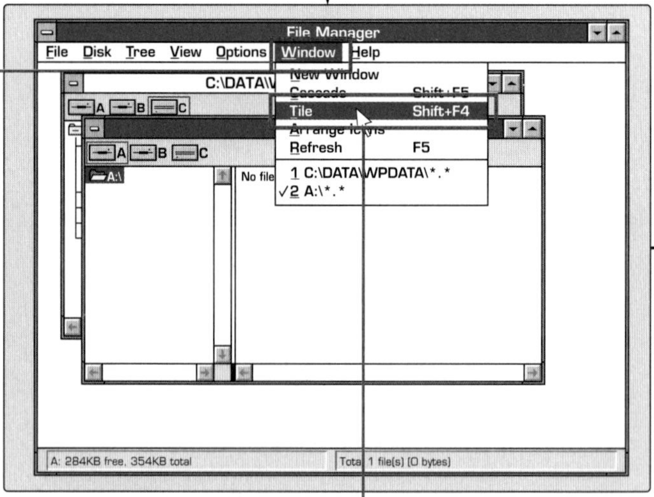

3 To tile the directory windows, click **Window** to open its menu.

4 Click **Tile**.

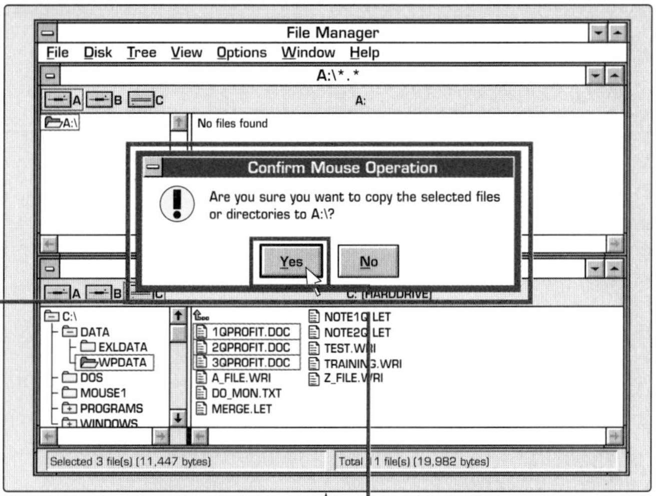

■ Windows offers you a final chance to copy or not copy the selected files to the drive.

6 Click the **Yes** button to copy the files.

Note: Click the ***No*** *button to cancel the copy.*

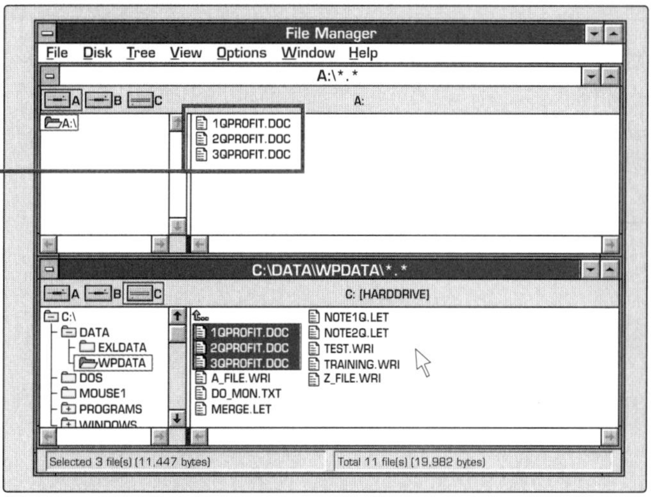

■ The files are copied to a different drive (example: drive **A:**).

Note: To close a window, double click its Control menu box ⊟ *.*

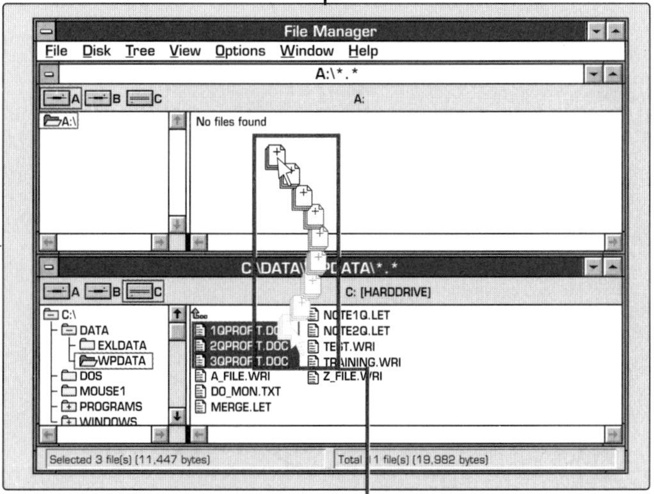

■ The windows are tiled.

5 Select the files you want to copy to the disk, then drag them into the new directory window. Release the mouse button.

Note: To select files, refer to pages 68-71.

TO MOVE FILES INSTEAD OF COPYING THEM

The same procedure applies, except hold down **Alt** before you drag the files as illustrated in step **5**. Release the mouse button and then release **Alt**.

Note: The ***Confirm Mouse Operation*** *dialog box displays "Are you sure you want to* ***move*** *the selected files or directories to* ***A:****?".*

COPY OR MOVE FILES

Copy Directories Containing Files to a Different Drive

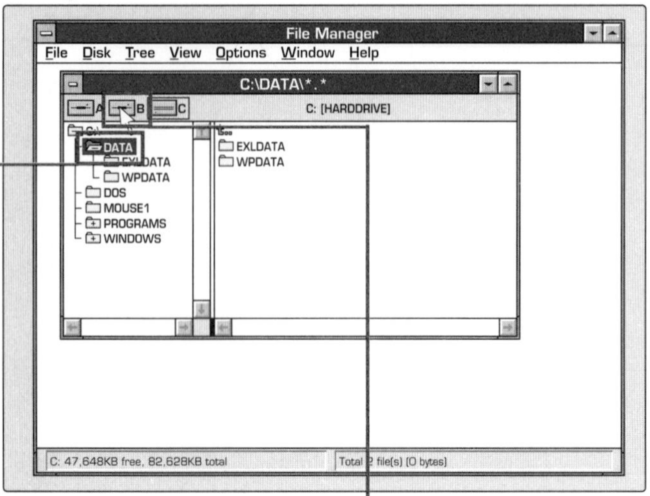

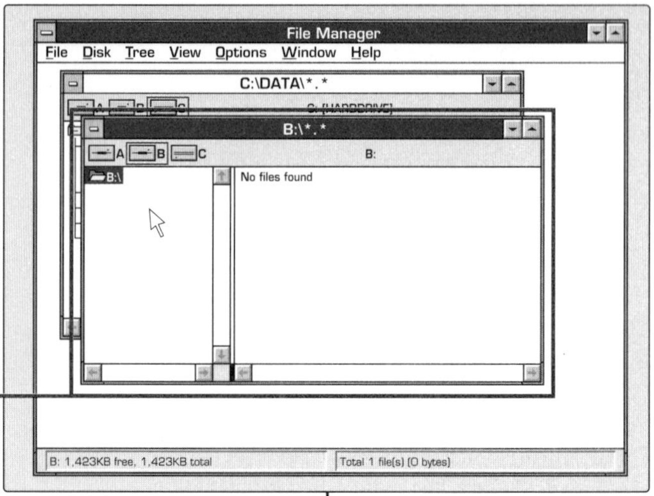

This is useful for backing up all your data files at the same time.

1 Click the directory (example: **DATA**) you want to copy to a disk.

2 Double click the drive icon (example: **B:**) you want to copy the directory to.

Note: Make sure you have a formatted disk in the drive you want to copy the directory to.

■ A new directory window appears, displaying the contents of the current drive (example: drive **B:**).

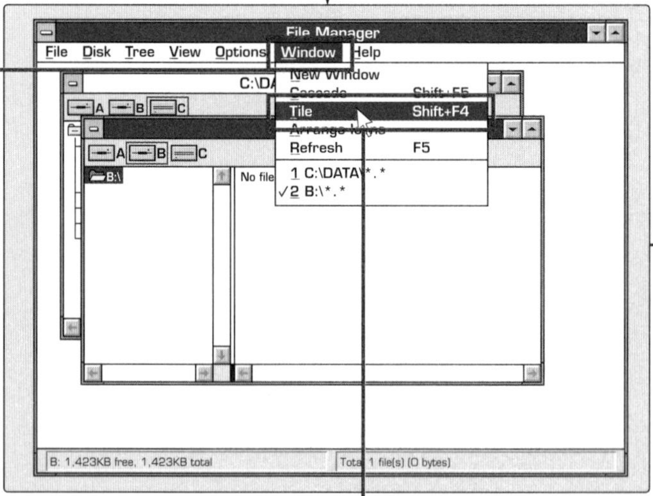

3 To tile the directory windows, click **Window** to open its menu.

4 Click **Tile**.

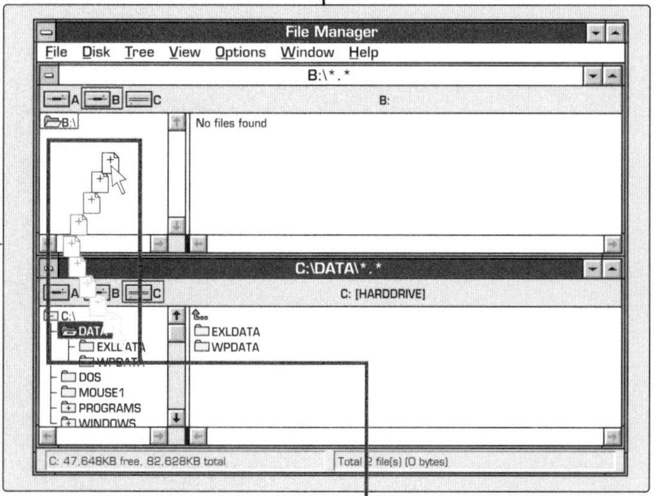

■ The windows are tiled.

5 Drag the directory (example: **DATA**) to the new directory window. Then release the mouse button.

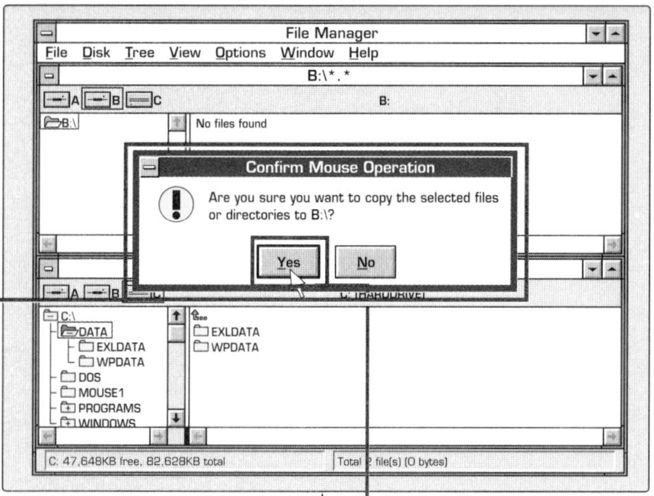

■ Windows offers you a final chance to copy or not copy the selected directory and its files to the drive.

6 Click the **Yes** button to copy the directory.

Note: Click the ***No*** *button to cancel the copy.*

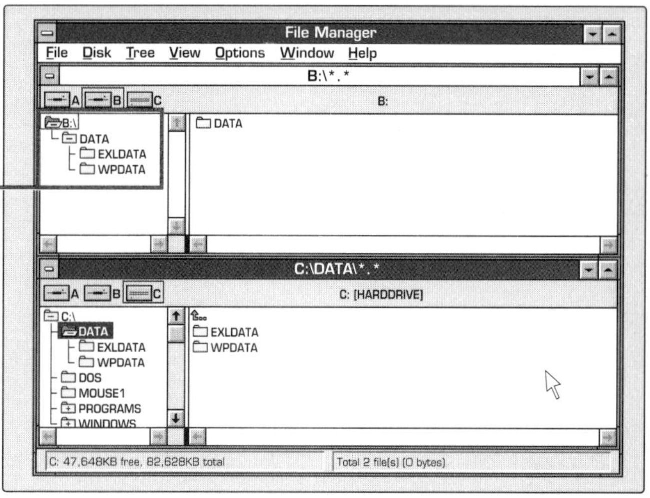

■ The directory is copied to a different drive (example: drive **B:**).

Note: If the copied directory contains subdirectories and/or data files, these are also copied to the drive.

Note: To close a window, double click its Control menu box ⊟ *.*

TO MOVE DIRECTORIES INSTEAD OF COPYING THEM

The same procedure applies, except hold down **Alt** before you drag the directory as illustrated in step **5**. Release the mouse button and then release **Alt**.

Note: The ***Confirm Mouse Operation*** *dialog box displays "Are you sure you want to* ***move*** *the selected files or directories to* ***B:****?".*

COPY OR MOVE FILES

Copy a File Within the Same Directory

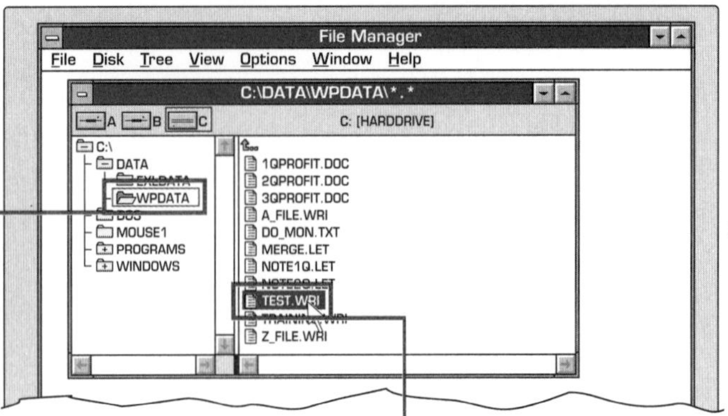

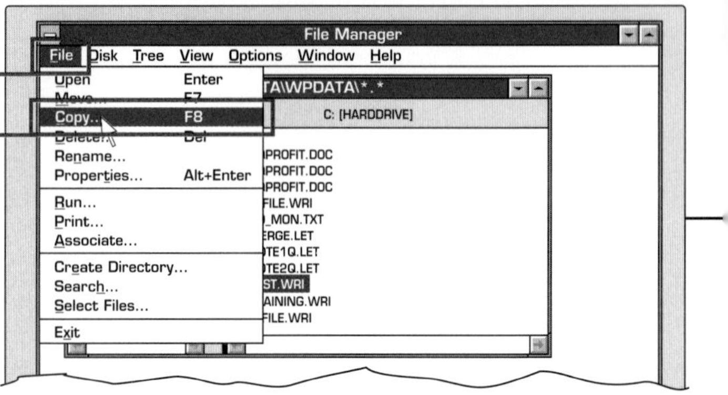

This is useful if you want to modify an existing file but still retain a copy of the original.

1 Click the directory (example: **WPDATA**) that contains the file you want to copy.

2 Click the file (example: **TEST.WRI**) you want to copy.

3 Click **File** to open its menu.

4 Click **Copy** and the **Copy** dialog box appears on the next screen.

Shortcut

Press **F8**

Move Files from One Directory to Another Within the Same Drive

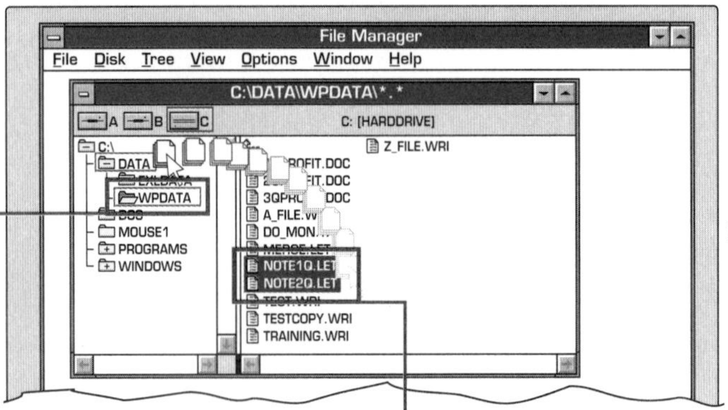

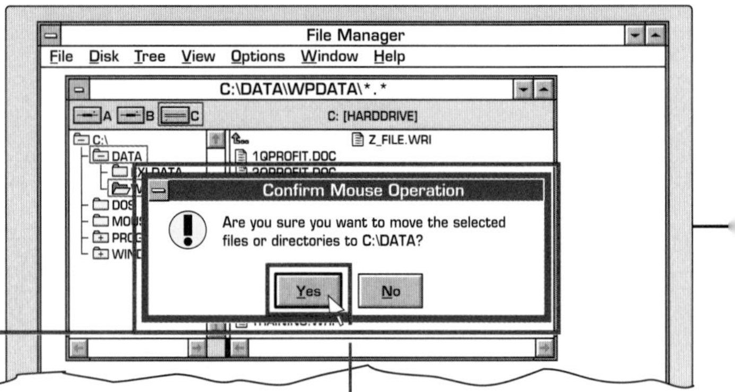

1 Click the directory (example: **WPDATA**) that contains the files you want to move.

2 Select the files (example: **NOTE1Q.LET** and **NOTE2Q.LET**) you want to move to another directory.

Note: To select files, refer to pages 68-71.

3 Drag the files to the new directory (example: **DATA**). Then release the mouse button.

■ Windows offers you a final chance to move or not move the selected files to the directory.

4 Click the **Yes** button to move the files.

*Note: Click the **No** button to cancel the move.*

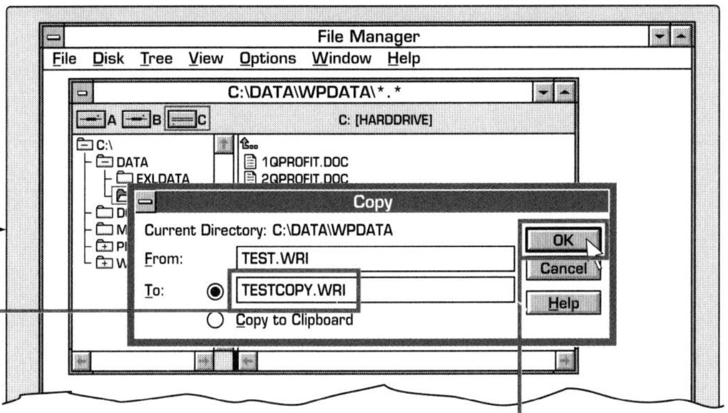

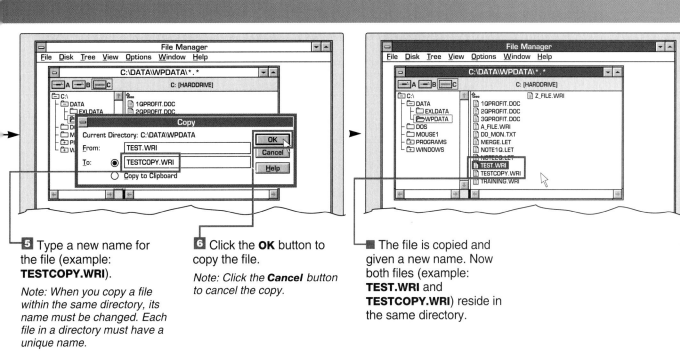

5 Type a new name for the file (example: **TESTCOPY.WRI**).

Note: When you copy a file within the same directory, its name must be changed. Each file in a directory must have a unique name.

6 Click the **OK** button to copy the file.

*Note: Click the **Cancel** button to cancel the copy.*

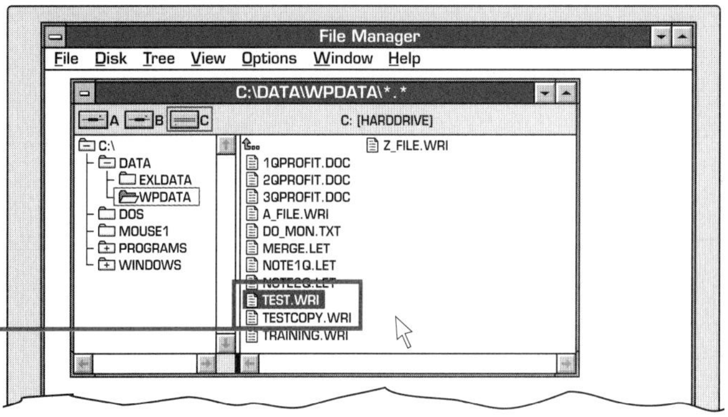

■ The file is copied and given a new name. Now both files (example: **TEST.WRI** and **TESTCOPY.WRI**) reside in the same directory.

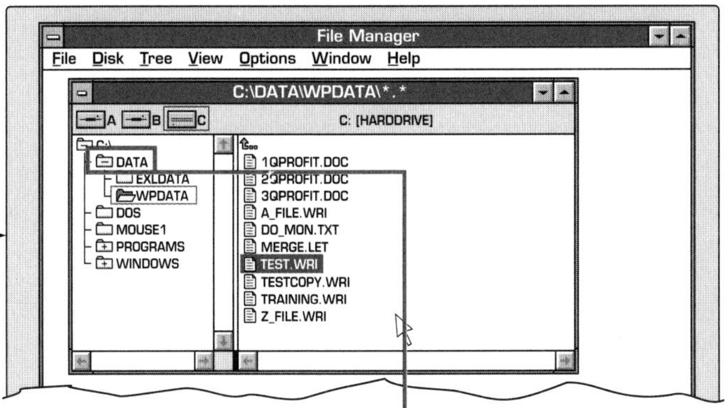

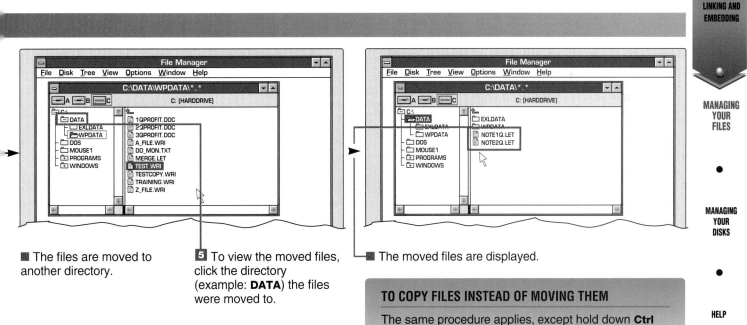

■ The files are moved to another directory.

5 To view the moved files, click the directory (example: **DATA**) the files were moved to.

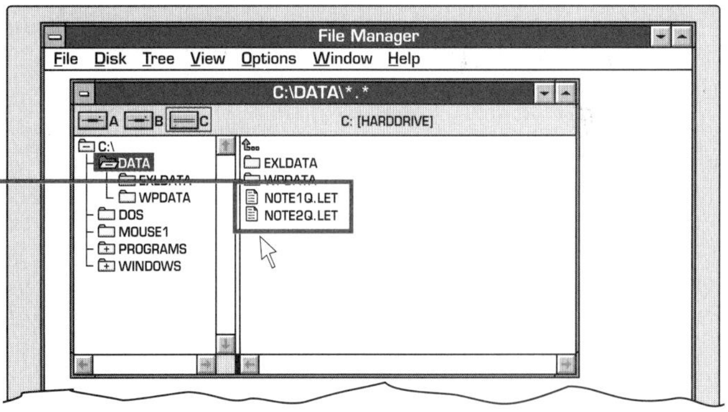

■ The moved files are displayed.

TO COPY FILES INSTEAD OF MOVING THEM

The same procedure applies, except hold down **Ctrl** before you drag the files as illustrated in step **3**. Release the mouse button and then release **Ctrl**.

*Note: The **Confirm Mouse Operation** dialog box displays "Are you sure you want to **copy** the selected files or directories to **C:\DATA?**".*

COPY OR MOVE FILES

Create a New Group Window

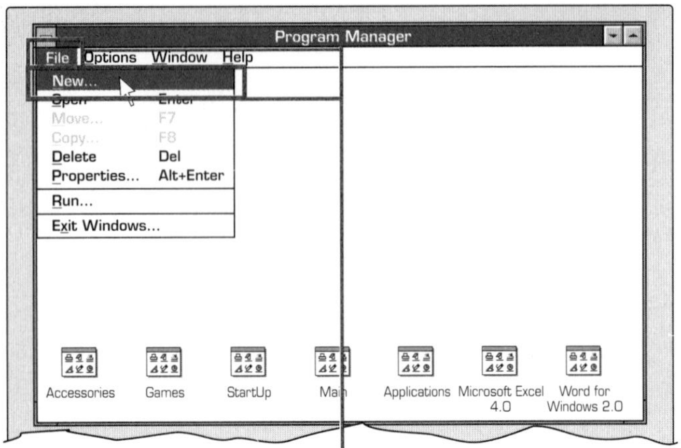

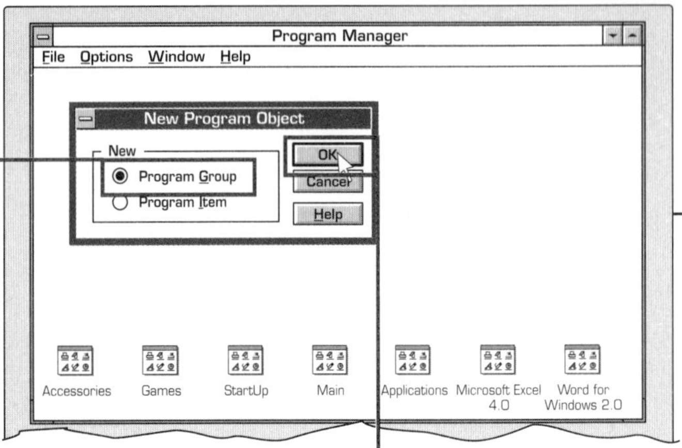

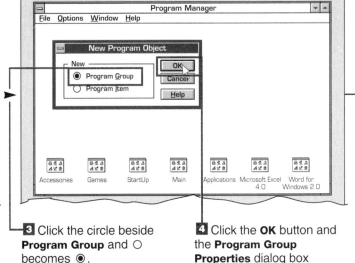

Suppose you are working on a project that uses several program and data files. A new Group window can be created to hold and manage these programs and files in one central location.

1 Click **File** to open its menu.

2 Click **New** and the **New Program Object** dialog box appears.

3 Click the circle beside **Program Group** and ○ becomes ◉.

4 Click the **OK** button and the **Program Group Properties** dialog box appears.

Copy Files to a Group Window

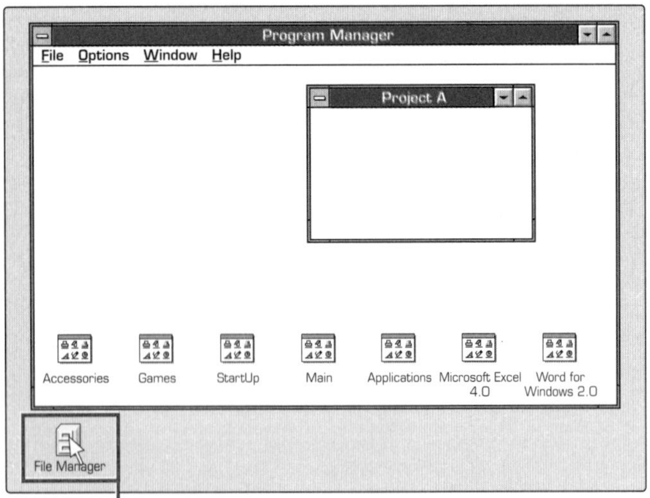

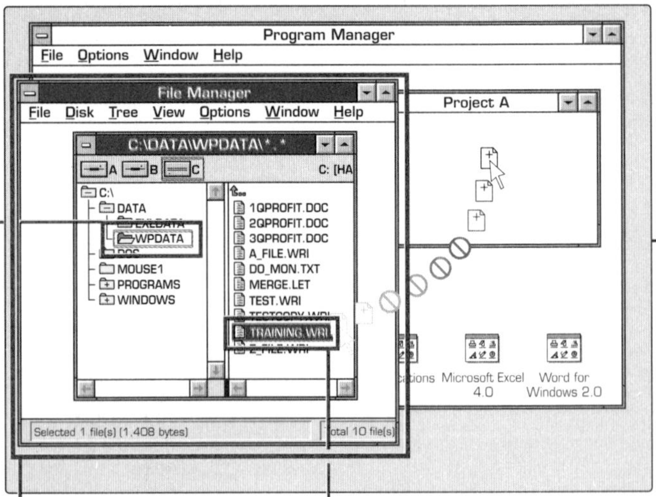

Files can be copied from any directory window into a Group window. These files can then be started from the Group window.

1 Double click the **File Manager** to start it.

2 Resize and move the **File Manager** as shown above.

3 Click the directory (example: **WPDATA**) that contains the file you want to copy.

4 Click on the file you want to copy (example: **TRAINING.WRI**) and drag it into the Group window (example: **Project A**).

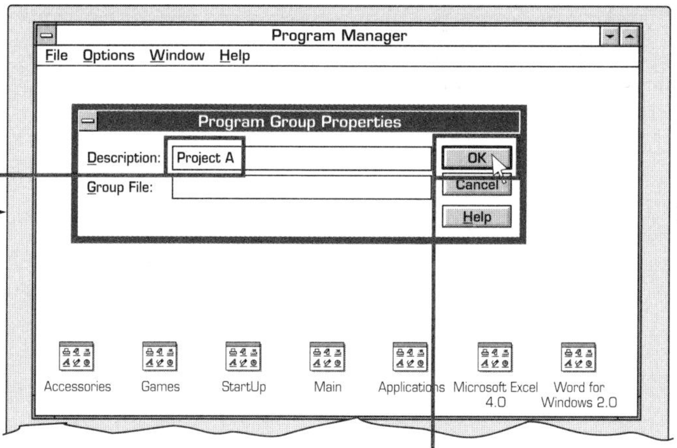

5 Type a name (example: **Project A**) for the new Group window.

6 Click the **OK** button.

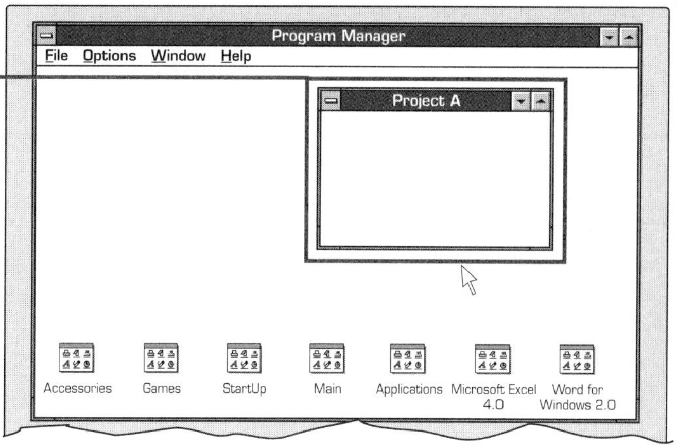

7 The new Group window appears (example: **Project A**). Resize the window as shown above.

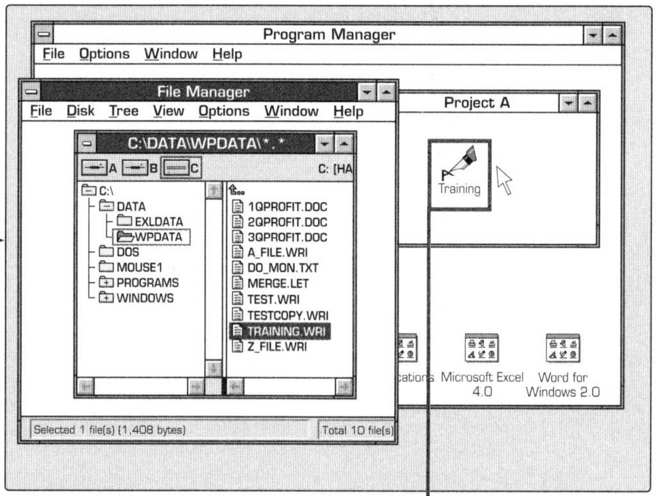

5 Release the mouse button and the file (example: **TRAINING.WRI**) appears as a Program item icon in the Group window (example: **Project A**).

Note: To close a window, double click its Control menu box ▭.

DELETE A PROGRAM ITEM ICON

1 Click the icon (example: **Training**) to select it.

2 Press **Delete** and the **Delete** dialog box appears.

3 To delete the icon, click the **Yes** button.

Open a File from the File Manager

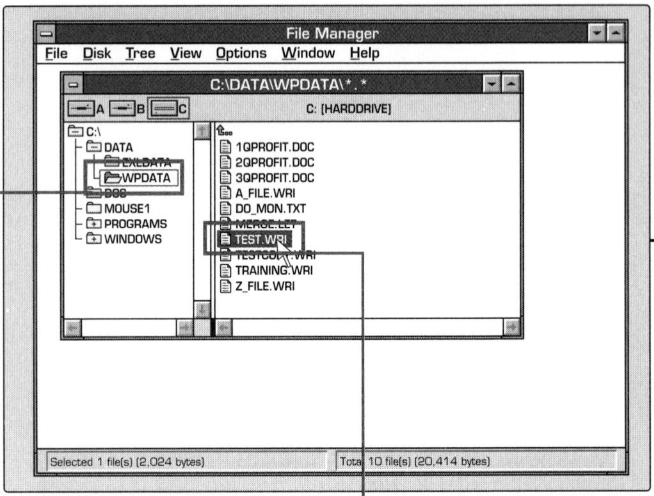

1 Click the directory (example: **WPDATA**) that contains the file you want to open.

2 Double click the file (example: **TEST.WRI**) you want to open.

Rename a File

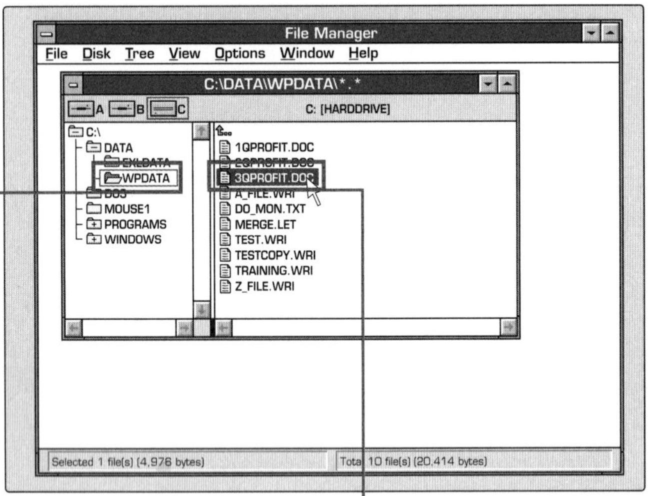

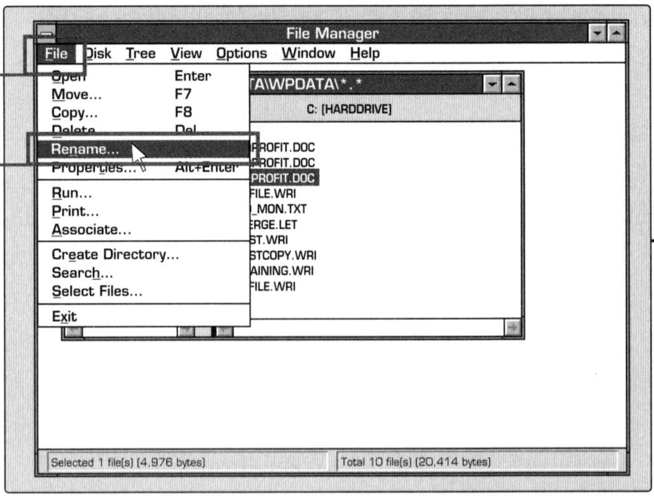

1 Click the directory (example: **WPDATA**) that contains the file you want to rename.

2 Click the file (example: **3QPROFIT.DOC**) you want to rename.

3 Click **File** to open its menu.

4 Click **Rename** and the **Rename** dialog box appears.

Shortcut

Press **Alt**,**F**,**N**

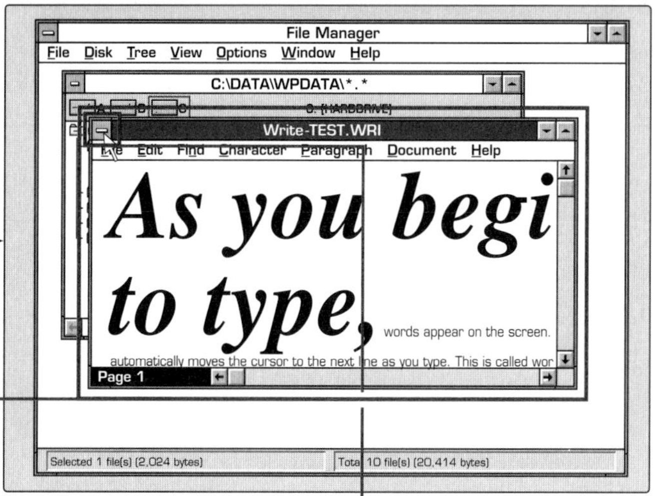

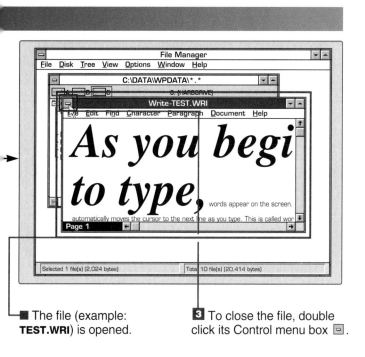

■ The file (example: **TEST.WRI**) is opened.

3 To close the file, double click its Control menu box ⊟.

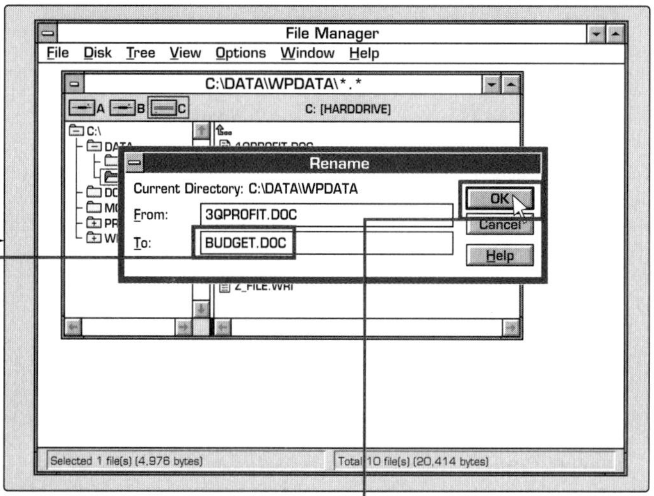

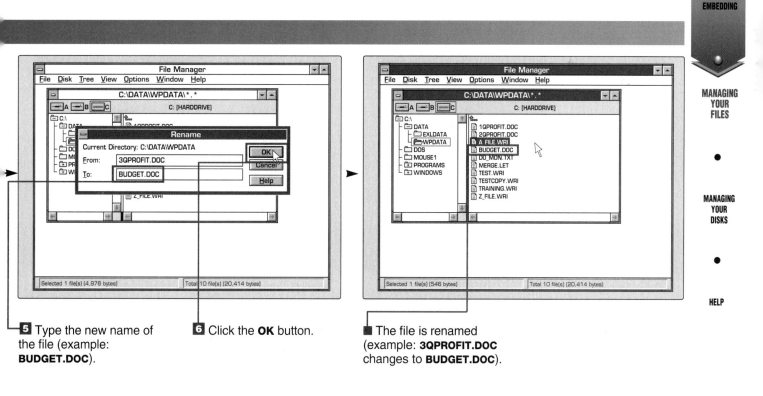

5 Type the new name of the file (example: **BUDGET.DOC**).

6 Click the **OK** button.

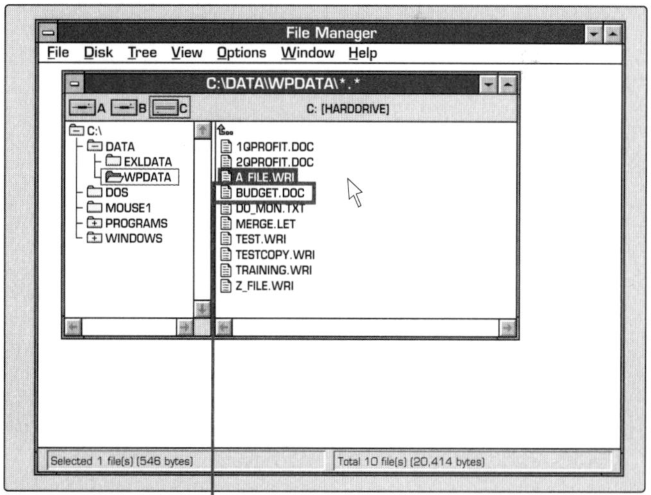

■ The file is renamed (example: **3QPROFIT.DOC** changes to **BUDGET.DOC**).

DELETE FILES

Delete a File

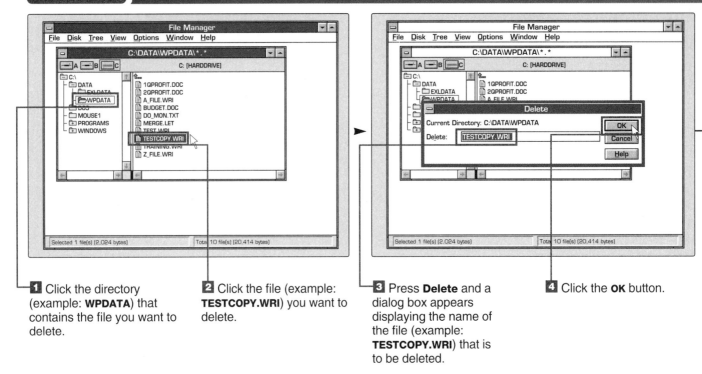

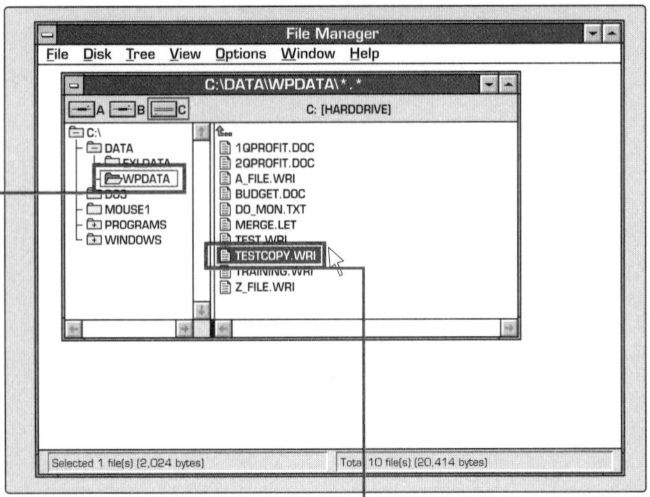

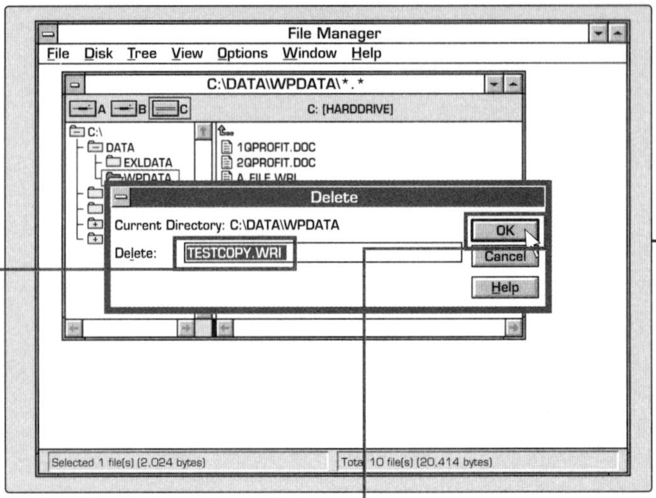

1 Click the directory (example: **WPDATA**) that contains the file you want to delete.

2 Click the file (example: **TESTCOPY.WRI**) you want to delete.

3 Press **Delete** and a dialog box appears displaying the name of the file (example: **TESTCOPY.WRI**) that is to be deleted.

4 Click the **OK** button.

Delete Multiple Files

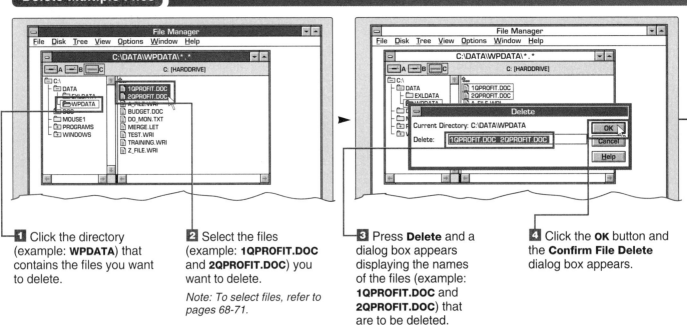

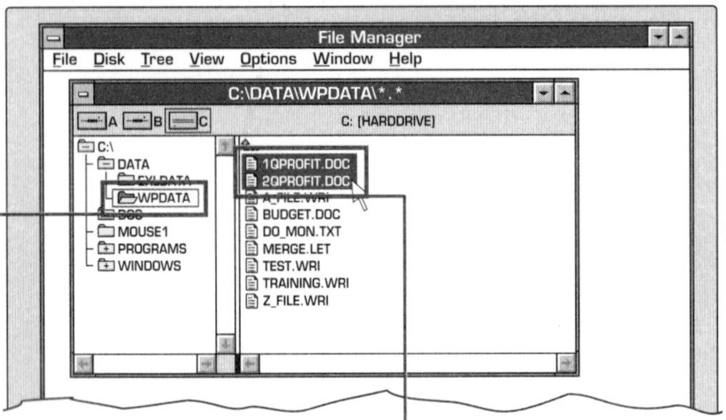

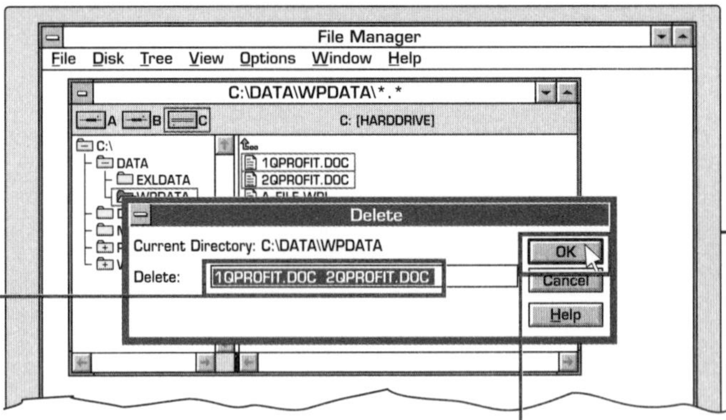

1 Click the directory (example: **WPDATA**) that contains the files you want to delete.

2 Select the files (example: **1QPROFIT.DOC** and **2QPROFIT.DOC**) you want to delete.

Note: To select files, refer to pages 68-71.

3 Press **Delete** and a dialog box appears displaying the names of the files (example: **1QPROFIT.DOC** and **2QPROFIT.DOC**) that are to be deleted.

4 Click the **OK** button and the **Confirm File Delete** dialog box appears.

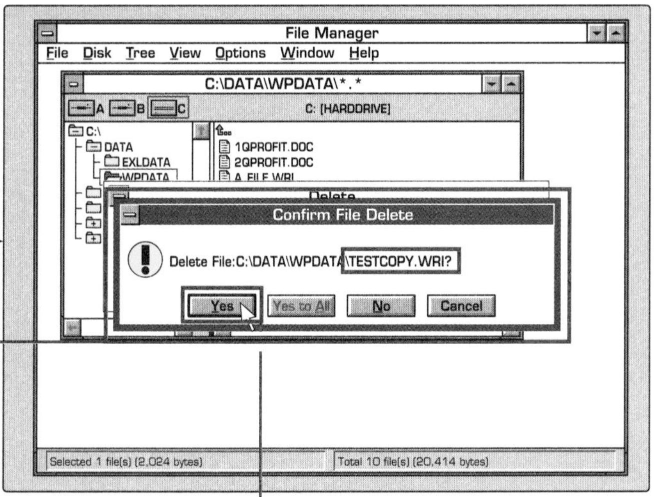

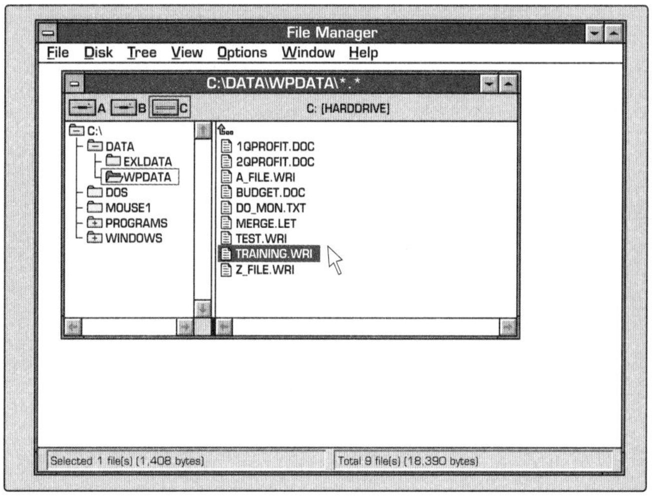

■ The **Confirm File Delete** dialog box appears, offering you one last chance to change your mind.

5 To delete the file, click the **Yes** button.

Note: If you do not want to delete the file, click the ***No*** *button.*

■ The file is deleted.

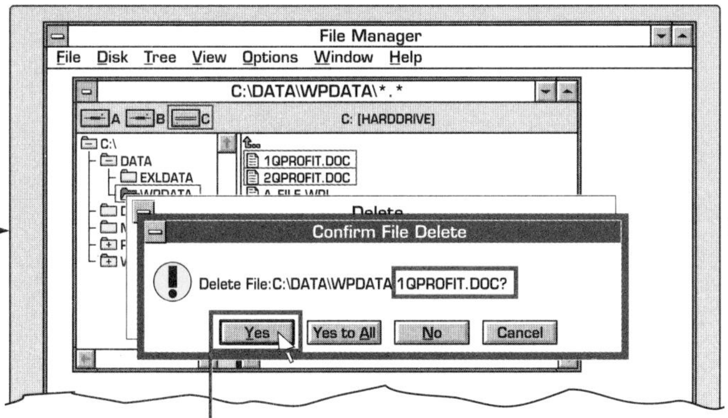

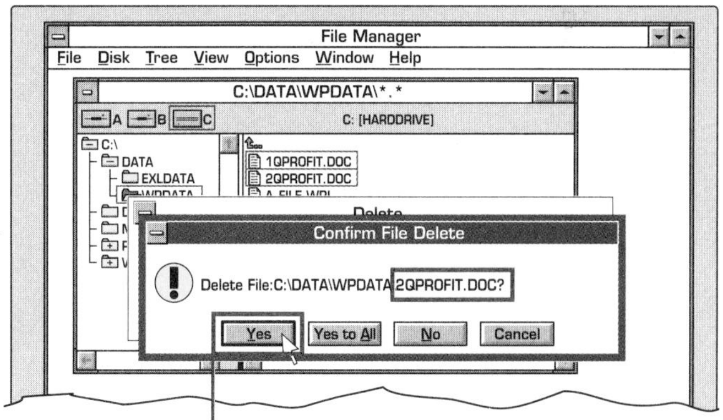

5 Click the **Yes** button to delete the first file (example: **1QPROFIT.DOC**).

Note: Click the ***Yes to All*** *button to delete all the files at one time.*

Click the ***No*** *button if you do not want to delete the file.*

Click the ***Cancel*** *button to cancel the Delete command.*

6 Click the **Yes** button to delete the next file (example: **2QPROFIT.DOC**).

Note: If more files were selected, this process continues until all selected files are deleted.

FORMAT A DISK

Format a Disk

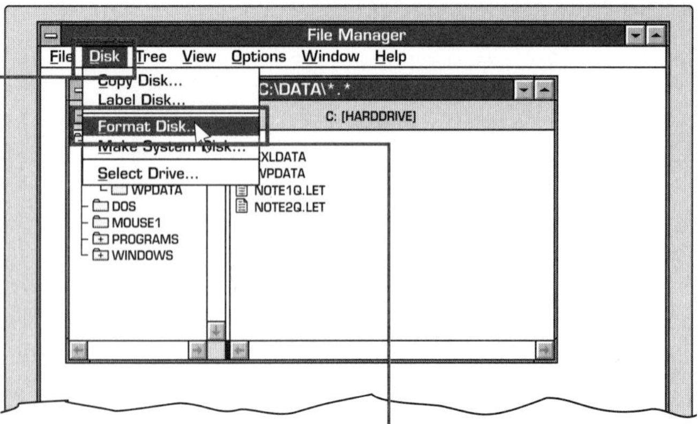

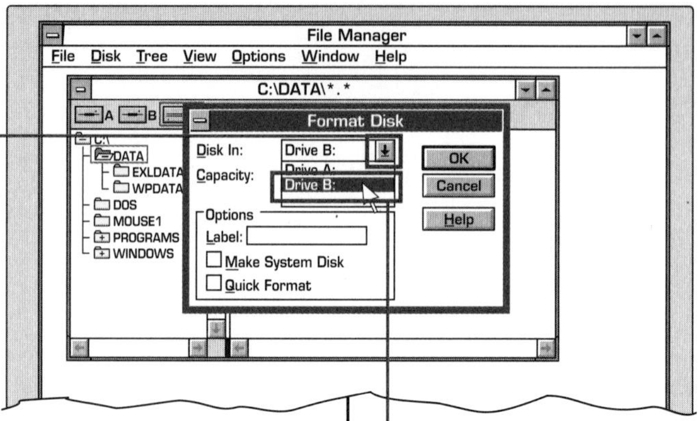

The Format Disk command prepares a new or previously formatted disk for storage of files.

1 Insert the disk to be formatted into a drive (example: drive **A:**).

2 Click **Disk** to open its menu.

3 Click **Format Disk** and the **Format Disk** dialog box appears on the next screen.

Shortcut

Press **Alt**,**D**,**F**

4 Click ⬇ beside **Disk In:** and a menu appears.

5 Click the drive (example: **Drive B:**) which contains the disk you want to format.

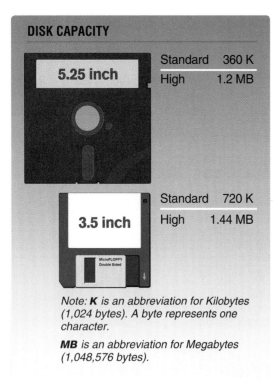

DISK CAPACITY

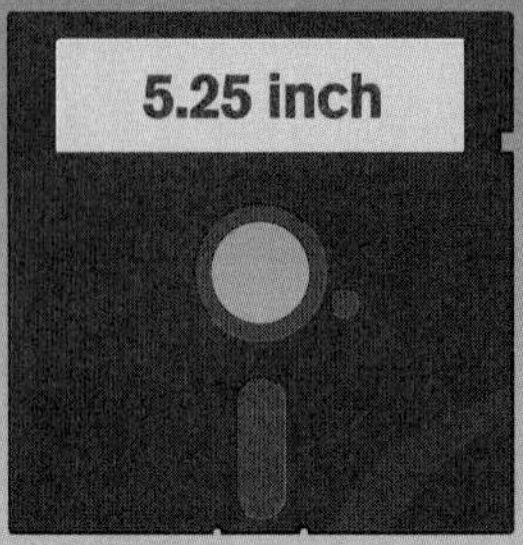

Standard	360 K
High	1.2 MB

Standard	720 K
High	1.44 MB

*Note: **K** is an abbreviation for Kilobytes (1,024 bytes). A byte represents one character.*

***MB** is an abbreviation for Megabytes (1,048,576 bytes).*

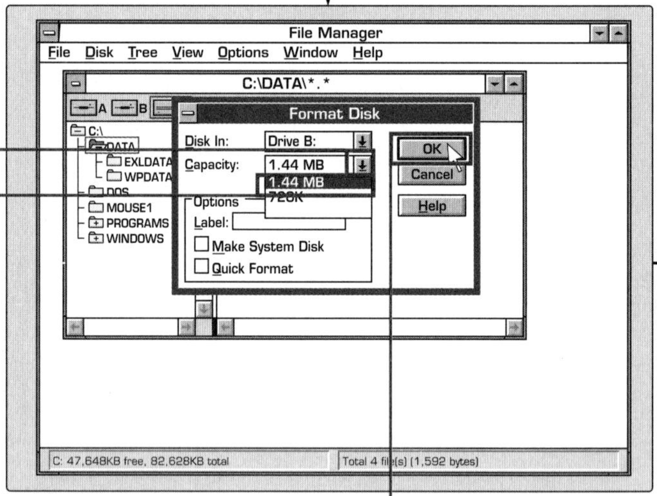

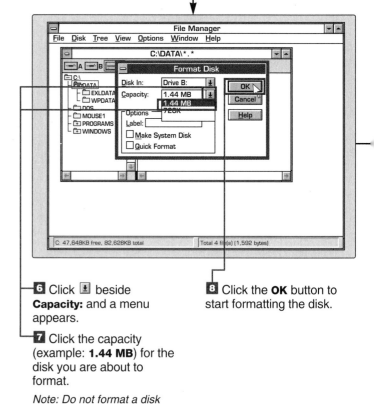

6 Click ⬇ beside **Capacity:** and a menu appears.

7 Click the capacity (example: **1.44 MB**) for the disk you are about to format.

Note: Do not format a disk to a size greater than its guaranteed capacity.

8 Click the **OK** button to start formatting the disk.

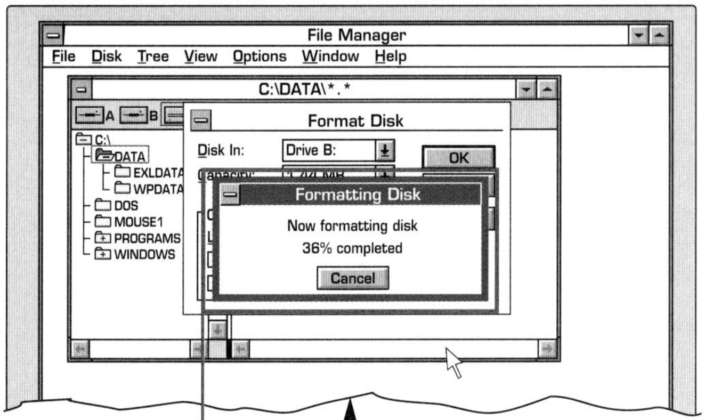

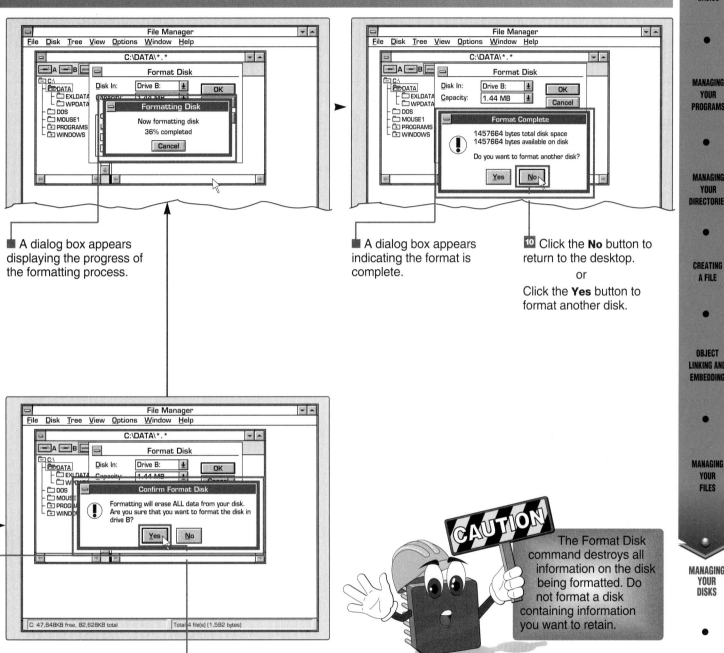

■ A dialog box appears displaying the progress of the formatting process.

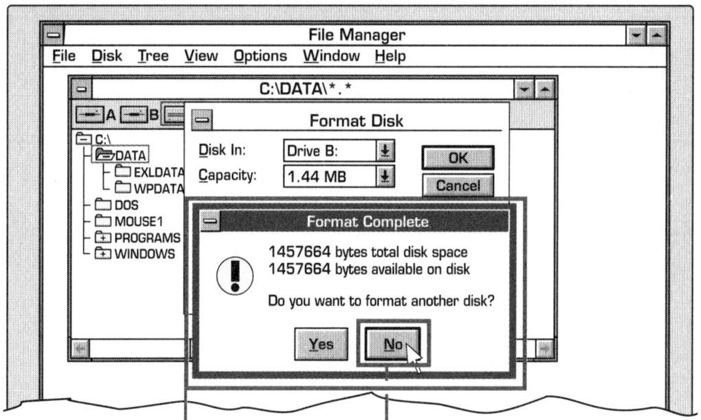

■ A dialog box appears indicating the format is complete.

10 Click the **No** button to return to the desktop.

or

Click the **Yes** button to format another disk.

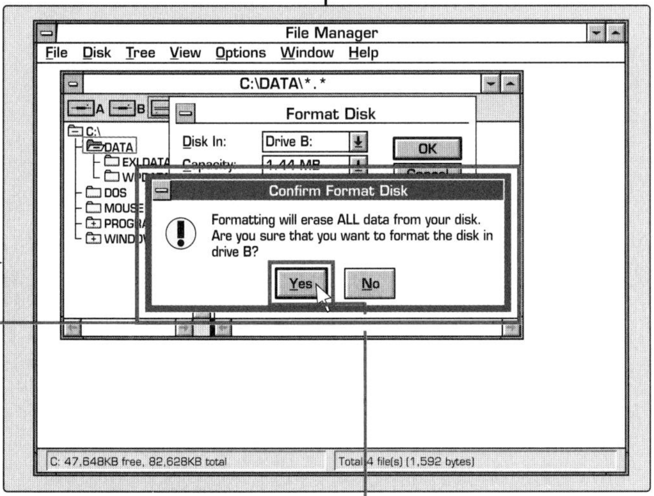

■ You are offered a final chance to change your mind.

9 Click the **Yes** button to proceed.

The Format Disk command destroys all information on the disk being formatted. Do not format a disk containing information you want to retain.

COPY A DISK

Copy a Disk

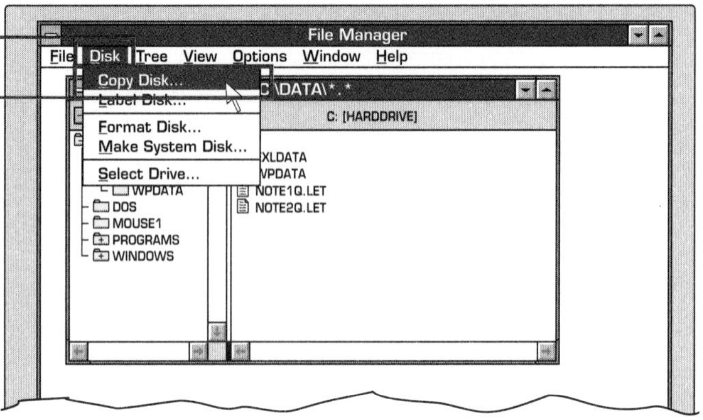

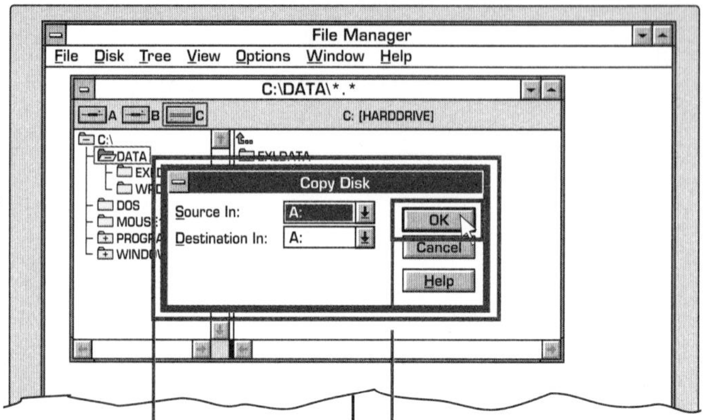

The Copy Disk command is used to copy the entire contents of one disk (the source) to another disk (the destination), so that the second disk is an exact copy of the first. This command only works on disks of the same size and capacity.

1 Click **Disk** to open its menu.

2 Click **Copy Disk**.

Shortcut

Press **Alt**,**D**,**C**

Note: To copy files between disks of different capacities, use the Copy command on page 72.

■ The **Copy Disk** dialog box only appears if your computer has two disk drives (A: and B:).

*Note: To change the source or destination drive, click ⬇ and a menu appears. Click the desired drive (example: **B:**).*

3 Click the **OK** button.

Note: For computers with one disk drive, drive A: is the source and destination drive.

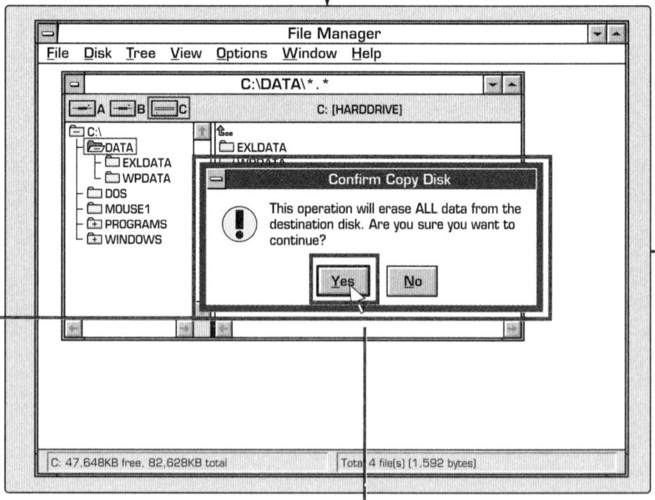

■ You are offered a final chance to change your mind.

4 Click the **Yes** button to continue.

*Note: Click the **No** button to cancel the copy.*

The Copy Disk command automatically formats the destination disk during the copy process. Make sure the destination disk does not contain any files you want to keep.

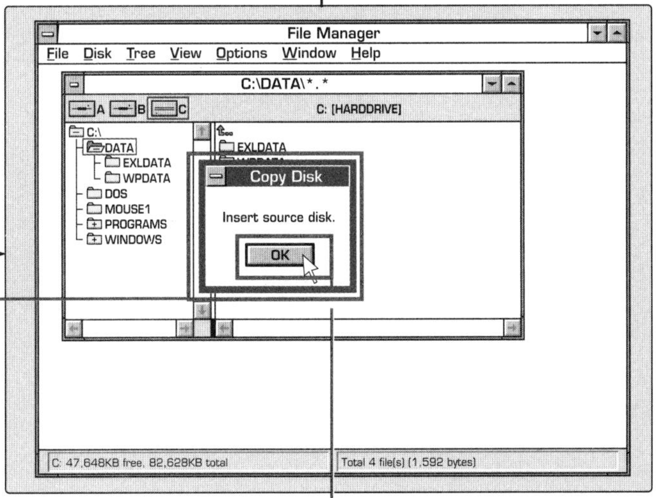

5 You are asked to insert the disk to be copied into the drive you specified (example: drive **A:**).

6 Click the **OK** button.

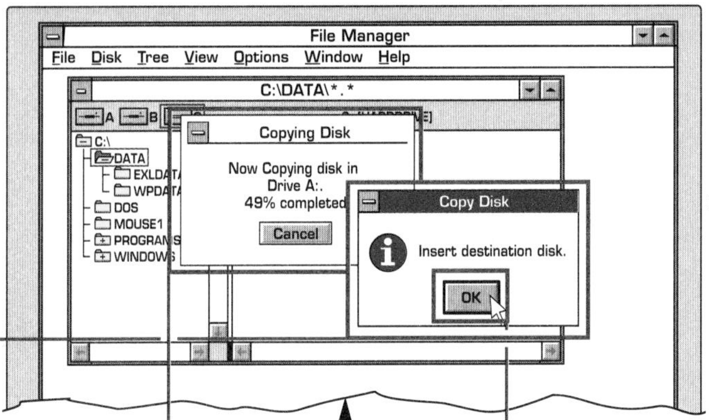

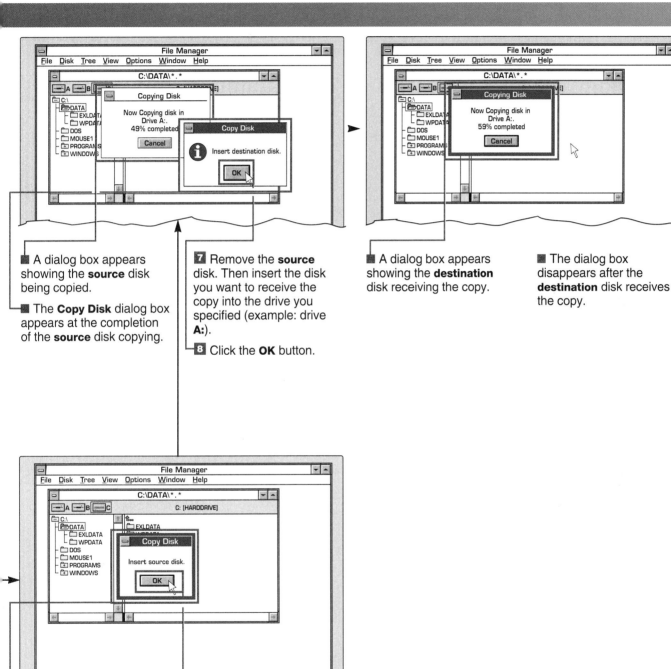

■ A dialog box appears showing the **source** disk being copied.

■ The **Copy Disk** dialog box appears at the completion of the **source** disk copying.

7 Remove the **source** disk. Then insert the disk you want to receive the copy into the drive you specified (example: drive **A:**).

8 Click the **OK** button.

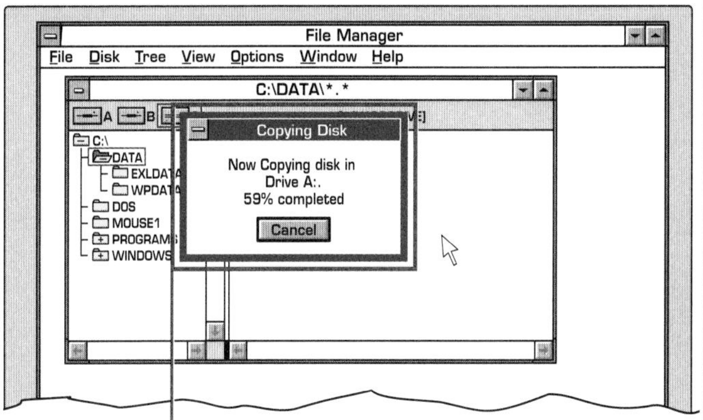

■ A dialog box appears showing the **destination** disk receiving the copy.

■ The dialog box disappears after the **destination** disk receives the copy.

Label a Disk

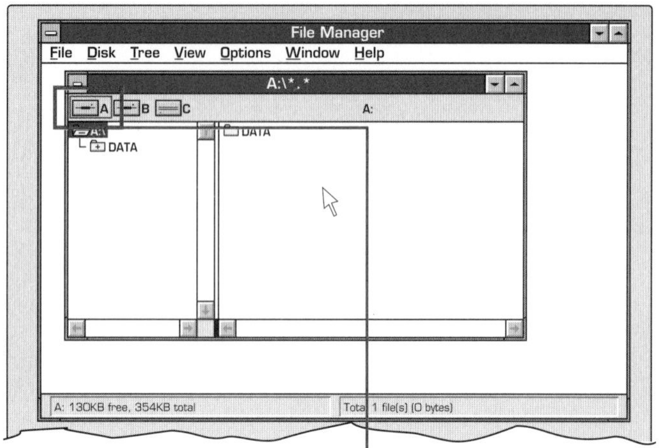

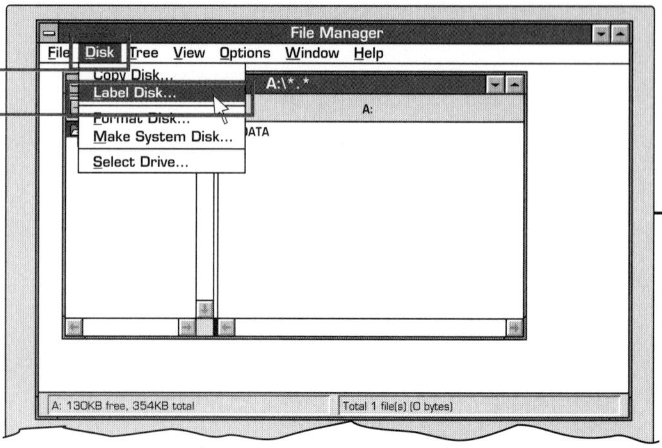

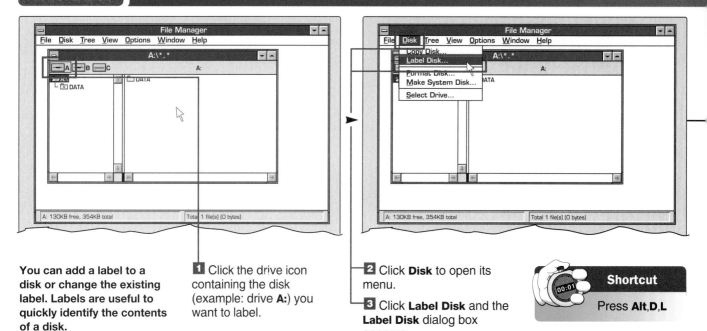

You can add a label to a disk or change the existing label. Labels are useful to quickly identify the contents of a disk.

1 Click the drive icon containing the disk (example: drive **A:**) you want to label.

2 Click **Disk** to open its menu.

3 Click **Label Disk** and the **Label Disk** dialog box appears.

Shortcut

Press **Alt**,**D**,**L**

Disk Protection

5.25 INCH DISK

Write Protect Notch

The open notch on the right side of the disk lets you copy information or delete information from the disk.

By placing a small piece of tape over the notch, the disk becomes write protected. You can still use the disk, but you cannot add or delete information to or from it.

Disks that do not have a notch are permanently write protected. Many programs are permanently write protected to guard their files from being deleted or modified.

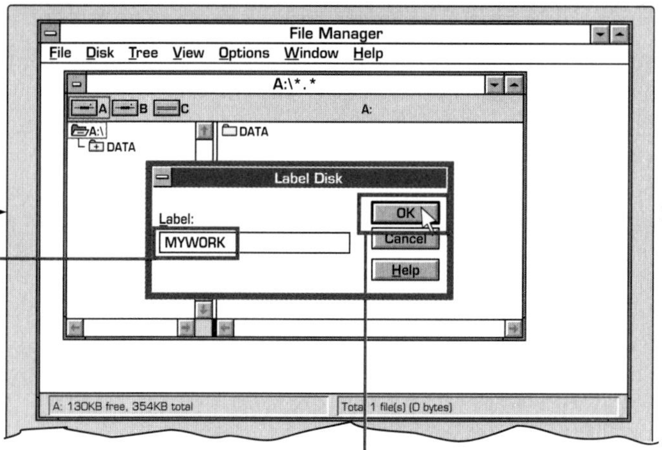

4 Type the label (example: **MYWORK**) for the disk.

Note: To change a label, type the new label name. It will replace the existing label.

The label can contain up to 11 characters including one blank space. Permissible characters are the letters A to Z, digits 0 through 9, and $ – ( ) _ { } #.

5 Click the **OK** button.

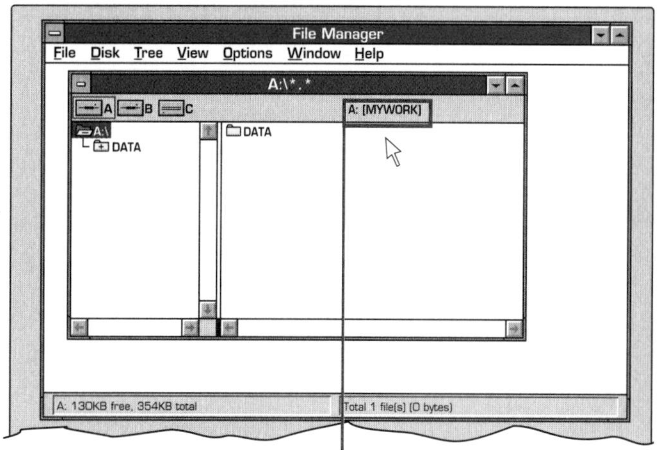

■ The new label (example: **MYWORK**) appears.

Note: You can also add a label or change an existing label on your hard drive using the same command.

3.5 INCH DISK

Write Protect Switch

The switch works similar to the notch on the 5.25 inch disk. With the switch in the closed position, you can erase, modify or add information to the disk.

With the switch in the open position, as illustrated to the left, the disk is write protected.

Note: Make sure your disks are properly labeled and protected from extreme heat or cold, humidity, food and drinks.

Keep disks away from magnetic influences such as telephones, magnetic paper clip holders, or the computer monitor.

CONTEXT SENSITIVE HELP

HELP CONTENTS

Context Sensitive Help

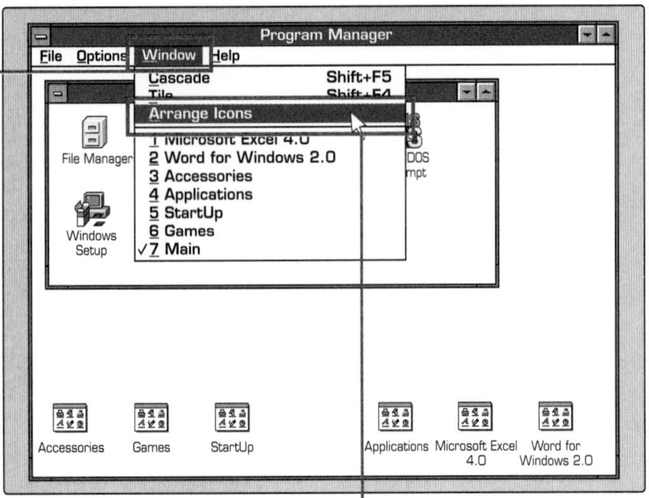

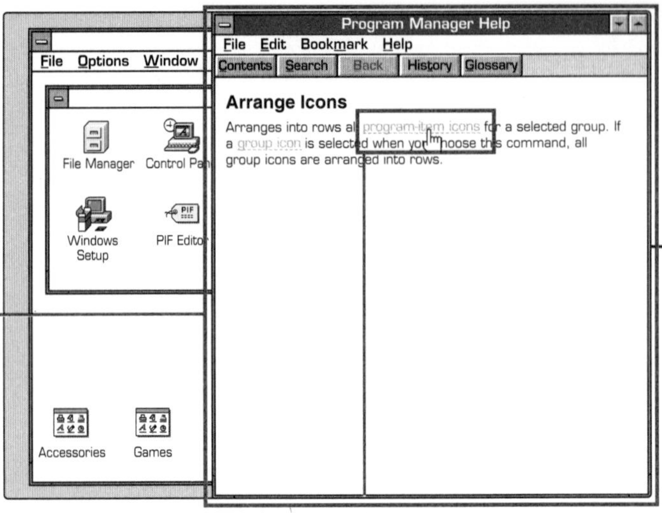

This feature permits you to receive detailed help information for any command or dialog box.

1 Click a menu title (example: **Window**) to open its menu.

2 Press ⬇ until the command you want help on is highlighted (example: **Arrange Icons**).

3 Press **F1** and the **Program Manager Help** window appears.

4 Move the mouse over a term (example: program-item icons) and it turns into a hand. Then click the left mouse button.

Note: This only applies to dotted, underlined text.

Help Contents

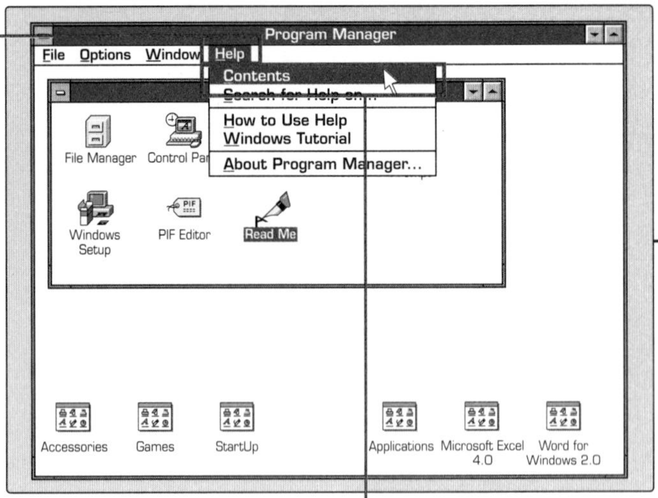

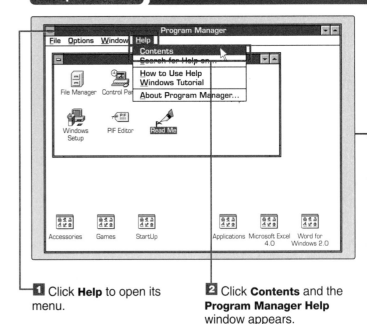

1 Click **Help** to open its menu.

2 Click **Contents** and the **Program Manager Help** window appears.

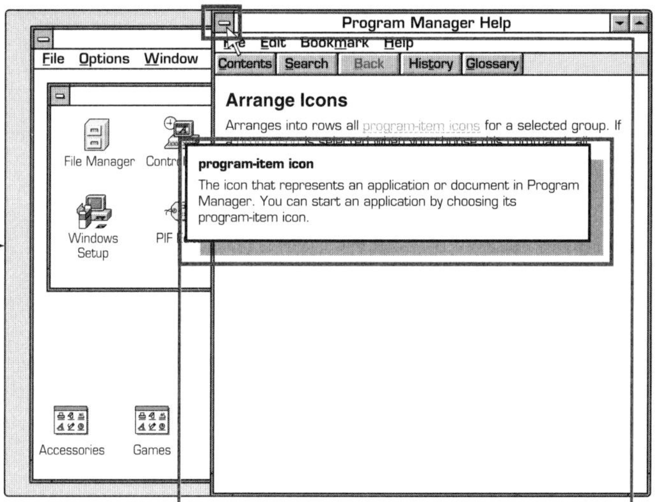

■ A detailed explanation of that term appears.

5 Click anywhere on the desktop to remove the explanation.

6 To exit **Program Manager Help**, double click its Control menu box ⊟.

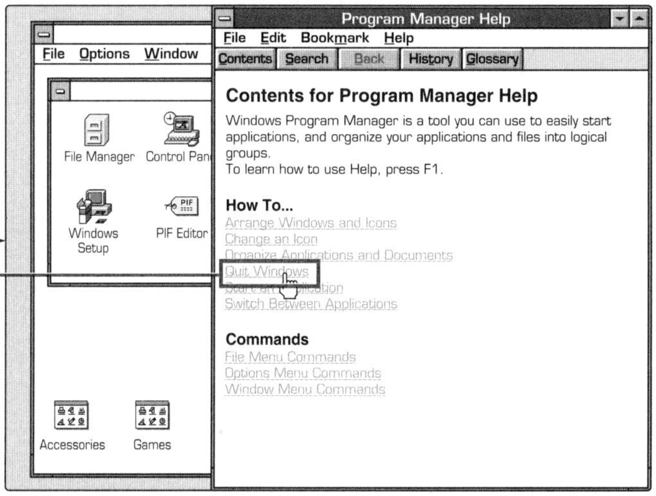

3 Move the mouse over a topic (example: Quit Windows) you want more information on, and it turns into a hand pointer. Then click the left mouse button.

Note: This only applies to underlined text.

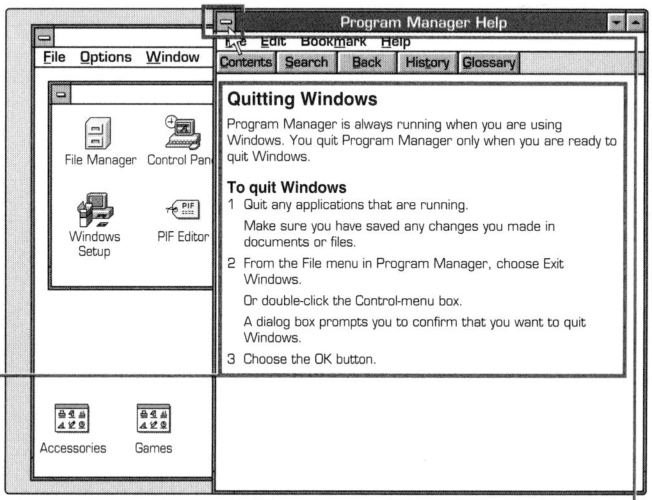

■ A detailed explanation of that topic appears.

4 To exit **Program Manager Help**, double click its Control menu box ⊟.

WINDOWS BASICS
MANAGING YOUR PROGRAMS
MANAGING YOUR DIRECTORIES
CREATING A FILE
OBJECT LINKING AND EMBEDDING
MANAGING YOUR FILES
MANAGING YOUR DISKS
HELP

Search for Help on a Specific Topic

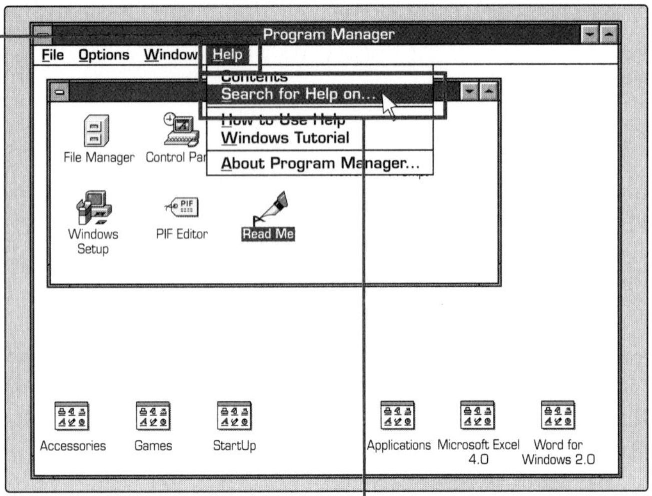

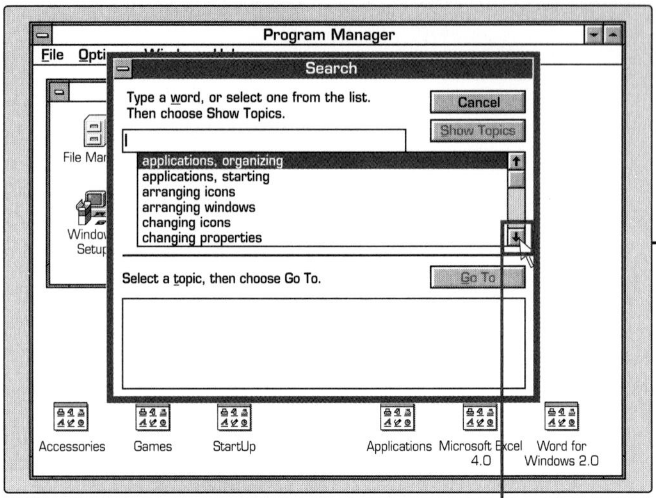

1 Click **Help** to open its menu.

2 Click **Search for Help on** and the **Search** dialog box appears.

3 To view more topics, click the down scroll arrow.

Glossary

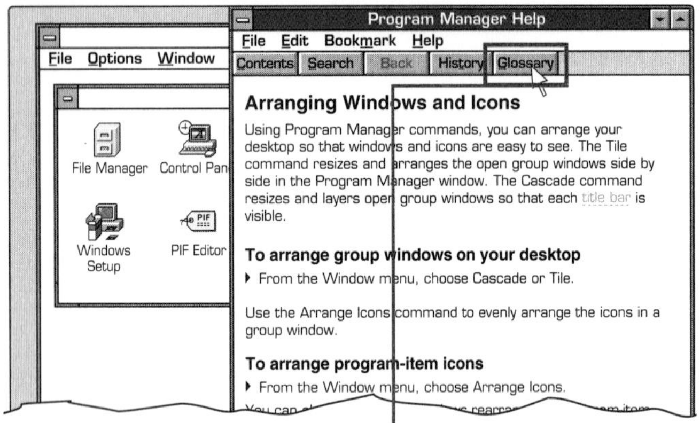

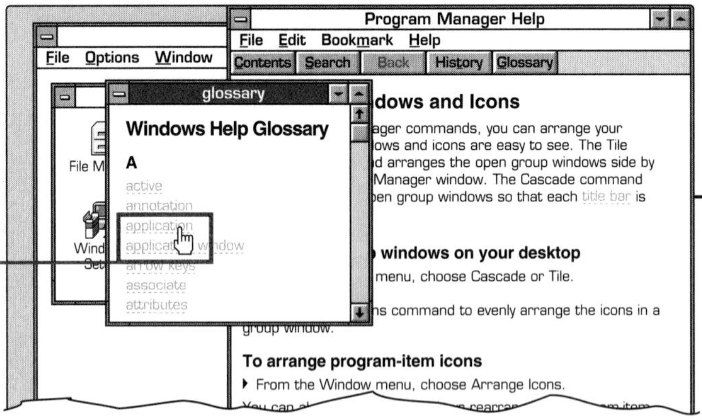

The Windows Help Glossary lists definitions of common words.

1 Click the **Glossary** button and the **Windows Help Glossary** appears.

2 Move the mouse over a term you want a definition for (example: application) and it turns into a hand pointer. Then click the left mouse button.

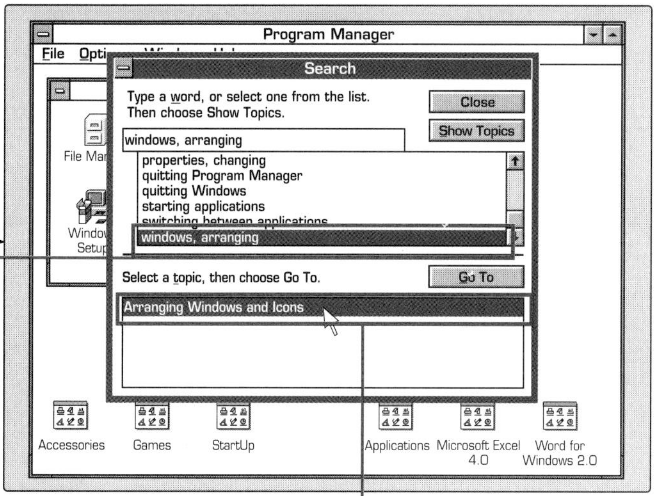

4 Double click the topic (example: **windows, arranging**) you want help on.

5 A list of available topics in that category appears. Double click the topic of interest (example: **Arranging Windows and Icons**).

Note: In this example, only one topic is displayed.

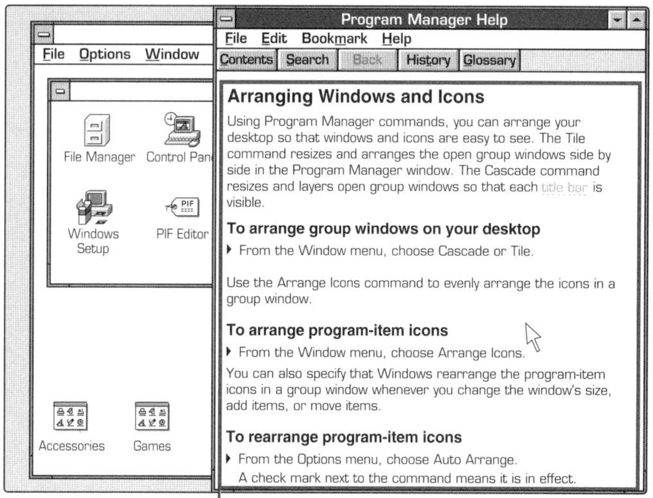

Help on the selected topic appears.

Note: You can also access the ***Search*** *dialog box by clicking* Search *when using* ***Program Manager Help****.*

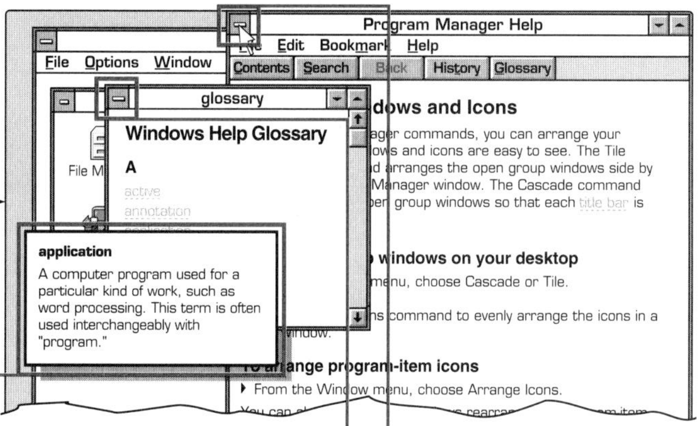

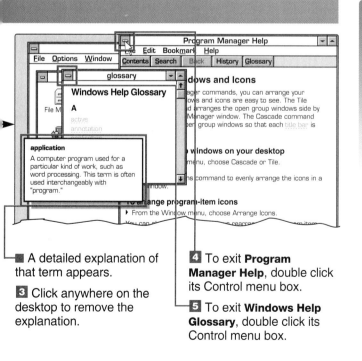

A detailed explanation of that term appears.

3 Click anywhere on the desktop to remove the explanation.

4 To exit **Program Manager Help**, double click its Control menu box.

5 To exit **Windows Help Glossary**, double click its Control menu box.

ADDITIONAL CHOICES

Back	Click this button to return to the last topic you displayed.
History	Click this button to view a list of the last topics you displayed. Then double click the topic you want to view again.

Index